HOW TO FORM A CORPORATION IN FLORIDA

Sixth Edition

Mark Warda
Attorney at Law

SPHINX® PUBLISHING
AN IMPRINT OF SOURCEBOOKS, INC.®
NAPERVILLE, ILLINOIS
www.SphinxLegal.com

Sixth Edition, 2003

Published by: **Sphinx® Publishing, An Imprint of Sourcebooks, Inc.®**

Naperville Office
P.O. Box 4410
Naperville, Illinois 60567-4410
630-961-3900
Fax: 630-961-2168
www.sourcebooks.com
www.SphinxLegal.com

This publication is designed to provide accurate and authoritative information in regard to the subject matter covered. It is sold with the understanding that the publisher is not engaged in rendering legal, accounting, or other professional service. If legal advice or other expert assistance is required, the services of a competent professional person should be sought.

From a Declaration of Principles Jointly Adopted by a Committee of the
American Bar Association and a Committee of Publishers and Associations

This product is not a substitute for legal advice.

Disclaimer required by Texas statutes.

Library of Congress Cataloging-in-Publication Data
Warda, Mark.
  How to form a corporation in Florida / Mark Warda.-- 6th ed.
    p. cm.
  Includes index.
  ISBN 1-57248-356-3
  1. Incorporation--Florida--Popular works. 2.
Incorporation--Florida--Forms. I. Title.

KFF213.5.Z9 W37 2003
346.759'065--dc22
                            2003016437

Printed and bound in the United States of America.

VHG Paperback — 10 9 8 7 6 5 4 3 2 1

To Alexandra my wife and partner
who helped me update everything
in this book

CONTENTS

Using Self-Help Law Books

Before using a self-help law book, you should realize the advantages and disadvantages of doing your own legal work and understand the challenges and diligence that this requires.

The Growing Trend

Rest assured that you won't be the first or only person handling your own legal matter. For example, in some states, more than seventy-five percent of the people in divorces and other cases represent themselves. Because of the high cost of legal services, this is a major trend and many courts are struggling to make it easier for people to represent themselves. However, some courts are not happy with people who do not use attorneys and refuse to help them in any way. For some, the attitude is, "Go to the law library and figure it out for yourself."

We write and publish self-help law books to give people an alternative to the often complicated and confusing legal books found in most law libraries. We have made the explanations of the law as simple and easy to understand as possible. Of course, unlike an attorney advising an individual client, we cannot cover every conceivable possibility.

Cost/Value Analysis

Whenever you shop for a product or service, you are faced with various levels of quality and price. In deciding what product or service to buy, you make a cost/value analysis on the basis of your willingness to pay and the quality you desire.

When buying a car, you decide whether you want transportation, comfort, status, or sex appeal. Accordingly, you decide among such choices as a Neon, a Lincoln, a Rolls Royce, or a Porsche. Before making a decision, you usually weigh the merits of each option against the cost.

When you get a headache, you can take a pain reliever (such as aspirin) or visit a medical specialist for a neurological examination. Given this choice, most people, of course, take a pain reliever, since it costs only pennies; whereas a medical examination costs hundreds of dollars and takes a lot of time. This is usually a logical choice because it is rare to need anything more than a pain reliever for a headache. But in some cases, a headache may indicate a brain tumor and failing to see a specialist right away can result in complications. Should everyone with a headache go to a specialist? Of course not, but people treating their own illnesses must realize that they are betting on the basis of their cost/value analysis of the situation. They are taking the most logical option.

The same cost/value analysis must be made when deciding to do one's own legal work. Many legal situations are very straight forward, requiring a simple form and no complicated analysis. Anyone with a little intelligence and a book of instructions can handle the matter without outside help.

But there is always the chance that complications are involved that only an attorney would notice. To simplify the law into a book like this, several legal cases often must be condensed into a single sentence or paragraph. Otherwise, the book would be several hundred pages long and too complicated for most people. However, this simplification necessarily leaves out many details and nuances that would apply to special or unusual situations. Also, there are many ways to interpret most legal questions. Your case may come before a judge who disagrees with the analysis of our authors.

Therefore, in deciding to use a self-help law book and to do your own legal work, you must realize that you are making a cost/value analysis. You have decided that the money you will save in doing it yourself outweighs the chance that your case will not turn out to your satisfaction. Most people handling their own simple legal matters never have a problem, but occasionally people find that it ended up costing them more to have an attorney straighten out the situation than it would have if they had hired an attorney in the beginning. Keep this in mind while handling your case, and be sure to consult an attorney if you feel you might need further guidance.

Local Rules

The next thing to remember is that a book which covers the law for the entire nation, or even for an entire state, cannot possibly include every procedural difference of every jurisdiction. Whenever possible, we provide the exact form needed; however, in some areas, each county, or even each judge, may require unique forms and procedures. In our state books, our forms usually cover the majority of counties in the state, or provide examples of the type of form which will be required. In our national books, our forms are sometimes even more general in nature but are designed to give a good idea of the type of form that will be needed in most locations. Nonetheless, keep in mind that your state, county, or judge may have a requirement, or use a form, that is not included in this book.

You should not necessarily expect to be able to get all of the information and resources you need solely from within the pages of this book. This book will serve as your guide, giving you specific information whenever possible and helping you to find out what else you will need to know. This is just like if you decided to build your own backyard deck. You might purchase a book on how to build decks. However, such a book would not include the building codes and permit requirements of every city, town, county, and township in the nation; nor would it include the lumber, nails, saws, hammers, and other materials and tools you would need to actually build the deck. You would use the book as your guide, and then do some work and research involving such matters as whether you need a permit of some kind, what type and grade of wood are available in your area, whether to use hand tools or power tools, and how to use those tools.

Before using the forms in a book like this, you should check with your court clerk to see if there are any local rules of which you should be aware, or local forms you will need to use. Often, such forms will require the same information as the forms in the book but are merely laid out differently or use slightly different language. They will sometimes require additional information.

Changes in the Law

Besides being subject to local rules and practices, the law is subject to change at any time. The courts and the legislatures of all fifty states are constantly revising the laws. It is possible that while you are reading this book, some aspect of the law is being changed.

In most cases, the change will be of minimal significance. A form will be redesigned, additional information will be required, or a waiting period will be extended. As a result, you might need to revise a form, file an extra form, or wait out a longer time period; these types of changes will not usually affect the outcome of your case. On the other hand, sometimes a major part of the law is changed, the entire law in a particular area is rewritten, or a case that was the basis of a central legal point is overruled. In such instances, your entire ability to pursue your case may be impaired.

Again, you should weigh the value of your case against the cost of an attorney and make a decision as to what you believe is in your best interest.

INTRODUCTION

Each year hundreds of thousands of corporations are registered in this country, tens of thousands in Florida alone. The corporation is the preferred way of doing business for most people because it offers many advantages over partnerships and sole proprietorships. It is not a coincidence that the largest businesses in the world are corporations.

The main reason people incorporate is to avoid personal liability. While sole proprietors and partners have all of their personal assets at risk, corporate shareholders risk only what they paid for their stock. With so many people ready to sue for any reason or for no reason, the corporation is one of the few inexpensive protections left.

Creating a simple corporation is very easy and it is the purpose of this book to explain, in simple language, how you can do it yourself. A simple corporation as used in this book is one in which there are five or fewer shareholders and all of them are active in the business.

Chapters 1 through 4 and Chapter 6 get you started. If you plan to sell stock to someone who is not active in the business or to have six or more shareholders, you should seek the advice of an attorney. However, some guidance is provided throughout this book as to what some of the concerns will be in these circumstances. (see Chapter 5.)

If your situation is in any way complicated or involves factors not mentioned in this book, you should seek the advice of an attorney practicing corporate law. The cost of a short consultation can be a lot cheaper than the consequences of violating the law.

If you plan to sell stock to outside investors, you should consult with a lawyer who specializes in securities laws. Selling a few thousand shares of stock to friends and neighbors may sound like an easy way to raise capital for your business, but it is not. Since the stock market crash of the 1930s there have been federal laws regulating the sale of securities. There are harsh criminal penalties for violators and the laws do not have many loopholes. The basic rules are explained in Chapter 5.

This book also explains the basics of corporate taxation, but you should discuss your own particular situation with your accountant before deciding what is best for you. He or she can also set you up with an efficient system of bookkeeping which can save both time and money.

Finally, if you need to amend or dissolve your corporation, Chapters 7 and 8 will help.

Good luck with your new business!

I ◼ CORPORATIONS IN GENERAL

A *corporation* is a legal "person" that can be created under state law. As a person, a corporation has certain rights and obligations, such as the right to do business and the obligation to pay taxes. Sometimes one hears of a law referring to *natural persons*, which are people. That is to differentiate them from corporations, which are *persons*, but not natural persons.

Business corporations were invented hundreds of years ago to promote risky ventures. Prior to the use of corporations, persons engaged in business faced the possibility of unlimited liability. By using a corporation, many people could put up a fixed sum of money for a new venture such as a voyage to explore the New World. If the venture made money, they shared the profits. If the venture went into debt, the most they could lose was the initial investment they put up.

The reasons for having a corporation are the same today. They allow investors to put up money for new ventures without risk of further liability. The corporation remains one of the few innovations that has not yet been abandoned.

Before forming a corporation, you should be familiar with the common corporate terms that will be used in the text.

Shareholders   A *shareholder* is a person who owns stock in a corporation. In most small corporations the shareholders are the same as the officers and directors, but in large corporations most shareholders are not officers or directors. Sometimes small corporations have shareholders who are not officers, such as when the stock is in one spouse's name and the other spouse runs the business. Specific laws regarding issuance of shares and shareholders' rights are in Florida Statutes (Fla. Stat.) Sections (Secs.) 607.0601 through 607.06401. (see Appendix B.)

Officers   *Officers* are usually the president, secretary, treasurer, and vice president. These persons run the day-to-day affairs of the business. They are elected each year by a vote of the board of directors. In Florida, one person can hold all of the offices of a corporation.

Board of Directors   The *board of directors* is the controlling body of a corporation that makes major corporate decisions and elects the officers. It usually meets just once a year. A corporation can have just one director (who can also hold all offices and own all the stock). In a small corporation the board members are usually also officers.

Registered Agent   The *registered agent* is the person designated by the corporation to receive legal papers that must be served on the corporation. The registered agent should be regularly available at the registered office of the corporation. The registered office can be the corporate office or the office of the corporation's attorney or other person who is the registered agent.

A person accepting the position as registered agent must sign a statement that he or she understands the duties and responsibilities of the position. These are spelled out in Florida Statutes, Sections 607.0501 through 607.0505. (See Appendix B.)

Articles of Incorporation   *Articles of Incorporation* is the name of the document that is filed with the Secretary of State to start the corporation. In most cases, it legally needs to contain only five basic statements. Some corporations have lengthy **ARTICLES OF INCORPORATION** (form 1, p.137). However, this makes it harder to make changes in the corporate structure. It is usually better to keep the articles short and put the details in the **BYLAWS** (form 8, p.159).

Bylaws   *Bylaws* are the rules governing the structure and operation of the corporation. Typically the **BYLAWS** will set out rules for the board of directors, officers, shareholders, and corporate formalities.

Florida Statutes Chapter 607 contains most of Florida's laws regarding general corporate activities. For example, it lists all of the powers of corporations so they do not have to be recited again in the articles or bylaws.

(Legal definitions of other corporate terms are included in Florida Statutes, Section 607.01401 contained in Appendix B.)

2 ADVANTAGES AND DISADVANTAGES OF INCORPORATING

Before forming a corporation, the business owner or prospective business owner should become familiar with the advantages and disadvantages of incorporating.

Advantages

The following are some of the advantages that a corporation has over other forms of businesses such as *sole proprietorships* and *partnerships*.

Limited Liability The main reason for forming a corporation is to *limit the liability* of the owners. In a sole proprietorship or partnership the owners are personally liable for the debts and liabilities of the business, and creditors can go after all of their assets to collect. If a corporation is formed and operated properly, the owners can be protected from all such liability.

Example 1: If several people are in partnership and one of them makes many large extravagant purchases in the name of the partnership, the other partners can be held liable for the full amount of all such purchases. The creditors can take the bank accounts, cars, real estate, and other property of any partner to pay the debts of the partnership. If only one partner has money, he or she may have to pay all of the debts accumulated by all the other partners. When doing business in the corporate form, the corporation may go bankrupt and the shareholders may lose their initial investment, but the creditors cannot touch the assets of the owners.

Example 2: If a person runs a taxi business and one of the drivers causes a terrible accident, the owner can be held liable for the full amount of the damages. If the taxi driver was on drugs and killed several people and the damages amount to millions of dollars more than the insurance coverage, the owner may lose everything he owns. With a corporation, only the corporation would be liable and if there was not enough money the owner still could not be touched. One true example is a business owner who owned hundreds of taxis. He divided the cabs among hundreds of different corporations that he owned. Each corporation only had minimum insurance, so when one taxi was involved in an accident the owner only lost the assets of that corporation.

NOTE: *If a corporate officer or shareholder does something negligent, signs a debt personally, or guarantees a corporate debt, the corporation will not provide protection from the consequences of the act or from the debt. Also, if a corporation does not follow the proper corporate formalities, it may be ignored by a court and the owners or officers may be held personally liable. The formalities include having separate bank accounts, holding meetings, and keeping minutes. When a court ignores a corporate structure and holds the owners or officers liable it is called piercing the corporate veil. A good explanation of Florida law on* piercing the corporate veil *is contained in the Florida Supreme Court case, Dania Jai-Alai Palace, Inc. v. Sykes, 450 So.2d 1114 (1984).*

Continuous Existence
A corporation may have a *perpetual* existence. When a sole proprietor or partner dies, the assets of their business may go to their heirs, but the business does not exist any longer. If the surviving spouse or other heirs of a business owner want to continue the business in their own names, they will be considered a new business even if they are using the assets of the old business. With a partnership, the death of one partner may cause a dissolution of the business.

Example 1: If a person dies owning a sole proprietorship, his or her spouse may want to continue the business. That person may inherit all of the assets but will have to start a new business. This means getting new licenses and tax numbers, registering the name, and establishing credit from scratch. With a corporation, the business continues with all of the same licenses, bank accounts, etc.

Example 2: If one partner dies, the partnership may be forced out of business. The heirs of the deceased partner can force the sale of their share of the assets of the partnership even if the surviving partner needs them to continue the business. If the surviving partners do not have the money to buy the heirs out, the business may have to be dissolved. With a corporation, the heirs would only inherit stock. With properly drawn documents, the business could continue.

Ease of Transferability

A corporation and all of its assets and accounts may be transferred by the simple assignment of a *stock certificate*. With a sole proprietorship or partnership, each of the individual assets must be transferred and the accounts, licenses, and permits must be individually transferred.

Example: If a sole proprietorship is sold, the new owner will have to get a new occupational license, set up a new bank account, and apply for a new taxpayer identification number. The title to any vehicles and real estate will have to be put in the new owner's name. All open accounts will have the name changed as well. He or she will probably have to submit new credit applications. With a corporation, all of these items remain in the same corporate name. For instance, if John Buyer purchased the corporation, as the new shareholder, he would elect himself director and as director, he would elect himself president, treasurer, and any other offices he wanted to hold.

NOTE: *In some cases, the new owners will have to submit personal applications for such things as credit lines or liquor licenses.*

Transfer of Ownership

By distributing stock, the owner of a business can share the profits of a business without giving up control. This is done by keeping a majority of stock or by issuing different classes of stock; some with voting rights and others without.

Example: If a person wants to give his or her children some of the profits of the business, he or she can give them stock and pay dividends to them without giving them any control over the management. This would not be practical with a partnership or sole proprietorship.

Ease of Raising Capital

A corporation may raise capital by selling stock or borrowing money. A corporation does not pay taxes on money it raises by the sale of stock.

Example: If a corporation wants to expand, the owners can sell off 10%, 50%, or 90% of the stock and still remain in control of the business. The people putting up the money may be more willing to invest if they know they will have a piece of the action than if they were making a loan with a limited return. They may not want to become partners in a partnership.

NOTE: *There are strict rules about the sale of stock with criminal penalties and triple damages for violators. (see Chapter 5.)*

Separate Record Keeping

A corporation has all its own bank accounts and records. A partner or sole proprietor may have trouble differentiating between expenses of the business and those for personal items.

Tax Advantages

There are some tax advantages that are available only to corporations, including the following.

✪ Medical insurance for your family may be fully deductible.

✪ A tax deferred trust can be set up for a retirement plan.

✪ Losses are fully deductible for a corporation whereas an individual must prove there was a profit motive before deducting losses.

Ease of Estate Planning

With a corporation, shares of a company can be distributed more than with a partnership. Different heirs can be given different percentages, and control can be limited to those who are most capable.

Prestige

The name of a corporation sounds more prestigious than the name of a sole proprietor to some people. "John Smith d/b/a Acme Builders" sounds like one lone guy. "Acme Builders, Incorporated," sounds like it might be a large operation.

Separate Credit Rating

A corporation has its own credit rating that can be better or worse than the owner's credit rating. A corporate business can go bankrupt while the owner's credit remains unaffected, or an owner's credit may be bad but the corporation may maintain a good rating.

Disadvantages

Extra Tax Return
A corporation is required to file its own tax return. This is a bit longer and more complicated than the form required by a sole proprietorship and may entail additional expenses if the services of an accountant are required. (A partnership must also file its own tax return, so there is no advantage or disadvantage over a partnership as far as tax returns are concerned.)

Annual Report
A corporation must file a one-page *annual report* with the state (that lists names and addresses of officers and directors) and pay a fee of $150. If you are late, there is a $400 penalty.

Separate Credit Rating
The owners of a corporation must be careful to keep their personal business separate from the business of the corporation. The corporation must have its own records and have minutes of meetings. Money must be kept separate. But in every business, records should be separate, so the corporate structure might make it easier to do so.

Extra Expenses
There are, of course, expenses in operating a corporation compared to not operating one. People who employ an attorney to form their corporation pay a lot more than people who use this book. A corporation owner will have to pay unemployment compensation for him or herself which a sole proprietor would not have to pay. The Florida unemployment tax starts at 2.7% of the first $7000 ($189 per year) and if there are no claims, it drops to 0.1% of $7000 ($7 per year).

Checking Accounts
Checks made out to a corporation cannot be cashed; they must be deposited into a corporate account. Some banks have higher fees just for businesses that are incorporated. See the section on *Bank Accounts* in Chapter 4 for tips on avoiding high bank fees.

3 | TYPES OF CORPORATIONS

Before forming a corporation, you must make a few choices. Will the corporation be based in Florida or elsewhere? Will it be an S or a C corporation? Will it be a closely held corporation? Professional service corporation? Not-for-profit corporation?

Florida Corporation v. Foreign Corporation

A person wishing to form a corporation must decide whether the corporation will be a Florida corporation or a *foreign* corporation. A foreign corporation is one incorporated in another state that does business in Florida.

Delaware Corporations   In the past, there was some advantage to incorporating in Delaware, since that state had very liberal laws regarding corporations, and many national corporations are incorporated there. However, in recent years most states have liberalized their corporation laws—so today there is no advantage to incorporating in Delaware for most people.

Nevada Corporations

Nevada has liberalized its corporation laws recently to attract businesses. It allows bearer stock and other rules that allow more privacy to corporate participants. It also does not share information with the Internal Revenue Service and does not have a state income tax.

Today Florida has very favorable corporate laws so out-of-state laws are not as big an advantage. If you form a corporation in a state other than Florida, you will probably have to have an agent or an office in that state and will have to register as a foreign corporation doing business in Florida. This is more expensive and more complicated than just registering as a Florida corporation to begin with. Also, if you are sued by someone who is not in your state, they can sue you in the state that you are incorporated in, and that would probably be more expensive for you than a suit filed in your local court. In some states, your corporation may be required to pay state income tax.

S Corporations

A corporation has a choice of how it wants to be taxed. It can make the election at the beginning of its existence or at the beginning of a new tax year. The choices follow.

S Corporations

Formerly called a *Subchapter S corporation*, an *S corporation* pays no income tax and may only be used for small businesses. All of the income or losses of the corporation for the year are passed through to the shareholders who report them on their individual returns. At the end of each year, the corporation files an *information return* listing all of its income, expenses, depreciation, etc., and sends to each shareholder a notice of his or her share as determined by percentage of stock ownership.

Advantages. Using this method avoids double taxation and allows pass-through of losses and depreciation. The business is treated like a partnership. Since many businesses have tax losses during the first years due to start-up costs, many businesses elect S status and switch over to C corporation status in later years. Once a corporation terminates its S status, there is a five year waiting period before it can switch back.

NOTE: *At the time of this book is being published, S corporations do not have to pay Florida corporate income tax. However, there are proposals to extend the corporate tax to S corporation, but to exempt profits of $15,000 or $25,000.*

Disadvantages. Profits and losses must be distributed according to stock ownership and losses cannot exceed basis. If stockholders are in high income brackets, their share of the profits will be taxed at those rates. Shareholders who do not *materially participate* in the business cannot deduct losses. Some *fringe benefits* such as health and life insurance may not be tax deductible in an S corporation.

Requirements. To qualify for S corporation status, the following must apply. The corporation must:

✪ have no more than seventy-five shareholders, none of whom are non-resident aliens or corporations, all of whom consent to the election (shares owned by a husband and wife jointly are considered owned by one shareholder);

✪ have only one class of stock;

✪ not be a member of an *affiliated group*;

✪ have only U.S. taxpayers or residents as shareholders; and,

✪ file **ELECTION BY A SMALL BUSINESS CORPORATION (IRS FORM 2553)** (see form 14, p.177) before the end of the 15th day of the third month of the tax year that it is to be effective and have it approved by the IRS.

Multiple Corporations. The IRS has approved the use of two or more S corporations in partnership to increase the number of allowable investors in a venture. It may also be possible for an S corporation to form a partnership with a C corporation.

C Corporations

A *C corporation* pays taxes on its net earnings at corporate tax rates. Salaries of officers, directors, and employees are deducted from income and are therefore not taxed to the corporation. However, money paid out in dividends is taxed twice. It is taxed at the corporation's rate as part of its profit, and then the stockholders must include the amounts they receive as dividends in their income.

Advantages. If taxpayers are in a higher tax bracket than the corporation and the money will be left in the company for expansion, taxes are saved. Fringe benefits such as health, accident, and life insurance are deductible expenses.

Disadvantages. Double taxation of dividends by the federal government is the biggest problem with a C corporation. Also, Florida has an income tax of 5.5% which only applies to C corporations and applies to all income over $5000.

NOTE: *Neither of these taxes applies to money taken out as salaries. Many small business owners take all profits out as salaries to avoid double taxation and the Florida income tax. But there are rules requiring that salaries be reasonable and if a stockholder's salary is deemed to be too high, relative to his or her job, the salary may be considered dividends and subject to the double taxation.*

Requirements. All corporations are C corporations, unless they specifically elect to become S corporations.

Closely Held Corporation Election

A *closely held corporation* election is beneficial for many small businesses. Its purpose is to place restrictions on the transferability of stock. Often it obligates a shareholder to offer to the corporation or the shareholders the opportunity to purchase the stock before offering it to any outside purchaser. If the corporation and shareholders reject the offer, they typically must still consent to who the transferee (buyer) of the shares will be.

To elect to have these restrictions, they should be included in the bylaws, printed on the certificates, and in many states they must be included in the **ARTICLES OF INCORPORATION** (see form 1, p.137).

Professional Service Corporations

Certain types of services can only be rendered by a corporation if it is a *Professional Service Corporation* or *Professional Association.* These are such businesses as attorneys, physicians, certified public accountants, veterinarians, architects, life insurance agents, chiropractors, and similarly *licensed* professionals. A professional service corporation comes under nearly all of the rules of Florida Statutes, Chapter 607 regarding corporations in general, unless they conflict with Chapter 621, which specifically governs professional service corporations. The major differences between the two are purpose, name, shareholder status, and merger.

Purpose

A professional service corporation must have one specific purpose spelled out in the **ARTICLES OF INCORPORATION** (see form 1, p.137), and that purpose must be to practice one of the professions. It may not engage in any other business, but it may invest its funds in real estate, stocks, bonds, mortgages, or other types of investments. A professional service corporation may change its purpose to another legal purpose, but it will then no longer be a professional service corporation. (Fla. Stat., Secs. 621.05 and 621.08.)

Name

The name of a professional service corporation must contain the word *chartered* or *professional association* or the abbreviation *P.A.* It may use its name without these words if it registers for a fictitious name (see Chapter 4). A professional service corporation may not use the words *company, corporation, incorporated,* or any abbreviation of these. It may contain the name of some or all of the shareholders and may contain the names of deceased or retired shareholders. (Fla. Stat. Sec. 621.12.)

Shareholder Status

Only persons licensed to practice the profession may be shareholders of a professional service corporation. A shareholder who loses his or her right to practice must immediately sever all employment with and financial interests in such corporation. If such a shareholder does not do so, the corporation may be dissolved by the Florida Department of Legal Affairs. No shareholder may enter into a voting trust or other similar arrangement with anyone. (Fla. Stat. Secs. 621.09, 621.10 and 621.11.)

Merger

A professional service corporation may not merge with any other corporation except a Florida professional service corporation that is licensed to perform the same type of services.

Not-for-Profit Corporations

Not-for-profit corporations are usually used for social clubs, churches, and charities, and are beyond the scope of this book. While they are similar to for-profit corporations in many aspects, such as limited liability and the required formalities, there are additional state and federal requirements that must be met.

In some cases, a business can be formed as a not-for-profit corporation. It would not be allowed to distribute profits to its founders but it could pay salaries and enjoy numerous tax advantages. For information on books dealing with not-for-profit corporations, check your local bookstore or library. Also, see the *For Further Reference* section at the end of this book.

4 START-UP PROCEDURES

The steps necessary to legally establish your corporation are not difficult, but still need to be followed closely. Such preliminary things as checking on available corporate names must be done, as well as filing the required paperwork and acquiring tax payer information. This chapter will take you through these steps.

Name Check

The very first thing to do before starting a corporation is to thoroughly check out the name you wish to use to be sure it is available. Many businesses have been forced to stop using their name after spending thousands of dollars promoting it.

The best way to check the availability of a corporate name is the Secretary of State's web site at:

www.sunbiz.org/corpweb/inquiry/corinam.html

If you do not have access to the Internet, you can have a name checked by telephone at 800-755-5111. The charge is $4.00.

Business Listings   Since some businesses neglect to properly register their name (yet still may have superior rights to the name), you should also check phone books and business directories. Many libraries have phone books from around the country as well as directories of trade names.

Yellow Page Listings   If you have a computer with Internet access, you can search every yellow pages listing for free. Just search for *yellow pages* with any web search engine. You can select a state, enter your business name, and it will tell you if any other companies are listed with that name. One site that allows you to search all states at once is:

www.switchboard.com

If you do not have access to a computer, you may be able to use one at your public library or have the search done at your library for a small fee.

Trademark Search   To be sure that your use of the name does not violate someone else's *trademark* rights, you should have a trademark search done of the mark in the *United States Patent and Trademark Office*. In the past this required a visit to their offices or the hiring of a search firm. Today, trademark records are online and you can now search them at:

www.uspto.gov

If you do not have access to the Internet, you might be able to do it at a public library or to have one of their employees order an online search for you for a small fee. If this is not available to you, you can have the search done through a firm. Some firms that do searches are:

Government Liaison Services, Inc.
200 N. Glebe Road, Suite 321
Arlington, VA 22203
GLS@Trademarkinfo.com
703-524-8200 or 800-642-6564
fax: 703-525-8451
www.trademarkinfo.com

Thomson & Thomson
500 Victory Road
North Quincy, MA 02171-3145
800-692-8833 or 617-479-1600
fax: 617-786-8273
www.thomson-thomson.com

Blumberg Excelsior Corporate Services, Inc.
4435 Old Winter Garden Road
P.O. Box 2122, Orlando, FL 32802
407-299-8220 or 800-327-9220
fax: 407-291-6912
www.blumberg.com.index2.html

Similar Names Sometimes it seems like every good name is taken. But a name can often be modified slightly or used on different types of goods. If there is a "TriCounty Painting, Inc." in Pensacola, it may be possible to use something like "TriCounty Painting of Tampa Bay, Inc." if you are in a different part of the state. Try different variations if your favorite is taken. Another possibility is to give the corporation one name and then do business under a fictitious name. (see *Fictitious Names* on page 20.)

Example: If you want to use the name "Flowers by Freida" in Miami and there is already a "Flowers by Freida, Inc." in Pensacola, you might incorporate under the name "Freida Jones, Inc." and then register the corporation as doing business under the fictitious name "Flowers by Freida." Unless "Flowers by Freida, Inc." has registered a trademark for the name either in Florida or nationally, you will probably be able to use the name. However, you should realize that you might run into complications later, especially if you or the other company decide to expand into other areas of the state. One protection available would be to register the name as a trademark. This would give you exclusive use of the name anywhere that someone else was not already using it.

Forbidden Names A corporation may not use certain words in its name if there would be a likelihood of confusion. There are state and federal laws that control the use of these words. In most cases, your application will be rejected if you use a forbidden word. Some of the words that may not be used without special licenses or registration are:

Assurance	Florida Spaceport
Bank	Insurance
Banker	Olympic
Banking	Spaceport Florida
Credit Union	Trust Company
Disney	

Trademarks

The name of a business cannot be registered as a trademark. If the name is used in connection with goods or services, it may be registered and such registration will grant the holder exclusive rights to use that name except in areas where someone else has already used the name. A trademark may be registered either in Florida or in the entire country.

Each trademark is registered for a certain *class* of goods. If you want to sell "Zapata" chewing gum, it does not matter that someone has registered the name "Zapata" for use on shoes. If you want to register the mark for several types of goods or services, you must register it for each different class into which the goods or services fall, and pay a separate fee for each category.

For protection within the state of Florida, the mark may be registered with the Florida Department of State. The cost is about $87.50. Application forms and instructions can be obtained from:

Trademark Registration Section
Division of Corporations
P. O. Box 6327
Tallahassee, FL 32314
www.dos.state.fl.us/doc/pdf/cr2e014.pdf

For protection across the entire United States the mark can be registered with the United States Patent and Trademark Office and the cost is $335. The procedure for federal registration is more complicated than state registration.

Fictitious Names

A corporation may operate under a *fictitious name* just as an individual can. This is done when a corporation wants to operate several businesses under different names or if the business name is not available as a corporate name. Fictitious names used to be registered in each county, but they are now registered statewide with the Secretary of State. However, registering a fictitious name does not give the registrant any rights to the name. While corporate names are carefully checked by the Secretary of State and disallowed if they are similar to others, fictitious names are filed without checking and any number of people may register the same name. The cost of registering a fictitious name is $50. Application forms and instructions can be obtained from your local courthouse or by writing:

Fictitious Name Section
Secretary of State
P. O. Box 6327
Tallahassee, FL 32314
850-245-6058
www.dos.state.fl.us/doc/corp_dir.htm

NOTE: *When a fictitious name is used by a corporation, the corporate name should also be used. If the public does not see that they are dealing with a corporation, they may be able to "pierce the corporate veil" and sue the stockholders individually.*

Articles of Incorporation

The act that creates a corporation is the filing with the Secretary of State of the **ARTICLES OF INCORPORATION**. Today, this can be done either electronically over the Internet or by mail. Both ways are explained below.

Electronic Filing   You can form your corporation in a matter on minutes on the Secretary of State's web site using a credit card to pay the fees. This is the easiest way for most small businesses. If you wish to have different classes of stock with different rights, you should file a paper copy of Articles as explained below.

To file electronically, go to **www.sunbiz.org**.

Click on "Electronic Filing" in the left hand column.

◈   Click on "On-line Filing" in the left column.

◈   Click the "Accept" button at the bottom.

◈   Select "Articles of Incorporation for Florida Profit Corporation."

◈   Click "Add filing."

You will get a screen that looks like this:

Division of Corporations

Florida Profit Corporation

Filing Information

Make sure that your corporate name is available. If you are unsure, press the search button below to perform a corporate name search.

[Corporate Name Search]

If an effective date is required for this filing, enter here **(month/day/year)** ☐ / ☐ / ☐

Number of Certificates of Status	0 ⬍ **(Optional)**
Number of Certified Copies	0 ⬍ **(Optional)**
Corporate Name **(Name must include suffix such as "Corp", "Inc.", "Incorporated", etc.)**	
Corporate Stock Shares **(Cannot be zero)**	

Principal Place of Business

Address	
Suite, Apt. #, etc.	
City, State	,
Zip Code & Country	

Mailing Address

If your corporate mailing address is the same as the principal address above, check the box below. Otherwise, enter your corporate mailing address.

Mailing address same as principal address.

Address	
Suite, Apt. #, etc.	
City, State	,
Zip Code & Country	

Name And Address of Registered Agent

Name (Last, First, Middle, Title) ☐ , ☐ , ☐ (Sr., Jr., etc...)

- OR -

RA Business Name	
Address	
Suite, Apt. #, etc.	
City, State	, FL
Zip Code & Country	US

The new Registered Agent must type their name in the 'Registered Agent Signature' block below. RA signature MUST be an individual name. If the RA is a business entity, an individual must sign on the entity's behalf. **Do not enter the corporate name that you are attempting to file as Registered Agent.** A business entity cannot serve as its own RA.

Registered Agent Signature [＿＿＿＿＿＿＿＿＿＿]

Incorporator Name And Address

Name [＿＿＿＿＿＿＿＿＿＿]
Address [＿＿＿＿＿＿＿＿＿＿]
[＿＿＿＿＿＿＿＿＿＿]
[＿＿＿＿＿＿＿＿＿＿]

Incorporator Signature [＿＿＿＿＿＿＿＿＿＿]

Corporate Purpose
Corporate purpose is 'Any and all lawful business'.
(Do not check this box if a "Professional Association". You must list specific purpose below.)
(Maximum of 240 characters.)

[＿＿＿＿＿＿＿＿＿＿]

Correspondence Name And E-mail Address
Name and e-mail address to whom correspondence pertaining to this filing should be e-mailed.
Name [＿＿＿＿＿＿＿＿]
E-mail Address [＿＿＿＿＿＿＿＿]

Name Information

Officer/Director Name And Address
Title [＿] (P, VP, etc...)
Name (Last, First, Middle, Title) [＿], [＿], [＿][＿] (Sr., Jr., etc...)
- OR -
Entity Name [＿＿＿＿＿＿]
Street Address [＿＿＿＿＿＿]
City, State [＿＿＿], [＿]
Zip Code & Country [＿] [＿]

Title [＿] (P, VP, etc...)
Name (Last, First, Middle, Title) [＿], [＿], [＿][＿] (Sr., Jr., etc...)
- OR -
Entity Name [＿＿＿＿＿＿]
Street Address [＿＿＿＿＿＿]
City, State [＿＿＿], [＿]
Zip Code & Country [＿] [＿]

Title [＿] (P, VP, etc...)
Name (Last, First, Middle, Title) [＿], [＿], [＿][＿] (Sr., Jr., etc...)

- OR -

Entity Name

Street Address

City, State   ,

Zip Code & Country

Title   (P, VP, etc...)

Name (Last, First, Middle, Title)   ,   ,   ,   (Sr., Jr., etc...)

- OR -

Entity Name

Street Address

City, State   ,

Zip Code & Country

Title   (P, VP, etc...)

Name (Last, First, Middle, Title)   ,   ,   ,   (Sr., Jr., etc...)

- OR -

Entity Name

Street Address

City, State   ,

Zip Code & Country

Title   (P, VP, etc...)

Name (Last, First, Middle, Title)   ,   ,   ,   (Sr., Jr., etc...)

- OR -

Entity Name

Street Address

City, State   ,

Zip Code & Country

Please carefully review the information that you have entered on this page before continuing. By clicking "Continue," you affirm that the information listed is what you desire to be reflected for the filing. As noted in the disclaimer, once the document is submitted, it cannot be changed or altered by our office or the remitter.

Continue   Reset

You should then fill in the information as follows:

- ◈ The effective date would usually be the date you are filing. If you are filing in late December, you might not want it to be effective until January 1st.

- ◈ You are not required to have a Certificate of Status (cost $8.75) or a Certified Copy (cost $8.75), and most people do not get them. However, if you need some kind of hard evidence of your filing (for example if you are applying for a franchise), you might want to order a Certificate of Status now.

- ◈ You should have already checked your corporate name on their search page. If not, you can click the button above to be sure it is available. Your name must include one of the following six words:

  Incorporated or Inc.

  Corporation or Corp.

  Company or Co.

  If you are starting a Professional Service Corporation, it must include the words "Professional Association," "P.A." or "Chartered."

- ◈ The number of shares of stock can be any number greater than zero. Most people use an even number like 100, 1,000 or 1,000,000. You should authorize more than you plan to issue so you can issue more later.

- ◈ The Principal Place of Business cannot be a post office box, or a commercial mail service. If you do not have a commercial location, this can be your home address.

- ◈ Your mailing address can be a post office box if you prefer to get your mail there.

- ◈ Registered Agent: The name of the registered agent and the address of the registered office along with the agents acceptance. Each corporation must have a registered agent and a registered office. The registered agent can by any individual or a corporation, the registered address can be the corporation's address. If the registered agent is another person, such as an attorney or accountant, then their return address would be the registered office.

The business address of the registered agent is considered the registered office of the corporation. Technically, it may not be a residence unless that address is also a business office of the corporation. Penalty for failure to comply is the inability to maintain a lawsuit and a fine of $5 per day up to $500.

→ The incorporator name, address, and signature, is the person filing the Articles of Incorporation. Usually it is the person forming the business, but it can be an attorney or other agent.

→ Normally your Corporate Purpose would be "any and all lawful business." (Why limit yourself?) However, if you are starting a Professional Service Corporation (doctor, lawyer, CPA, etc.), you need to limit the purpose to that profession.

→ The Correspondence Name and e-mail address is the person the Secretary of State will contact with your filing receipt and questions about your filing, if any.

→ You do not have to enter any officers or directors at this time. You can elect them later and list them next year on your annual business report. However, if you think that someone you will be dealing with may want to see some proof of who the officers are, then you can list them now.

Filing by Mail   You can file your **ARTICLES OF INCORPORATION** by mail as well as over the Internet. It usually takes at least a week to get them back. The one advantage is that you can include a photocopy and they return it with the filing date stamped on it. Some businesses consider this better proof of your existence than printing the web page off your computer.

You can use form 1, p.137 in Appendix C for a regular corporation or form 2, p.141 for a professional corporation. Fill in each item of information the same as explained above under electronic filing.

The **ARTICLES OF INCORPORATION** must be filed with the Secretary of State of Florida by sending them to:

Division of Corporations
Department of State
P. O. Box 6327
Tallahassee, FL 32314

You should mail them along with a **TRANSMITTAL LETTER** (form 1, p.137) and the filing fees. The fees are $70.00, including the filing fee ($35.00) and the designation of registered agent fee ($35.00). If you wish to receive a certified copy of the articles, the cost is $8.75. (This covers up to eight pages.) A certificate of status is available for an additional $8.75.

The return time for the articles is usually a week or two. If there is a need to have them back quickly, they may be sent by a courier, such as FedEx, with prepaid return. In such cases, they are filed the day received and returned shortly thereafter. The address for courier delivery is:

Secretary of State of Florida
Division of Corporations
Department of State
409 E. Gaines St.
Tallahassee, FL 32399

Articles of Correction

If you find you have made an error in the **ARTICLES OF INCORPORATION** you filed either online or by mail, you can correct it within ten business days by filing **ARTICLES OF CORRECTION** (see form 3, p.142). The filing fee is $35. It is $8.75 for a certified copy or certificate of status. (If you wait more than ten days, you must file **ARTICLES OF AMENDMENT TO ARTICLES OF INCORPORATION**. See Chapter 7 and form 4, p.145).

Shareholder Agreement

Whenever there are two or more shareholders in a corporation, they should consider drawing up a **SHAREHOLDER AGREEMENT** (form 35, p.217). This is a document that spells out the rights and obligations of the parties in the event disagreements come up. Even family corporations should consider a **SHAREHOLDER AGREEMENT**, since it could settle some issues without the expense of litigation.

Since a **SHAREHOLDER AGREEMENT** is a fairly complicated document, you should consider having one drafted by an attorney. (Be sure the attorney drafts it to fit your needs and does not just have an assistant print out a standard form.)

Some of the issues that are usually included in a **SHAREHOLDER AGREEMENT** are discussed below and a simple **SHAREHOLDER AGREEMENT** form is included in Appendix C. (see form 35, p.217.) This might suit your needs while your corporation is small. Be sure to review it as your company grows to be sure it still fits your needs.

When deciding on a **SHAREHOLDER AGREEMENT**, you will consider your options during the expansion of your company, but be sure to also consider the possibility of negative events, such as bankruptcy or death of a participant. These are the times when a **SHAREHOLDER AGREEMENT** is most needed.

Rights of Minority

The biggest risk in a small corporation with unequal ownership is that an owner of a minority interest will be shut out of decision-making. Unless some rights are spelled out in a **SHAREHOLDER AGREEMENT**, any shareholder with less than 50% interest risks having his or her investment tied up indefinitely. Many of the clauses in a **SHAREHOLDER AGREEMENT** address various rights (salary, withdrawal) of shareholders with a minority interest.

Supermajority Vote or Unanimous Consent

In order to allow shareholders with minority interests to have a say in major changes in the corporation, you can require unanimous consent or a larger than simple majority vote (*supermajority*) on such issues. One danger to keep in mind is that requiring unanimous consent can allow one disgruntled shareholder to sabotage the efforts of the majority.

Example: If the majority wants to sell the company, you would not want one shareholder with 10% interest to kill the deal. You should seek an agreement that can balance the rights of the majority and the minority. If a 10% owner is the only one who does not want to sell, then he or she can be given the right to buy out the other 90%.

Devoting Best Efforts

One problem that sometimes comes up in the life of a corporation is that one shareholder loses interest and no longer contributes the time that was originally expected. Or, a shareholder might become a part of a competing enterprise. To avoid disagreements you should spell out what is expected of each shareholder. You could spell out how many hours a week each person is expected to work, or you could just have a general agreement that each shareholder will devote his or her best efforts to the company.

Right to Serve as Director

A very effective protection for minority shareholders is the right of each to serve as a director. This enables them to take part in directors' meetings without being elected and to stay informed of activities of the corporation. However, being a director alone does not guarantee a right to control decisions.

Salary

If there is a chance that some of the shareholders will later vote themselves higher salaries than others, you can include an agreement as to what the salaries will be and include a requirement that any change must be agreed to by everyone or by more than a simple majority.

Nominating Officers and Employees

One common provision in a **SHAREHOLDER AGREEMENT** is to agree as to what office will be held by each shareholder. Any change could require unanimous consent or a supermajority vote. However, be sure to provide for the possibility that someone may become unable or unwilling to do the job.

Compulsory Buy-Out

A way to end a dispute between shareholders is to provide for a compulsory buy-out. This can be open-ended in which either party can buy out the other, or it can be specific in which one persons shares are subject to a buy-out. A formula for determining the buy-out price should be in the agreement to avoid disagreements later.

Transfer of Shares

Most small corporations limit the ability of shareholders to sell their shares. This protects the corporation from violations of securities laws and from persons whom they might not want as shareholders. A limitation on the ability to sell shares is usually combined with a buy-out plan.

Additional Shares   To maintain a balance of power among the shareholders it is important to have provisions covering the issuance of new shares or a merger with another corporation. Besides a clause that provides a majority or unanimous consent for decisions concerning these events, a provision to issue new shares on a *pro rata* basis can solve some situations.

Transfer of Substantial Assets   To protect the shareholder's value, a clause should be added that any transfer of substantial assets for any consideration other than cash is not allowed.

Endorsement   An *endorsement* on the shares that informs a potential transferee about the circumstance that the shares are subject to certain restrictions concerning their transfer. It warns the transferee and betters the chances of the corporation in case of a lawsuit on account of a transfer not being in accordance with the provisions of the **SHAREHOLDER AGREEMENT.**

Formalities   To avoid any misunderstanding, the formalities as to how the **SHAREHOLDER AGREEMENT** should be complied with can be included.

Arbitration   Because going to court is so expensive and can take years, it is a good idea to put an *arbitration* clause in your agreement. Arbitrators are often lawyers or former judges, so you get a decision similar to what you would have gotten court without the expense or delay.

Boilerplate   Most **SHAREHOLDER AGREEMENTS** contain standard legal *boilerplate* language, such as *Entire Agreement* (there are no verbal additions to this agreement), *Severability* (if one clause is invalid that would not be reason to throw out the entire agreement), and *Choice of Law* (which state's laws will be used to interpret the agreement).

Florida has specific rules on shareholder agreements. (Fla. Stat. Secs. 607.0731 and 607.0732.) The most important of these is that the existence of a **SHAREHOLDER AGREEMENT** must be noted on the stock certificates to make it binding on future transferees of the stock.

Organizational Paperwork

Every corporation must have **BYLAWS** and must maintain a set of minutes of its meetings. The **BYLAWS** must be adopted at the first meeting and the first minutes of the corporation will be of the organizational meeting.

Bylaws The **BYLAWS** (form 8, p.159)are the rules for organization and operation of the corporation and are required by Fla. Stat. Sec. 607.0206. Two sets of **BYLAWS** are included with this book. Form 8 is for simple corporations, and form 9 is for professional associations.

To complete form 8:

◈   Fill in the name of the corporation at the top blank.

◈   Write the city of the main office of the corporation, and the state in the Article I blanks.

◈   Write the proposed date and time of the annual meeting (this can be varied each year as needed) in Article II, Section 1.

◈   Fill in the number of directors to be on the board in Article III, Section 1.

◈   In Article VI, Section 1, fill in the blank for how many months the board has to issue a report.

◈   Articles XI and XII both require a state in the blanks. Most likely you will fill in Florida because you incorporated in Florida.

◈   The secretary will date and sign the form.

To complete form 9:

◈   Fill in the name of the corporation in the top blank.

◈   Write in the city of the corporation's main office in Article I.

◈   Write in the profession in Article II.

◈ Fill in the proposed date and time of the annual meeting in Article III, Section 2.

◈ Write the number of directors in Article IV, Section 2.

◈ Fill in the number of shares and the par value at Article VIII, Section 1.

◈ The secretary will sign and date the form.

Waiver of Notice

Before a meeting of the incorporators, the board of directors, or the shareholders can be held to transact lawful business, formal notice must be given to the parties ahead of time. Since small corporations often need to have meetings on short notice and do not want to be bothered with formal notices, it is customary to have all parties sign written **WAIVERS OF NOTICE**. Florida law allows the waiver to be signed at any time, even after the meeting has taken place, for both shareholders and for directors. (Fla. Stat., Secs. 607.0706 and 607.0823.) **WAIVERS OF NOTICE** are included in this book for the organizational meeting (form 6 for the shareholders), for the annual meetings (form 17 for directors and form 18 for shareholders), and special meetings (form 20 for the directors and form 22 for the shareholders).

Minutes

As part of the formal requirements of operating a corporation, a record of **MINUTES** must be kept of the meetings of shareholders and the board of directors. Usually only one meeting of each is required per year (the annual meeting) unless there is some special need for a meeting in the interim (such as the resignation of an officer). The first **MINUTES** that will be needed are the **MINUTES OF THE ORGANIZATIONAL MEETING OF INCORPORATORS AND DIRECTORS** of the corporation. (see form 7, p.156.) At this meeting, the officers and directors are elected; the Bylaws, corporate seal and stock certificates are adopted; and, other organizational decisions are made.

To complete form 7:

◈ Fill in the name of the corporation at the top blank.

◈ Write the date, address, and time of the meeting in the first blank.

◈ Write the names of all attendees in the second paragraph.

◈   In the fourth paragraph, write the name of the Incorporator that called the meeting, and the names of the elected chairperson and temporary secretary.

◈   In the fifth paragraph, write what state (most likely Florida) in which the articles were filed and the date they were filed.

◈   Next, write the names of the Board of Directors next to their respective titles of President, Vice President, Secretary and Treasurer.

◈   On page two, affix the corporate seal at the top right side.

◈   In the paragraph beginning with RESOLVED, write in the blanks the bank that will hold the corporate accounts. In the last blank of that paragraph write in how many signatures of authority are required to make transactions with the bank account. Then list in the blanks below that all those that potentially has the authority to make transactions.

◈   In the second to the last paragraph on that page, check one of the boxes at item 2. Indicating C or S status of the corporation.

◈   On page 3, list the names of the board of directors.

◈   Next, list in the three columns who wants to buy shares, how many shares, and the total of what they will owe. (Example: John Smith, 100 shares, $100 if the shares were $1.00 each.)

◈   The President and Secretary (not the chairperson and temporary secretary) should sign and date the form.

Resolutions   When the board of directors or shareholders make major decisions, it is usually done in the form of a resolution. At the organizational meeting ,one important resolution is choosing a bank with a **Banking Resolution.** (see form 10, p.169.) Another is **Resolution (Adopting S Corporation Status).** (see form 15, p.183.) If the organizers have spent their own money to organize the corporation, a **Resolution to Reimburse Expenses** can be used to allow the corporation, to repay them. (see form 12, p.173.)

Waiver of Meeting   Florida law allows corporate officers to execute incorporation papers without a meeting. It is better to have a formal meeting to prove to possible future creditors that you conducted the corporation in a formal manner. (Fla. Stat., Sec. 607.0205(2))

Tax Forms

IRS Form SS-4 (Employer Identification Number)   Prior to opening a bank account for the corporation, you will need to obtain an **EMPLOYER IDENTIFICATION NUMBER (EIN)** (form 5, p.147) that is the corporate equivalent of a social security number. You can do so by mail, fax, over the phone, or over the Internet. By mail it takes weeks, by fax you may never hear from them, and the Internet filing is not always working, so the most reliable way is over thc phone. Depending on who answers the phone at the IRS, you may get your number in twenty minutes or within a couple days.

However you obtain your EIN, you will need to supply the information on **IRS FORM SS-4** (see form 5, p.147). You need to fill it out even if you phone, because they may ask you to fax it to them.

The contacts for obtaining the EIN are:

EIN Operation
Holtsville, NY 00501
866-816-2065
631-447-8960
www.irs.gov/businesses/small/article/0,,id=102767,00.html

When you apply for this number, you will probably be put on the mailing list for other corporate tax forms. If you do not receive these, you should call your local IRS forms number and request the forms for new businesses. These include Circular E explaining the taxes due, the IRS W-4 forms for each employee, the tax deposit coupons, and the IRS Form 941 quarterly return for withholding.

Form 2553 (S Corporation)   If you wish to elect S corporation tax status for your corporation (see Chapter 3), you must file **ELECTION BY A SMALL BUSINESS CORPORATION (IRS FORM 2553)** with the IRS within seventy-five days of incorporation. (see form 14, p.177.) As a practical matter you should sign and file this at your incorporation meeting; otherwise, you may forget. To make the S corporation status *official* you should also adopt a corporate **RESOLUTION (ADOPTING S CORPORATION STATUS)** and keep it in your minute book. (see form 15, p.183.)

***Form DR-1
(States Sales Tax
Registration)***

If you will be selling or renting goods or services at retail, you must collect Florida Sales and Use Tax. Some services such as doctors' and lawyers' fees and newspaper advertising are not taxed, but most others are. If you have any doubt, check with the Florida Department of Revenue.

First you must register to collect the tax. This is done by filing form DR-1 with the Florida Department of Revenue. You can obtain the form by calling 850-488-8422, or from this website:

www.myflorida.com/dor/forms/

You can also file electronically at this website:

www.myflorida.com/dor/forms/register.html

After you obtain your tax number, you will be required to collect sales tax on all purchases. In some cases, new businesses are required to post a bond to insure taxes are paid. Tax returns must be filed monthly. After a year, if your taxes are low, you may be allowed to remit only quarterly.

***Florida Income
Tax***

Florida has a state income tax that applies to corporations that are not S corporations, but you must let the Florida Department of Revenue know that your corporation is an S corporation or they will assume that you are not. To do this, you must file a Florida corporate tax return for the first year the corporation is in business and include the statement that you are an S corporation.

Corporate Supplies

Corporate Kits

A corporation needs to keep a permanent record of its legal affairs. This includes:

✪ the original charter;

✪ minutes of all meetings;

✪ records of the stock issued, transferred, and cancelled;

✪ fictitious names registered; and,

✪ any other legal matters.

The records are usually kept in a ring binder. Any ring binder will do, but it is possible to purchase a specially prepared corporate kit that has the name of the corporation printed on it and usually contains forms such as minutes, stock certificates, etc. Most of these items are included with this book, so purchasing such a kit is unnecessary unless you want to have a fancy leather binder or specially printed stock certificates.

Some sources for corporate kits are:

Blumberg Excelsior
4435 Old Winter Garden Road
P. O. Box 2122, Orlando, FL 32802
407- 299-8220
800-327-9220
Fax: 407-291-6912
www.blumberg.com/index2.html

Corpex
1440 Fifth Avenue
Bay Shore, NY 11706
800-221-8181
631-968-0277
Fax: 800-826-7739
631-968-0397
Email: Corpex@CorpexNet.com
www.corpexnet.com

CorpKit Legal Supplies
46 Taft Avenue
Islip, NY 11751-2112
888-888-9120
Fax: 888-777-4617
Email: info@corpkit.com
www.corpkit.com

Corporate Seal   One thing that is not included with this book is a *corporate seal*. This must be specially made for each corporation. Most corporations use a metal seal like a notary's seal to emboss the paper. These can be ordered from many office supply companies. In recent years, many have been using rubber stamps for corporate seals. These are cheaper, lighter, and easier to read. Rubber stamp seals can also be ordered from office supply stores, printers, and specialized rubber stamp companies. The corporate seal should contain the full, exact name of the corporation, the word "SEAL" and the year of incorporation. It may be round or rectangular.

Stock Florida corporations are no longer required to issue **STOCK CERTIFICATES** (see
Certificates and form 34, p.207) to represent shares of ownership. (Fla. Stat., Sec. 607.0625.)
Offers to However, as a practical matter, it is a good idea to do so. Doing so shows some
Purchase Stock formality and gives each person tangible evidence of ownership. If you do issue shares, the face of each certificate must show:

✪   the corporate name;

✪   that the corporation was organized under Florida law;

✪   the name of the shareholder(s); and,

✪   the number, class, and series of the stock.

The certificate must be signed by one or more officers designated by the **BYLAWS** or the board of directors.

If there are two or more classes or series of stock, the front or back of the certificate must disclose that upon request and without charge the corporation will provide to the shareholder the preferences, limitations, and relative rights of each class or series; the preferences of any preferred stock; and the board of directors' authority to determine rights for any subsequent classes or series. If there are any restrictions, they must be stated on the certificate, or a statement must be included that they are available without charge.

The **STOCK CERTIFICATES** can be fancy, with engraved eagles for example, or they can be typed or even handwritten. **STOCK CERTIFICATE** forms are included at the end of this book. (see form 34, p.207.) For professional associations, the following statement should be typed on the certificate:

"The transfer of the shares represented by this certificate is restricted by the bylaws of the corporation."

Before any stock is issued, the purchaser should submit an **OFFER TO PURCHASE STOCK.** (see form 11, p.171.) The offer states that it is made pursuant to IRS Code 1244. The advantage of this section is that in the event the business fails or the value of the stock drops, the shareholder can write-off up to $50,000 ($100,000 for married couples) as ordinary income, rather than as a long term capital lose which would be limited to $3,000 a year.

Some thought should be given to the way in which the ownership of the stock will be held. Stock owned in one person's name alone is subject to probate upon death. Making two persons joint owners of the stock (joint tenants with full rights of survivorship) would avoid probate upon the death of one of them. However, taking a joint owner's name off in the event of a disagreement (such as divorce) could be troublesome.

Where a couple jointly operates a business, joint ownership would be best. But where one person is the sole party involved in the business the desire to avoid probate should be weighed against the risk of losing half the business in a divorce. Another way to avoid probate is to put ownership of the stock in a living trust.

Organizational Meeting

The real birth of the corporation takes place at the initial meeting of the incorporators and the original board of directors. At this meeting the stock is issued and the officers and board of directors are elected. Other business may also take place, such as opting for S corporation status or adopting employee benefit plans.

Usually **MINUTES, STOCK CERTIFICATES**, tax, and other forms are prepared before the organizational meeting and used as a script for the meeting. They are then signed at the end of the meeting. Otherwise, they may be forgotten until it is too late.

The agenda for the initial meeting is usually as follows:

✪ signing the **WAIVER OF NOTICE OF THE ORGANIZATIONAL MEETING** (form 6);

✪ noting persons present;

✪ presentation and acceptance of articles of incorporation (the copy returned by the Secretary of State);

✪ election of Directors;

✪ adoption of **BYLAWS** (form 8 or form 9);

✪ election of officers;

✪ presentation and acceptance of corporate seal;

✪ presentation and acceptance of **STOCK CERTIFICATE** (form 34);

✪ designation of bank with **BANKING RESOLUTION** (form 10);

✪ acceptance of **OFFERS TO PURCHASE STOCK** (form 11);

✪ (Use form 13, **BILL OF SALE**, if property is traded for stock.);

✪ resolution to pay expenses;

✪ adoption of special resolutions such as S corporation status (form 15); and,

✪ adjournment.

At the end of the meeting, the stock certificates are usually issued, but in some cases, such as when a prospective shareholder does not yet have money to pay for them, they are issued when paid for.

To issue the stock, the certificates at the end of this book should be completed by adding the name of the corporation, a statement that the corporation is organized under the laws of Florida, the number of shares the certificate represents, and the person to whom the certificate is issued. Each certificate should be numbered in order to keep track of them.

A record of the stock issuance should be made on the **STOCK TRANSFER LEDGER**. (see form 32, p.203.) It should also be made on the **STOCK CERTIFICATE STUBS**. (see form 33, p.205) The **STOCK CERTIFICATE STUBS** should be cut apart on the dotted lines, punched and inserted in the ring binder.

Minute Book

After the organizational meeting, you should set up your minute book. As noted on page _, this can be a fancy leather book or a simple ring binder. The minute book usually contains the following:

- ✪   a title page ("Corporate Records of _____");

- ✪   a table of contents;

- ✪   the letter from the Secretary of State acknowledging receipt and filing of the articles of incorporation;

- ✪   copy of the **ARTICLES OF INCORPORATION**;

- ✪   copy of any fictitious name registration;

- ✪   copy of any trademark registration;

- ✪   **WAIVER OF NOTICE OF THE ORGANIZATIONAL MEETING**;

- ✪   **MINUTES OF THE ORGANIZATIONAL MEETING OF INCORPORATORS AND DIRECTORS**;

- ✪   **BYLAWS**;

- ✪   sample **STOCK CERTIFICATE**;

- ✪   **OFFER TO PURCHASE STOCK**;

✪ tax forms:

•**IRS FORM SS-4** and Employer Identification Number certificate,

•**IRS FORM 2553** and acceptance, and

•Florida Form DR-1 and state tax number certificate;

✪ **STOCK TRANSFER LEDGER**; and,

✪ **STOCK CERTIFICATE STUBS**.

Bank Accounts

A corporation must have a bank account. Checks payable to a corporation cannot be cashed. They must be deposited into an account.

Fees   Unfortunately, many banks charge higher rates to corporations for the right to put their money in the bank. You can tell how much extra a corporation is being charged when you compare a corporate account to a personal account with similar activity.

Example: For similar balance and activity, an individual might earn $6.00 interest for the month while a corporation pays $40.00 in bank fees. Surely the bank is not losing money on every personal account. Therefore, the corporate account is simply generating $46.00 more in profit for the bank.

Fortunately, some banks have set up reasonable fees for small corporations such as charging no fees if a balance of $1000 or $2500 is maintained. Because the fees can easily amount to hundreds of dollars a year, it pays to shop around.

Another way to save money in bank charges is to order checks from a private source rather than through the bank. These are usually much cheaper than those the bank offers because the bank makes a profit on the check printing. If the bank officer does not like the idea when you are opening the account, just wait until your first batch runs out and switch over without telling the bank. They probably will not even notice, as long as you get the checks printed correctly.

While most *business checks* are large (and expensive), there is no reason you cannot use small *personal size* checks for your business.

Documents All you should need to open a corporate bank account is a copy of your **ARTICLES OF INCORPORATION** (see form 1, p.137) and your federal tax identification number. Some banks, however, want more.

If you have trouble opening the account, you can use the **BANKING RESOLUTION** included with this book, or you can make up a similar form. (see form 10, p.169.)

Licenses

Counties and municipalities are authorized to levy a license tax on the *privilege* of doing business. Before opening your business, you should obtain a *county occupational license*, and if you will be working within a city, a *city occupational license*. Businesses that perform work in several cities, such as builders, must obtain a license from each city they work in. This does not have to be done until you actually begin a job in a particular city.

County occupational licenses can be obtained from the tax collector in the county courthouse. City licenses are usually available at city hall. Be sure to find out if zoning allows your type of business before buying or leasing property because the licensing departments will check the zoning before issuing your license.

Problems occasionally arise when persons attempt to start a business in their home. Small new businesses cannot afford to pay rent for commercial space and cities often try to forbid business in residential areas. Getting a county occupational license often gives notice to the city that a business is being conducted in a residential area.

Some people avoid the problem by starting their businesses without occupational licenses, figuring that the penalties are nowhere near the cost of office space. Others get the county license and ignore the city rules. If a person has commercial trucks and equipment parked on his property, there will probably be complaints by neighbors and the city will most likely take legal action. But if a person's business consists merely of making phone calls out of the home and keeping supplies inside the house, the problem may never come up.

Home Businesses

However, court battles with a city are expensive and probably not worth the effort for a small business. The best course of action is to keep a low profile. Using a post office box is sometimes helpful in diverting attention away from the residence. However, the Secretary of State and the occupational license administrator will want a street address. There should be no problem using a residential address and explaining to the city that it is merely the corporate address and that no business is conducted on the premises.

5 SELLING CORPORATE STOCK

Securities Laws

The issuance of securities is subject to both federal and state securities laws. A *security* is stock in the company (*common* and *preferred*) and debt (notes, bonds, etc.). The laws covering securities are so broad that any instrument that represents an investment in an enterprise, where the investor is relying on the efforts of others for profit, is considered a security. Even a *promissory note* has been held to be a security. Once an investment is determined to involve a security, strict rules apply. There can be criminal penalties, and civil damages can also be awarded to purchasers, if the rules are not followed.

The rules are designed to protect people who put up money as an investment in a business. In the stock market crash in the 1930s, many people lost their life savings in swindles, and the government wants to be sure that it will not happen again. Unfortunately, the laws can also make it difficult to raise capital for many honest businesses.

The goal of the laws covering sales of securities is that investors be given full disclosure of the risks involved in an investment. To accomplish this, the law usually requires that the securities must either be registered with the federal

Securities and Exchange Commission (SEC) and/or a similar state regulatory body, and that lengthy disclosure statements be compiled and distributed.

The law is complicated and strict compliance is required. The penalties are so harsh that some lawyers will not handle securities matters. You most likely would not be able to get through the registration process on your own. But, like your decision to incorporate without a lawyer, you may wish to consider some alternatives when attempting to raise capital without a lawyer.

One option is to borrow the money as a personal loan from friends or relatives. The disadvantage is that you will have to pay them back personally if the business fails. However, you may have to do that anyway if they are close relatives or if you don't follow the securities laws.

Another option is to tailor your stock issuance to fall within the exemptions in the securities laws. There are some exemptions in the securities laws for small businesses that may apply to your transaction. (The anti-fraud provisions always apply, even if the transaction is exempt from registration.) Some exemptions are explained below, but you should make at least one appointment with a securities lawyer to be sure you have covered everything and that there have not been any changes in the law. Often you can pay for an hour or so of a securities lawyer's time for $100 or $200 and just ask questions about your plans. He or she can tell you what not to do and what your options are. Then you can make an informed decision.

For an explanation of Florida Securities law, a good book is *Florida Small Business Practice*, published by the Florida Bar CLE division. It should be available in most law libraries. For technical laws and regulations of all fifty states, see the *Blue Sky Reporter* also available at most law libraries.

Federal Exemptions from Securities Laws

In most situations where one person, a husband and wife, or a few partners run a business, and all parties are active in the enterprise, securities laws do not apply to their issuance of stock to themselves. These are the simple corporations that are the subject of this book. As a practical matter, if your father or aunt wants to put up some money for some stock in your business, you probably will not get in trouble. They probably will not seek triple damages and criminal penalties if your business fails.

However, you may wish to obtain money from additional investors to enable your business to grow. This can be done in many circumstances as long as you follow the rules carefully. In some cases, you do not have to file anything with the SEC but in others you must file some sort of notice.

Private Offering

If in selling stock you meet any of the following guidelines, your business may fall into the *private offering* exemption.

✪ All persons to whom offers are made are financially astute, are participants in the business, or have a substantial net worth.

✪ No advertising or general solicitation is used to promote the stock.

✪ The number of persons to whom the offers are made is limited.

✪ The shares are purchased for investment and not for immediate resale.

✪ The persons to whom the stock is offered are given all relevant information (including financial information) regarding the corporation and the issuance of stock.

✪ A filing claiming the exemption is made upon the United States Securities and Exchange Commission.

There are numerous court cases explaining each aspect of these rules, including such questions as what is a *financially astute* person.

Intrastate Offering

If you only offer your securities to residents of one state, you may be exempt from federal securities laws. This is because federal laws usually only apply to interstate commerce. Intrastate offerings are covered by SEC Rule 147 and if it is followed carefully, your sale will be exempt from federal registration.

Small Offerings

In recent years the SEC has liberalized the rules in order to make it easier for businesses to grow. Under *Regulation D*, adopted by the Securities and Exchange Commission, there are three types of exemptions under Rules 504, 505, and 506:

✪ The offering of securities of up to $1,000,000 in a twelve-month period can be exempt under SEC Rule 504. Offers can be made to any number of persons, no specific information must be provided, and investors do not have to be sophisticated.

✪ Under Rule 505, the offering of up to $5,000,000 can be made in a twelve-month period, but no public advertising may be used and only thirty-five non-accredited investors may purchase stock. Any number of accredited investors may purchase stock. Accredited investors are sophisticated individuals with high net worth or high income, large trusts or investment companies, or persons involved in the business.

✪ Rule 506 has no limit on the amount of money that may be raised. Like Rule 505, it does not allow advertising and limits non-accredited investors to thirty-five.

Florida Securities Laws

Unfortunately, the simplification of federal requirements has not been accompanied by similar changes at the state level. Florida and most states still have much stricter requirements for the issuance of securities. There is a movement to change the laws, but for now the only way to avoid the Florida registration procedures is to qualify for the Florida private placement.

Private Placement Exemption

Private placement exemption can apply if *all* of the following conditions are true:

✪ there are thirty-five or fewer purchasers of shares;

✪ no commissions are paid to anyone to promote the stock unless that person is a registered securities dealer;

✪ no advertising or general solicitation is used to promote the stock;

✪ all material information (including financial information) regarding the stock issuance and the company is given to or accessible to all shareholders; and,

✪ when sales are made to five or more persons, a three day right of recision is given.

These rules may sound simple on the surface, but there are many more rules, regulations, and court cases explaining each one in more detail. For example, what does *thirty-five persons* mean? Sounds simple, but it can mean more than thirty-five persons. Spouses, persons whose net worth exceeds a million dollars, and founders of the corporation may not be counted in some circumstances. Each state has its own *blue sky* requirements and exemptions. If you are going to raise money from investors, check with a qualified securities lawyer.

As you can see, the exemption does not give you much latitude in raising money. Therefore, for most issuances you will have to register.

Internet Stock Sales

With the Internet, promoters of stock have a new way of reaching large numbers of people, most of whom are financially able to afford investments in securities. However, all securities laws also apply to the Internet and they are being enforced. Recently state attorneys general have issued cease and desist orders to promoters not registered in their states.

Under current law, you must be registered in a state in order to sell stock to its residents. If you are not registered in a state, you must turn down any residents from that state who want to buy your stock.

Payment for Shares

When issuing stock, it is important that full payment be made by the purchasers. If the shares have a par value and the payment is in cash, then the cash must not be less than the par value. In most states, promissory notes cannot be used in payment for shares. The shares must not be issued until the payment has been received by the corporation.

Trading Property for Shares

In many cases, organizers of a corporation have property they want to contribute for use in starting up the business. This is often the case where an on-going business is incorporated. To avoid future problems, the property should be traded at a fair value for the shares. The directors should pass a resolution stating that they agree with the value of the property. When the stock certificate is issued in exchange for the property, a **BILL OF SALE** (see form 13, p.175.) should be executed by the owner of the property detailing everything that is being exchanged for the stock.

Taxable Transactions

In cases where property is exchanged for something of value, such as stock, there is often income tax due as if there had been a sale of the property. Fortunately, Section 351 of the IRS Code allows tax-free exchange of property for stock if the persons receiving the stock for the property or for cash *end up owning* at least 80% of the voting and other stock in the corporation. If more than 20% of the stock is issued in exchange for services instead of property and cash, then the transfers of property will be taxable and treated as a sale for cash.

Trading Services for Shares

In some cases, the founders of a corporation wish to issue stock to one or more persons in exchange for their services to the corporation. It has always been possible to issue shares for services that have previously been performed. Some states make it unlawful to issue shares for promises to perform services in the future. Check your corporation's statutes with regard to this.

Florida's Division of Securities

For answers to specific questions on Florida securities registration you can contact:

Florida Department of Financial Services
Division of Securities
200 East Gaines Street
Tallahassee, FL 32399-0300
850-413-9805
www.fldfs.com/Consumers/Local_Offices

6 RUNNING A CORPORATION

Day-to-Day Activities

There are not many differences between running a corporation and any other type of business. The most important point to remember is to keep the corporation separate from your personal affairs. Do not be continuously making loans to yourself from corporate funds and do not commingle funds.

Another important point to remember is to always refer to the corporation as a corporation. Always use the designation *Inc.* or *Corp.* on everything. Always sign corporate documents with your corporate title. If you do not, you may lose your protection from liability. There have been many cases where a person forgot to put *pres.* after his name and was held personally liable for a corporate debt.

Corporate Records

Minutes   Florida Statutes require that a corporation keep a permanent record of minutes of the proceedings of its shareholders and board of directors, a record of all actions taken by the shareholders or board of directors without a meeting, and a record of all actions taken by a committee of the board of directors on behalf of the corporation." (Fla. Stat. Sec. 607.1601(l).)

Accounting Records

Accurate accounting records must be kept by the corporation. (Fla. Stat. Sec. 607.1601(2).)

Record of Shareholder

The corporation must also keep a record of its shareholders including the names and addresses and the number, class, and series of shares owned. (Fla. Stat. Sec. 607.1601(3).) This can be kept at the registered office, principal place of business or office of its stock transfer agent (if any). **THE STOCK TRANSFER LEDGER** form 32, p.203, can be used for this purpose.

Corporate Documents

The corporation must maintain copies of its **ARTICLES OF INCORPORATION**, form 1, p.137 and all amendments, **BYLAWS** (see form 8, p.159) and all amendments, resolutions regarding stock rights, minutes of shareholders' meetings and records of actions taken without a meeting for the last three years, written communications to all shareholders for the last three years, financial statements furnished to shareholders for the last three years, names and addresses of all current directors and officers, and the most recent annual report.

Form of Records

The minutes may be in writing or in any other form capable of being converted into written form within a reasonable time. This would mean that they could be kept in a computer or possibly on a videotape. However, it is always best to keep at least one written copy. Accidents can easily erase magnetic media.

Examination of Records

Any shareholder of a corporation has the right to examine and copy the corporation's books and records after giving written notice at least five business days before the date on which he or she wishes to inspect and copy them. (Fla. Stat. Sec. 607.1602.)

The shareholder may have an attorney or agent examine the records and may receive photocopies of the records. (Fla. Stat. Sec. 607.1603.) The corporation may charge a reasonable fee for making photocopies. If the records are not in written form, the corporation must convert them to written form. The corporation must bear the cost of:

✪ converting the **ARTICLES OF INCORPORATION** and any amendments, Bylaws, and amendments;

✪ resolutions by the board of directors creating different rights in the stock;

✪ minutes of all shareholders' meetings and records of any action taken by the shareholders without a meeting for the past three years;

✪ written communications to all shareholders generally or of any class, names and addresses of all officers and directors; and,

✪ the most recent annual report filed with the Secretary of State.

The shareholder must pay for converting any other records.

If the corporation refuses to allow a shareholder to examine the records, then the shareholder may get an order from the Circuit Court, and in such case the corporation would have to pay the shareholder' costs and attorney fees. (Fla. Stat., Sec. 607.1604.)

Balance Sheet   Unless the shareholders pass a resolution to the contrary within 120 days of the close of each fiscal year, the corporation must furnish its shareholders with financial statements including an end of the year balance sheet and yearly income and cash flow statements. (Fla. Stat. Sec. 607.1620.)

Shareholder Meetings

Each year the corporation must hold an annual meeting of the shareholders. These meetings may be formal and held in a restaurant or they may be informal and held in the swimming pool. A sole officer and director can hold the meeting without reciting all the verbiage or taking a formal vote. But the important thing is that the meetings are held and that minutes are kept. Regular minutes and meetings are evidence that the corporation is legitimate if the issue ever comes up in court. **MINUTE** forms for the annual meetings are included with this book. (see form 19, p.187.) You can use them as master copies to photocopy each year, changing the date and other old information.

Special Meetings   When important decisions must be made by the shareholders between the annual meetings, the corporation can hold special meetings. For these you can use **MINUTES OF SPECIAL MEETING OF SHAREHOLDERS.** (see form 21, p.189.)

Under the procedures of Florida Statutes, Section 607.0704, action may be taken by the shareholders without a formal meeting. However, for a small corporation it is best to use formal meetings in case someone later tries to *pierce the corporate veil.*

Notice of Meetings

Under Florida law, shareholders with voting rights must be notified of the date, time, and place of annual and special meetings at least ten but not more than sixty days prior. (Fla. Stat., Secs. 607.0705 and 607.0706.) No description of the purpose of an *annual* meeting need be given, but the purpose for a *special* meeting must be stated in the notice.

A shareholder may waive notice either before or after the meeting if done in writing and included in the minutes. Unless a shareholder objects, attendance at a meeting waives objection to the notice or lack thereof. Use **WAIVER OF NOTICE OF SPECIAL MEETING OF SHAREHOLDERS.** (see form 22, p.190.)

Voting

The following rules apply to voting at the shareholders' meeting:

- ✪ unless otherwise provided in the articles of incorporation or bylaws, a quorum consists of a majority of the shares entitled to vote (Fla. Stat., Sec. 607.0725(1));

- ✪ once a share is represented at a meeting for any purpose it is deemed present for quorum purposes for the rest of the meeting (Fla. Stat., Sec. 607.0725(2));

- ✪ holders of a majority of the shares represented may adjourn the meeting (Fla. Stat., Sec. 607.0725(4)); and,

- ✪ the **ARTICLES OF INCORPORATION** may authorize a quorum of less than a majority but it may not be less than one-third (Fla. Stat., Sec. 607.0725(5)).

Voting for Directors

Unless otherwise provided in the **ARTICLES OF INCORPORATION**, directors are elected by a plurality of votes. Shareholders do not have a right to cumulative voting unless provided in the articles.

Board of Directors' Meetings

Normally, a corporation's board of directors must hold a meeting once each year. These meetings may be formal or informal. A sole officer and director can hold the meeting without reciting all the verbiage or taking a formal vote. But the important thing is that the meetings are held and that minutes are kept. Regular minutes and meetings are evidence that the corporation is legitimate if the issue ever comes up in court. A **MINUTES OF THE ANNUAL MEETINGS OF THE BOARD OF DIRECTORS** is included with this book. (see form 17, p.185.) You can use it as a master copy to photocopy each year. All that needs to be changed is the date, unless you change officers or directors or need to take some other corporate action.

Special Meetings

When important decisions must be made by the board of directors between the annual meetings, the corporation can hold special meetings. **MINUTES OF SPECIAL MEETING OF THE BOARD OF DIRECTORS** is in Appendix C. (see form 20, p.188.)

Action without a Meeting

Under the procedures of Florida Statutes, Section 607.0821, action may be taken by the directors without a formal meeting as long as there are written consents to the action taken. However, for a small corporation it is best to use formal meetings in case someone later tries to *pierce the corporate veil*.

Notice of Meetings

Under Florida law, regular meetings of the board of directors may be held without notice unless the **ARTICLES OF INCORPORATION** or **BYLAWS** provide otherwise. (Fla. Stat. Secs. 607.0822 and 607.0823) Special meetings must be preceded by at least two days notice of the time, date, and place unless the articles or bylaws provide for a longer or shorter period. Use **WAIVER OF NOTICE OF SPECIAL MEETING OF THE BOARD OF DIRECTORS.** (see form 21, p.189.)

Voting

The following rules apply to voting at the directors' meeting.

✪ Unless otherwise provided in the **ARTICLES OF INCORPORATION** or **BYLAWS**, a quorum consists of a majority of the number of directors prescribed in the articles or bylaws.

✪ The **ARTICLES OF INCORPORATION** may authorize a *quorum* of less than a majority but it may not be less than one-third. (A quorum is the number of people necessary for business to be conducted.)

✪ If a quorum is present for a vote, a vote by a majority of those present constitutes an act of the board of directors unless otherwise provided in the articles or bylaws.

✪ A director present at a meeting of the board or a committee is deemed to have assented to an action taken unless he or she objects at the beginning of the meeting or the vote to the meeting or the business, or votes against or abstains from voting.

Committees   Unless prohibited by the **BYLAWS**, the board of directors may designate a committee of its members that can exercise all authority of the board except that it may not:

✪ approve or recommend actions which by law must be approved by the shareholders;

✪ fill vacancies on the board or committees thereof;

✪ adopt, repeal, or amend the bylaws;

✪ authorize reacquisition of shares except under a formula approved by the board; or,

✪ authorize sale of shares or shareholder rights except within limits set by the board.

Also, meeting rules of committees must comply with the rules for the board itself. Each committee must have at least two members and alternate members may be designated. Setting up a committee does not relieve a member of his or her duty to act in good faith and in the best interests of the corporation.

Annual Reports

Each year every corporation must file an annual report. The name of this form was recently changed to the *Uniform Business Report*. Fortunately, this is a simple one-page form that is sent to the corporation by the Secretary of State and usually merely has to be signed. It contains such information as the federal tax identification number, officers' and directors' names and addresses, the registered agent's name and the address of the registered office. It must be signed and returned by May 1st. If you fail to return the report by the due date, then the corporation is dissolved after notice is given by the Secretary of State.

The fee at the time of this publication is $150. Be sure to file your report on time. The penalty for late filing is $400. If your corporation has been dissolved and must be reinstated, there is a $600 reinstatement fee.

Tax Returns

A complete explanation of all of the tax filing requirements is beyond the scope of this book, but the following chart will help you keep track of most of the deadlines:

Florida Taxes

Requirements	Deadlines
✗ Sales and Use:	20th of each month
✗ Intangible:	June 30th
✗ Tangible Payment:	March 31st
✗ Tangible Report:	April 1st
✗ Corporate Income: (C corporations)	April 1st
✗ Unemployment:	Jan. 31st, April 30th, July 31st, Oct. 31st

Federal Taxes

Requirements	Deadlines
✗ Withholding: (Form 941)	Jan. 31st, April 30th, July 31st, Oct. 31st
✗ Income Tax: (Form 1120 or 1120S)	March 15th
✗ Unemployment: (Form 940)	Jan. 31st
(Form 508):	Jan. 31st, April 30th, July 31st, Oct. 31st
✗ Annual Reports: (Form W-2, 1099):	Jan. 31st
(Form W-3):	Feb. 28th

7 | AMENDING A CORPORATION

Occasionally, a corporation will find that its documents do not meet its current needs. To solve this, they can be amended, but the amendments must be done in compliance with Florida law.

Articles of Incorporation

Because the **ARTICLES OF INCORPORATION** included in this book are so basic, they will rarely have to be amended. The only reasons for amending them would be to change the name or the number of shares of stock, or to add some special clause such as a higher than majority voting requirement for directors as provided in Florida Statutes, Section 607.0728(1).

If the amendment is made before any shares are issued, it may be done by the incorporator or directors by filing *articles of amendment* signed by the incorporators or director stating the name of the corporation, the amendment and date adopted, and a statement that it is made before any shares were issued.

If the amendment is made after shares have been issued, the articles of amendment must be signed by the president or vice president, and the secretary or assistant secretary. The articles of amendment must contain the name of the corporation, the amendments, the date of adoption by the shareholders, and, if the change affects the outstanding shares, a statement of how the change will be effected.

The **ARTICLES OF AMENDMENT TO ARTICLES OF INCORPORATION** (form 1, p.137)must be filed with the Secretary of State along with the filing fee of $35. The procedure for amending corporate articles depends upon who is doing the amending and at what point in time the amendment is adopted. For more information, refer to Florida Statutes, Sections 607.1001 through 607.1009, included in Appendix B of this book.

Bylaws

The shareholders may always amend the **BYLAWS**. The board of directors may amend the **BYLAWS** unless the **ARTICLES OF INCORPORATION** state otherwise or unless the shareholders provide that the **BYLAWS** may not be amended by the board. (Fla. Stat., Sec. 607.1020.)

The **ARTICLES OF INCORPORATION** may allow a bylaw that requires a greater quorum or voting requirement for shareholders but such a requirement may not be adopted, amended, or repealed by the board of directors. (Fla. Stat., Sec. 607.1021.)

A bylaw that fixes a greater quorum or voting requirement for the board of directors that was adopted by the shareholders may be amended or repealed only by the shareholders, but if it was adopted by the board, it may be amended or repealed by the board. (Fla. Stat., Sec. 607.1022.)

Registered Agent
or Registered Office

To change the registered agent or registered office, a form must be sent to the Secretary of State with the fee of $35. This form called **STATEMENT OF CHANGE OF REGISTERED OFFICE OR REGISTERED AGENT OR BOTH FOR CORPORATIONS** is included in this book. (see form 31, p.202.) This form can be used to change both the registered agent and the registered office, or to just change one of them. If you are changing just one, such as the agent, then list the registered office as both the old address and the new address. If a registered agent wishes to resign even if no replacement has been named, he or she can use the **RESIGNATION OF REGISTERED AGENT**. (see form 29, p.200.)

NOTE: *The fee for this is $87.50. That is much more than replacing the registered agent.*

Officers and Directors

Usually officers and directors are replaced by having an election for new ones. But if an officer or director wishes to resign before the end of a term, you can use the **OFFICER/DIRECTOR RESIGNATION**. (see form 27, p.198.)

8 | DISSOLVING A CORPORATION

Automatic Dissolution

If your corporation has ceased to do business and you no longer need to keep it active, there is no reason to take any special action to dissolve it, because it will be automatically dissolved if you fail to file your annual report. Be sure that you will not need the corporation again, because the fees for reinstatement are very high.

If your corporation has some debts that it is unable to pay at the time of dissolution, then you would be better off formally dissolving the corporation or having it file bankruptcy.

Formal Dissolution

An advantage of formal dissolution is that if you give proper notice to creditors, after a period of time there is no risk that they can come back against the directors.

To formally dissolve a corporation, **ARTICLES OF DISSOLUTION** (see form 24, p.193)must be filed with the Secretary of State. If the corporation has not issued shares or commenced business, the **ARTICLES OF DISSOLUTION** must be authorized by a majority of the incorporators or directors and signed by the chairman or vice chairman of the board of directors, or by an officer. If there are no officers or directors, then by an incorporator. If shares have been issued, then the **ARTICLES OF DISSOLUTION** must be authorized by the shareholders and signed by the chairman or vice chairman of the board of directors, or by an officer. (see form 25, p.195.)

Bankruptcy

If your corporation is in debt beyond its means, it can file for bankruptcy. Chapter 7 bankruptcy is for liquidation and Chapter 11 for reorganization of debts.

If the debts are small and there is little chance the creditors will pursue collection, then bankruptcy is unnecessary. You can allow the state to dissolve the corporation for failure to file the annual report. However, if the debts are large and you fear the creditors will attempt to collect the debt from the officers or directors, you should go through formal bankruptcy and/or dissolution. Such a scenario is beyond the scope of this book. You should consult an attorney or bankruptcy text for further guidance. (See also *For Further Reference.*)

Glossary

A

annual report. A document filed by a corporation or limited liability company each year usually listing the officers, directors, and registered agent.

articles of incorporation. The document that demonstrates the organization of a corporation, called certificate of incorporation in some states.

articles of organization. The document that demonstrates the organization of a limited liability company.

B

blue sky laws. Laws governing the sales of securities.

bylaws. Rules governing the conduct of affairs of a corporation.

C

C corporation. A corporation that pays taxes on its profits.

common stock. The basic ownership shares of a corporation.

contract. An agreement between two or more parties.

corporation. An organization recognized as a person in the law that is set up to conduct a business owned by shareholders and run by officers and directors.

D

distributions. Money paid out to owners of a corporation or limited liability company.

E

employee. Person who works for another under that person's control and direction.

employer identification number (EIN). Number issued by the Internal Revenue Service to identify taxpayers who do not have social security numbers.

estate planning. Preparing such documents as a will, trust and other arrangements to control the passing of one's property at death.

exemption. The ability to sell certain limited types of securities without full compliance with securities registration laws.

F

fictitious name. A name used by a business that is not its personal or legal name.

G

general partnership. A business that is owned by two or more persons.

I

intangible property. Personal property that does not have physical presence, such as the ownership interest in a corporation.

intellectual property. Legal rights to the products of the mind, such as writings, musical compositions, formulas and designs.

L

liability. The legal responsibility to pay for an injury.

limited liability company. An entity recognized as a legal "person" that is set up to conduct a business owned and run by members.

limited liability partnership. An entity recognized as a legal "person" that is set up to conduct a business owned and run by professionals, such as attorneys or doctors.

limited partnership. A business that is owned by two or more persons of which one or more is liable for the debts of the business and one or more has no liability for the debts.

M

membership agreement. A contract controlling the operation of a limited liability company in which the company is run by members.

management agreement. A contract controlling the operation of a limited liability company in which the company is run by its managers.

minutes. Records of the proceedings of corporate meetings.

N

nonprofit corporation. An entity recognized as a legal "person" that is set up to run an operation in which none of the profits are distributed to controlling members.

O

occupational license. A government-issued permit to transact business.

operating agreement. A contract among members of a limited liability company spelling out how the company is to be run.

option. The right to buy stock at a future date, usually at a predetermined price.

organizational meeting. The meeting of the founders of a corporation or limited liability company in which the company is structured and ready to begin business.

P

par value.   A value given to newly-issued stock, which used to have legal significance, but now usually does not relate to anything except, in some states, taxation.

partnership.   A business formed by two or more persons.

personal property.   Any type of property other than land and the structures attached to it.

piercing the corporate veil.   When a court ignores the structure of a corporation and holds its owners responsible for its debts or liabilities.

professional association.   An entity recognized as a legal "person" that is set up to conduct a business of professionals such as attorneys or doctors.

promoters.   Persons who start a business venture and usually offer interests for sale to investors.

proprietorship.   A business that is owned by one person.

R

registered agent.   The person authorized to accept legal papers for a corporation or limited liability company, sometimes called a resident agent.

resident agent.   *See registered agent.*

S

S corporation.   A corporation in which the profits are taxed to the shareholders.

securities.   Interests in a business such as stocks or bonds.

shareholder agreement. A contract among the owners of a corporation that spells out their rights.

shares. Units of stock in a corporation.

stock. Ownership interests in a corporation.

T

tangible property. Physical personal property such as desks and tables.

trademark. A name or symbol used to identify the source of goods or services.

transferability. The ability to sell shares of stock in a corporation.

U

usury. Charging an interest rate higher than that allowed by law.

W

withholding. Money taken out of an employee's salary and remitted to the government.

Z

zoning. Governmental regulation controlling the use of a piece of real property.

For Further Reference

The following books will provide valuable information to those who are starting new businesses and corporations. Some are out of print, but they are classics that are worth tracking down.

For inspiration to give you the drive to succeed:

>Hill, Napoleon, *Think and Grow Rich*. New York: Fawcett Books, 1990, 233 pages.

>Karbo, Joe, *The Lazy Man's Way to Riches*. Sunset Beach: F P Publishing, 1974, 156 pages.

>Schwartz, David J., *The Magic of Thinking Big*. Fireside, 1987, 234 pages.

For hints on what it takes to be successful:

>Carnegie, Dale, *How to Win Friends and Influence People*. New York: Pocket Books, 1994, 276 pages.

>Ringer, Robert J., *Looking Out for #1*. New York: Fawcett Books, 1993.

Ringer, Robert J., *Million Dollar Habits*. New York: Fawcett Books, 1991.

Ringer, Robert J., *Winning Through Intimidation*. New York: Fawcett Books, 1993.

For advice on bookkeeping and organization:

Kamoroff, Bernard, *Small Time Operator (25th Edition)*. Bell Springs Publishing, 2000, 200 pages.

For a very practical guide to investing:

Tobias, Andrew, *The Only Investment Guide You'll Ever Need*. Harvest Books, 1999, 239 pages.

For advice on how to avoid problems with government agencies:

Browne, Harry, *How I Found Freedom in an Unfree World*. Great Falls: Liam Works, 1998, 387 pages.

The following are other books published by **Sphinx Publishing** that may be helpful to your business:

Eckert, W. Kelsea, Sartorius, Arthur, III, & Warda, Mark, *How to Form Your Own Corporation*. 2003.

Haman, Edward A., *How to Form Your Own Partnership*. 2002.

Ray, James C., *The Most Valuable Business Legal Forms You'll Ever Need*. 2001.

Ray, James C., *The Complete Book of Corporate Forms*. 2001.

Warda, Mark, *How to Form a Delaware Corporation from Any State*. 2002.

Warda, Mark, *Incorporate in Nevada from Any State*. 2001.

Warda, Mark, *How to Form a Limited Liability Company.* 2003.

Warda, Mark, *How to Register Your Own Copyright.* 2002.

Warda, Mark, *How to Register Your Own Trademark.* 2000.

The following are books published by ***Sourcebooks, Inc.*** that may be helpful to your business:

Covello, Joseph and Hazelgren, Mark. *Your First Business Plan.* 2002

Wendover, Robert W. *Smart Hiring.* 2002

The following websites provide information that may be useful to you in starting your business:

Internal Revenue Service: http://www.irs.gov

Small Business Administration: http://www.sba.gov

Social Security Administration: http://www.ssa.gov

U. S. Business Advisor: http://www.business.gov

Appendix A
Checklist

The following checklist includes the steps necessary to form a simple, *for-profit* corporation in Florida. All of these points are covered within the text of this book.

Checklist for Forming a Florida For-Profit Corporation

❏   Decide on corporate name

❏   Prepare and file Articles of Incorporation

❏   Send for Federal Employer Identification Number
(IRS Form SS-4)

❏   Prepare Shareholders' Agreement, if necessary

❏   Meet with accountant to discuss capitalization and tax planning

❏   If necessary, meet with securities lawyer regarding stock sales

❏   Obtain corporate seal and ring binder for minutes

❏   Hold organizational meeting

        ❏   Complete Bylaws, Waiver, Minutes,
Offers to Purchase Stock

        ❏   Sign all documents and place in minute book

❏   Issue stock certificates

        ❏   Be sure consideration is paid

        ❏   Complete Bill of Sale if property is traded for stock

        ❏   Fill in Transfer ledger

❏   File fictitious name if one will be used

❏   Get city or county licenses, if needed

❏   Open bank account

❏   For S corporation status, file IRS Form 2553

APPENDIX B
SELECTED FLORIDA
CORPORATION STATUTES

Included in this appendix are the Florida corporation statutes that will be most useful in organizing your corporation. There are other statutes that cover such things as mergers, buy-back of shares, share dividends, proxies, voting trusts and other matters that might come up at a future time. You can obtain a full copy of the statutes from the Secretary of State. Ask for their booklet, *Florida Business Corporation Act*.

To check future changes in the law, you can find Florida statutes at:

www.leg.state.fl.us/statutes/index.cfm

This appendix includes the following:

✪   Selections from Florida Statutes Chapter 607

✪   Florida Statutes Chapter 621 complete

CHAPTER 607

CORPORATIONS

607.0101 Short title.—This act shall be known and may be cited as the "Florida Business Corporation Act."

607.0102 Reservation of power to amend or repeal.—The Legislature has power to amend or repeal all or part of this act at any time, and all domestic and foreign corporations subject to this act shall be governed by the amendment or repeal.

607.0120 Filing requirements.

(1) A document must satisfy the requirements of this section and of any other section that adds to or varies these requirements to be entitled to filing by the Department of State.

(2) This act must require or permit filing the document in the office of the Department of State.

(3) The document must contain the information required by this act. It may contain other information as well.

(4) The document must be typewritten or printed, or, if electronically transmitted, the document must be in a format that can be retrieved or reproduced in typewritten or printed form, and must be legible.

(5) The document must be in the English language. A corporate name need not be in English if written in English letters or Arabic or Roman numerals, and the certificate of status required of foreign corporations need not be in English if accompanied by a reasonably authenticated English translation.

(6) The document must be executed:

(a) By a director of a domestic or foreign corporation, or by its president or by another of its officers;

(b) If directors or officers have not been selected or the corporation has not been formed, by an incorporator; or

(c) If the corporation is in the hands of a receiver, trustee, or other court-appointed fiduciary, by that fiduciary.

(7) The person executing the document shall sign it and state beneath or opposite his or her signature his or her name and the capacity in which he or she signs. The document may, but need not, contain the corporate seal, an attestation, an acknowledgment, or a verification.

(8) If the Department of State has prescribed a mandatory form for the document under s. 607.0121, the document must be in or on the prescribed form.

(9) The document must be delivered to the office of the Department of State for filing. Delivery may be made by electronic transmission if and to the extent permitted by the Department of State. If it is filed in typewritten or printed form and not transmitted electronically, the Department of State may require one exact or conformed copy, to be delivered with the document, (except as provided in s. 607.1509).

(10) When the document is delivered to the Department of State for filing, the correct filing fee, and any other tax, license fee, or penalty required to be paid by this act or other law shall be paid or provision for payment made in a manner permitted by the Department of State.

607.0121 Forms.

(1) The Department of State may prescribe and furnish on request forms for:

(a) An application for certificate of status,

(b) A foreign corporation's application for certificate of authority to transact business in the state,

(c) A foreign corporation's application for certificate of withdrawal, and

(d) The annual report, for which the department may prescribe the use of the uniform business report, pursuant to s. 606.06.

If the Department of State so requires, the use of these forms shall be mandatory.

(2) The Department of State may prescribe and furnish on request forms for other documents required or permitted to be filed by this act, but their use shall not be mandatory.

607.0122 Fees for filing documents and issuing certificates.— The Department of State shall collect the following fees when the documents described in this section are delivered to the department for filing:

(1) Articles of incorporation: $35.

(2) Application for registered name: $87.50.

(3) Application for renewal of registered name: $87.50.

(4) Corporation's statement of change of registered agent or registered office or both if not included on the annual report: $35.

(5) Designation of and acceptance by registered agent: $35.

(6) Agent's statement of resignation from active corporation: $87.50.

(7) Agent's statement of resignation from an inactive corporation: $35.

(8) Amendment of articles of incorporation: $35.

(9) Restatement of articles of incorporation with amendment of articles: $35.

(10) Articles of merger or share exchange for each party thereto: $35.

(11) Articles of dissolution: $35.

(12) Articles of revocation of dissolution: $35.

(13) Application for reinstatement following administrative dissolution: $600.

(14) Application for certificate of authority to transact business in this state by a foreign corporation: $35.

(15) Application for amended certificate of authority: $35.

(16) Application for certificate of withdrawal by a foreign corporation: $35.

(17) Annual report: $61.25.

(18) Articles of correction: $35.

(19) Application for certificate of status: $8.75.

(20) Certificate of domestication of a foreign corporation: $50.

(21) Certified copy of document: $52.50.

(22) Serving as agent for substitute service of process: $87.50.

(23) Supplemental corporate fee: $88.75.

(24) Any other document required or permitted to be filed by this act: $35.

607.0123 Effective time and date of document.—

(1) Except as provided in subsections (2) and (4) and in s. 607.0124(3), a document accepted for filing is effective on the date and at the time of filing, as evidenced by such means as the Department of State may use for the purpose of recording the date and time of filing.

(2) A document may specify a delayed effective date and, if desired, a time on that date, and if it does the document shall become effective on the date and at the time, if any, specified. If a delayed effective date is specified without specifying a time on that date, the document shall become effective at the start of business on that date. Unless otherwise permitted by this act, a delayed effective date for a document may not be later than the 90th day after the date on which it is filed.

(3) If a document is determined by the Department of State to be incomplete and inappropriate for filing, the Department of State may return the document to the person or corporation filing it, together with a brief written explanation of the reason for the refusal to file, in accordance with s. 607.0125(3). If the applicant returns the document with corrections in accordance with the rules of the department within 60 days after it was mailed to the applicant by the department and if at the time of return the

applicant so requests in writing, the filing date of the document will be the filing date that would have been applied had the original document not been deficient, except as to persons who relied on the record before correction and were adversely affected thereby.

(4) Corporate existence may predate the filing date, pursuant to s. 607.0203(1).

607.0124 Correcting filed document.—

(1) A domestic or foreign corporation may correct a document filed by the Department of State within 30 days after filing if the document:

(a) Contains an inaccuracy;

(b) Was defectively executed, attested, sealed, verified, or acknowledged; or

(c) The electronic transmission was defective.

(2) A document is corrected:

(a) By preparing articles of correction that:

1. Describe the document (including its filing date);

2. Specify the inaccuracy or defect to be corrected; and

3. Correct the inaccuracy or defect; and

(b) By delivering the articles of correction to the Department of State for filing, executed in accordance with s. 607.0120.

(3) Articles of correction are effective on the effective date of the document they correct except as to persons relying on the uncorrected document and adversely affected by the correction. As to those persons, articles of correction are effective when filed.

607.0125 Filing duties of Department of State.—

(1) If a document delivered to the Department of State for filing satisfies the requirements of s. 607.0120, the Department of State shall file it.

(2) The Department of State files a document by recording it as filed on the date of receipt. After filing a document, the Department of State shall deliver an acknowledgment or certified copy to the domestic or foreign corporation or its representative.

(3) If the Department of State refuses to file a document, it shall return it to the domestic or foreign corporation or its representative within 15 days after the document was received for filing, together with a brief, written explanation of the reason for refusal.

(4) The Department of State's duty to file documents under this section is ministerial. The filing or refusing to file a document does not:

(a) Affect the validity or invalidity of the document in whole or part;

(b) Relate to the correctness or incorrectness of information contained in the document;

(c) Create a presumption that the document is valid or invalid or that information contained in the document is correct or incorrect.

(5) If not otherwise provided by law and the provisions of this act, the Department of State shall determine, by rule, the appropriate format for, number of copies of, manner of execution of, method of electronic transmission of, and amount of and method of payment of fees for, any document placed under its jurisdiction.

607.0126 Appeal from Department of State's refusal to file document.—If the Department of State refuses to file a document delivered to its office for filing, within 30 days after return of the document by the department by mail, as evidenced by the postmark, the domestic or foreign corporation may:

(1) Appeal the refusal pursuant to s. 120.68; or

(2) Appeal the refusal to the circuit court of the county where the corporation's principal office (or, if none in this state, its registered office) is or will be located. The appeal is commenced by petitioning the court to compel filing the document and by attaching to the petition the document and the Department of State's explanation of its refusal to file. The matter shall promptly be tried de novo by the court without a jury. The court may summarily order the Department of State to file the document or take other action the court considers appropriate. The court's final decision may be appealed as in other civil proceedings.

607.0127 Evidentiary effect of copy of filed document.--A certificate from the Department of State delivered with a copy of a document filed by the Department of State is conclusive evidence that the original document is on file with the department.

607.0128 Certificate of status.—

(1) Anyone may apply to the Department of State to furnish a certificate of status for a domestic corporation or a certificate of authorization for a foreign corporation.

(2) A certificate of status or authorization sets forth:

(a) The domestic corporation's corporate name or the foreign corporation's corporate name used in this state;

(b)1. That the domestic corporation is duly incorporated under the law of this state and the date of its incorporation, or

2. That the foreign corporation is authorized to transact business in this state;

(c) That all fees and penalties owed to the department have been paid, if:

1. Payment is reflected in the records of the department, and

2. Nonpayment affects the existence or authorization of the domestic or foreign corporation;

(d) That its most recent annual report required by s. 607.1622 has been delivered to the department; and

(e) That articles of dissolution have not been filed.

(3) Subject to any qualification stated in the certificate, a certificate of status or authorization issued by the department may be relied upon as conclusive evidence that the domestic or foreign corporation is in existence or is authorized to transact business in this state.

607.0129 Penalty for signing false document.—A person who signs a document she or he knows is false in any material respect with intent that the document be delivered to the Department of State for filing is personally liable to any person who to her or his detriment reasonably relied on the document or information contained therein and is guilty of a misdemeanor of the second degree, punishable as provided in s. 775.083.

607.0130 Powers of Department of State.—

(1) The Department of State may propound to any corporation subject to the provisions of this act, and to any officer or director thereof, such interrogatories as may be reasonably necessary and proper to enable it to ascertain whether the corporation has complied with all applicable provisions of this act. Such interrogatories must be answered within 30 days after mailing or within such additional time as fixed by the department. Answers to interrogatories must be full and complete, in writing, and under oath. Interrogatories directed to an individual must be answered by the individual, and interrogatories directed to a corporation must be answered by the president, vice president, secretary, or assistant secretary.

(2) The Department of State is not required to file any document:

(a) To which interrogatories, as propounded pursuant to subsection (1), relate, until the interrogatories are answered in full;

(b) When interrogatories or other relevant evidence discloses that such document is not in conformity with the provisions of this act; or

(c) When the department has determined that the parties to such document have not paid all fees, taxes, and penalties due and owing this state.

(3) The Department of State may, based upon its findings hereunder or as provided in s. 213.053(14), bring an action in circuit court to collect any penalties, fees, or taxes determined to be due and owing the state and to compel any filing, qualification, or registration required by law. In connection with such proceeding the department may, without prior approval by the court, file a lis pendens against any property owned by the corporation and may further certify any findings to the Department of Legal Affairs for the initiation of any action permitted pursuant to s. 607.0505 which the Department of Legal Affairs may deem appropriate.

(4) The Department of State shall have the power and authority reasonably necessary to enable it to administer this act efficiently, to perform the duties herein imposed upon it, and to promulgate reasonable rules necessary to carry out its duties and functions under this act.

607.01401 Definitions.—As used in this act, unless the context otherwise requires, the term:

(1) "Articles of incorporation" includes original, amended, and restated articles of incorporation, articles of share exchange, and articles of merger, and all amendments thereto.

(2) "Authorized shares" means the shares of all classes a domestic or foreign corporation is authorized to issue.

(3) "Business day" means Monday through Friday, excluding any day a national banking association is not open for normal business transactions.

(4) "Conspicuous" means so written that a reasonable person against whom the writing is to operate should have noticed it. For example, printing in italics, boldface, or a contrasting color or typing in capitals or underlined is conspicuous.

(5) "Corporation" or "domestic corporation" means a corporation for profit, which is not a foreign corporation, incorporated under or subject to the provisions of this act.

(6) "Day" means a calendar day.

(7) "Deliver" or "delivery" means any method of delivery used in conventional commercial practice, including delivery by hand, mail, commercial delivery, and electronic transmission.

(8) "Distribution" means a direct or indirect transfer of money or other property (except its own shares) or incurrence of indebtedness by a corporation to or for the benefit of its shareholders in respect of any of its shares. A distribution may be in the form of a declaration or payment of a dividend; a purchase, redemption, or other acquisition of shares; a distribution of indebtedness; or otherwise.

(9) "Electronic transmission" or "electronically transmitted" means any process of communication not directly involving the physical transfer of paper that is suitable for the retention, retrieval, and reproduction of information by the recipient. For purposes of proxy voting in accordance with ss. 607.0721, 607.0722, and 607.0724, the term includes, but is not limited to, telegrams, cablegrams, telephone transmissions, and transmissions through the Internet.

(10) "Employee" includes an officer but not a director. A director may accept duties that make him or her also an employee.

(11) "Entity" includes corporation and foreign corporation; unincorporated association; business trust, estate, partnership, trust, and two or more persons having a joint or common economic interest; and state, United States, and foreign governments.

(12) "Foreign corporation" means a corporation for profit incorporated under laws other than the laws of this state.

(13) "Governmental subdivision" includes authority, county, district, and municipality.

(14) "Includes" denotes a partial definition.

(15) "Individual" includes the estate of an incompetent or deceased individual.

(16) "Insolvent" means the inability of a corporation to pay its debts as they become due in the usual course of its business.

(17) "Mail" means the United States mail, facsimile transmissions, and private mail carriers handling nationwide mail services.

(18) "Means" denotes an exhaustive definition.

(19) "Person" includes individual and entity.

(20) "Principal office" means the office (in or out of this state) where the principal executive offices of a domestic or foreign corporation are located as designated in the articles of incorporation or other initial filing until an annual report has been filed, and thereafter as designated in the annual report.

(21) "Proceeding" includes civil suit and criminal, administrative, and investigatory action.

(22) "Record date" means the date on which a corporation determines the identity of its shareholders and their share holdings for purposes of this act. The determination shall be made as of the close of the business on the record date unless another time is fixed.

(23) "Secretary" means the corporate officer to whom the board of directors has delegated responsibility under s. 607.08401 for custody of the minutes of the meetings of the board of directors and of the shareholders and for authenticating records of the corporation.

(24) "Shareholder" or "stockholder" means one who is a holder of record of shares in a corporation or the beneficial owner of shares to the extent of the rights granted by a nominee certificate on file with a corporation.

(25) "Shares" means the units into which the proprietary interests in a corporation are divided.

(26) "Sign" or "signature" means any symbol, manual, facsimile, conformed, or electronic signature adopted by a person with the intent to authenticate a document.

(27) "State," when referring to a part of the United States, includes a state and commonwealth (and their agencies and governmental subdivisions) and a territory and insular possession (and their agencies and governmental subdivisions) of the United States.

(28) "Subscriber" means a person who subscribes for shares in a corporation, whether before or after incorporation.

(29) "Treasury shares" means shares of a corporation that belong to the issuing corporation, which shares are authorized and issued shares that are not outstanding, are not canceled, and have not been restored to the status of authorized but unissued shares.

(30) "United States" includes district, authority, bureau, commission, department, and any other agency of the United States.

(31) "Voting group" means all shares of one or more classes or series that under the articles of incorporation or this act are entitled to vote and be counted together collectively on a matter at the meeting of shareholders. All shares entitled by the articles of incorporation or this act to vote generally on the matter are for that purpose a single voting group.

607.0140.

607.0141 Notice.—

(1) Notice under this act must be in writing, unless oral notice is:

(a) Expressly authorized by the articles of incorporation or the bylaws, and

(b) Reasonable under the circumstances.

Notice by electronic transmission is written notice.

(2) Notice may be communicated in person; by telephone, voice mail (where oral notice is permitted), or other electronic means; or by mail or other method of delivery.

(3)(a) Written notice by a domestic or foreign corporation authorized to transact business in this state to its shareholder, if in a comprehensible form, is effective:

1. Upon deposit into the United States mail, if mailed postpaid and correctly addressed to the shareholder's address shown in the corporation's current record of shareholders; or

2. When electronically transmitted to the shareholder in a manner authorized by the shareholder.

(b) Unless otherwise provided in the articles of incorporation or bylaws, and without limiting the manner by which notice otherwise may be given effectively to shareholders, any notice to shareholders given by the corporation under any provision of this chapter, the articles of incorporation, or the bylaws, shall be effective if given by a single written notice to shareholders who share an address if consented to by the shareholders at that address to whom such notice is given. Any such consent shall be revocable by a shareholder by written notice to the corporation.

(c) Any shareholder who fails to object in writing to the corporation, within 60 days after having been given written notice by the corporation of its intention to send the single notice permitted under paragraph (b), shall be deemed to have consented to receiving such single written notice.

(d) This subsection shall not apply to s. 607.0620, s.

607.1402, or s. 607.1404.

(4) Written notice to a domestic or foreign corporation authorized to transact business in this state may be addressed:

(a) To its registered agent at its registered office; or

(b) To the corporation or its secretary at its principal office or electronic mail address as authorized and shown in its most recent annual report or, in the case of a corporation that has not yet delivered an annual report, in a domestic corporation's articles of incorporation or in a foreign corporation's application for certificate of authority.

(5) Except as provided in subsection (3) or elsewhere in this act, written notice, if in a comprehensible form, is effective at the earliest date of the following:

(a) When received;

(b) Five days after its deposit in the United States mail, if mailed postpaid and correctly addressed; or

(c) On the date shown on the return receipt, if sent by registered or certified mail, return receipt requested, and the receipt is signed by or on behalf of the addressee.

(6) Oral notice is effective when communicated if communicated directly to the person to be notified in a comprehensible manner.

(7) If this act prescribes notice requirements for particular circumstances, those requirements govern. If articles of incorporation or bylaws prescribe notice requirements not less stringent than the requirements of this section or other provisions of this act, those requirements govern.

607.0201 Incorporators.—One or more persons may act as the incorporator or incorporators of a corporation by delivering articles of incorporation to the Department of State for filing.

607.0202 Articles of incorporation; content.—

(1) The articles of incorporation must set forth:

(a) A corporate name for the corporation that satisfies the requirements of s. 607.0401;

(b) The street address of the initial principal office and, if different, the mailing address of the corporation;

(c) The number of shares the corporation is authorized to issue;

(d) If any preemptive rights are to be granted to shareholders, the provision therefore;

(e) The street address of the corporation's initial registered office and the name of its initial registered agent at that office together with a written acceptance as required in s. 607.0501(3); and

(f) The name and address of each incorporator.

(2) The articles of incorporation may set forth:

(a) The names and addresses of the individuals who are to serve as the initial directors;

(b) Provisions not inconsistent with law regarding:

1. The purpose or purposes for which the corporation is organized;

2. Managing the business and regulating the affairs of the corporation;

3. Defining, limiting, and regulating the powers of the corporation and its board of directors and shareholders;

4. A par value for authorized shares or classes of shares;

5. The imposition of personal liability on shareholders for the debts of the corporation to a specified extent and upon specified conditions; and

(c) Any provision that under this act is required or permitted to be set forth in the bylaws.

(3) The articles of incorporation need not set forth any of the corporate powers enumerated in this act.

607.0203 Incorporation.—

(1) Unless a delayed effective date is specified, the corporate existence begins when the articles of incorporation are filed or on a date specified in the articles of incorporation, if such date is within 5 business days prior to the date of filing.

(2) The Department of State's filing of the articles of incorporation is conclusive proof that the incorporators satisfied all conditions precedent to incorporation except in a proceeding by the state to cancel or revoke the incorporation or involuntarily dissolve the corporation.

607.0204 Liability for preincorporation transactions—All persons purporting to act as or on behalf of a corporation, having actual knowledge that there was no incorporation under this chapter, are jointly and severally liable for all liabilities created while so acting except for any liability to any person who also had actual knowledge that there was no incorporation.

607.0205 Organizational meeting of directors.—

(1) After incorporation:

(a) If initial directors are named in the articles of incorporation, the initial directors shall hold an organizational meeting, at the call of a majority of the directors, to complete the organization of the corporation by appointing officers, adopting bylaws, and carrying on any other business brought before the meeting;

(b) If initial directors are not named in the articles, the incorporators shall hold an organizational meeting at the call of a majority of the incorporators:

1. To elect directors and complete the organization of the corporation; or

2. To elect a board of directors who shall complete the organization of the corporation.

(2) Action required or permitted by this act to be taken by incorporators or directors at an organizational meeting may be taken without a meeting if the action taken is evidenced by one or more written consents describing the action taken and signed by each incorporator or director.

(3) The directors or incorporators calling the organizational meeting shall give at least 3 days' notice thereof to each director or incorporator so named, stating the time and place of the meeting.

(4) An organizational meeting may be held in or out of this state.

607.0206 Bylaws.—

(1) The incorporators or board of directors of a corporation shall adopt initial bylaws for the corporation unless that power is reserved to the shareholders by the articles of incorporation.

(2) The bylaws of a corporation may contain any provision for managing the business and regulating the affairs of the corporation that is not inconsistent with law or the articles of incorporation.

607.0207 Emergency bylaws.—

(1) Unless the articles of incorporation provide otherwise, the board of directors of a corporation may adopt bylaws to be effective only in an emergency defined in subsection (5). The emergency bylaws, which are subject to amendment or repeal by the shareholders, may make all provisions necessary for managing the corporation during an emergency, including:

(a) Procedures for calling a meeting of the board of directors;

(b) Quorum requirements for the meeting; and

(c) Designation of additional or substitute directors.

(2) The board of directors, either before or during any such emergency, may provide, and from time to time modify, lines of succession in the event that during such emergency any or all officers or agents of the corporation are for any reason rendered incapable of discharging their duties.

(3) All provisions of the regular bylaws consistent with the emergency bylaws remain effective during the emergency. The emergency bylaws are not effective after the emergency ends.

(4) Corporate action taken in good faith in accordance with the emergency bylaws:

(a) Binds the corporation; and

(b) May not be used to impose liability on a corporate director, officer, employee, or agent.

(5) An emergency exists for purposes of this section if a quorum of the corporation's directors cannot readily be assembled because of some catastrophic event.

607.0301 Purposes and application.—Corporations may be organized under this act for any lawful purpose or purposes, and the provisions of this act extend to all corporations, whether chartered by special acts or general laws, except that special statutes for the regulation and control of types of business and corporations shall control when in conflict herewith.

607.0302 General powers.—Unless its articles of incorporation provide otherwise, every corporation has perpetual duration and succession in its corporate name and has the same powers as an individual to do all things necessary or convenient to carry out its business and affairs, including without limitation power:

(1) To sue and be sued, complain, and defend in its corporate name;

(2) To have a corporate seal, which may be altered at will and to use it or a facsimile of it, by impressing or affixing it or in any other manner reproducing it;

(3) To purchase, receive, lease, or otherwise acquire, own, hold, improve, use, and otherwise deal with real or personal property or any legal or equitable interest in property wherever located;

(4) To sell, convey, mortgage, pledge, create a security interest in, lease, exchange, and otherwise dispose of all or any part of its property;

(5) To lend money to, and use its credit to assist, its officers and employees in accordance with s. 607.0833;

(6) To purchase, receive, subscribe for, or otherwise acquire; own, hold, vote, use, sell, mortgage, lend, pledge, or otherwise dispose of; and deal in and with shares or other interests in, or obligations of, any other entity;

(7) To make contracts and guarantees, incur liabilities, borrow money, issue its notes, bonds, and other obligations (which may be convertible into or include the option to purchase other secu-

rities of the corporation), and secure any of its obligations by mortgage or pledge of any of its property, franchises, and income and make contracts of guaranty and suretyship which are necessary or convenient to the conduct, promotion, or attainment of the business of a corporation the majority of the outstanding stock of which is owned, directly or indirectly, by the contracting corporation; a corporation which owns, directly or indirectly, a majority of the outstanding stock of the contracting corporation; or a corporation the majority of the outstanding stock of which is owned, directly or indirectly, by a corporation which owns, directly or indirectly, the majority of the outstanding stock of the contracting corporation, which contracts of guaranty and suretyship shall be deemed to be necessary or convenient to the conduct, promotion, or attainment of the business of the contracting corporation, and make other contracts of guaranty and suretyship which are necessary or convenient to the conduct, promotion, or attainment of the business of the contracting corporation;

(8) To lend money, invest and reinvest its funds, and receive and hold real and personal property as security for repayment;

(9) To conduct its business, locate offices, and exercise the powers granted by this act within or without this state;

(10) To elect directors and appoint officers, employees, and agents of the corporation and define their duties, fix their compensation, and lend them money and credit;

(11) To make and amend bylaws, not inconsistent with its articles of incorporation or with the laws of this state, for managing the business and regulating the affairs of the corporation;

(12) To make donations for the public welfare or for charitable, scientific, or educational purposes;

(13) To transact any lawful business that will aid governmental policy;

(14) To make payments or donations or do any other act not inconsistent with law that furthers the business and affairs of the corporation;

(15) To pay pensions and establish pension plans, pension trusts, profit-sharing plans, share bonus plans, share option plans, and benefit or incentive plans for any or all of its current or former directors, officers, employees, and agents and for any or all of the current or former directors, officers, employees, and agents of its subsidiaries;

(16) To provide insurance for its benefit on the life of any of its directors, officers, or employees, or on the life of any shareholder for the purpose of acquiring at his or her death shares of its stock owned by the shareholder or by the spouse or children of the shareholder; and

(17) To be a promoter, incorporator, partner, member, associate, or manager of any corporation, partnership, joint venture, trust, or other entity.

607.0303 Emergency powers.—

(1) In anticipation of or during any emergency defined in subsection (5), the board of directors of a corporation may:

(a) Modify lines of succession to accommodate the incapacity of any director, officer, employee, or agent; and

(b) Relocate the principal office or designate alternative principal offices or regional offices or authorize the officers to do so.

(2) During an emergency defined in subsection (5), unless emergency bylaws provide otherwise:

(a) Notice of a meeting of the board of directors need be given only to those directors whom it is practicable to reach and may be given in any practicable manner, including by publication and radio;

(b) One or more officers of the corporation present at a meeting of the board of directors may be deemed to be directors for the meeting, in order of rank and within the same rank in order of seniority, as necessary to achieve a quorum; and

(c) The director or directors in attendance at a meeting, or any greater number affixed by the emergency bylaws, constitute a quorum.

(3) Corporate action taken in good faith during an emergency under this section to further the ordinary business affairs of the corporation:

(a) Binds the corporation; and

(b) May not be used to impose liability on a corporate director, officer, employee, or agent.

(4) No officer, director, or employee acting in accordance with any emergency bylaws shall be liable except for willful misconduct.

(5) An emergency exists for purposes of this section if a quorum of the corporation's directors cannot readily be assembled because of some catastrophic event.

(6) To the extent not inconsistent with any emergency bylaws so adopted, the bylaws of the corporation shall remain in effect during any emergency, and upon termination of the emergency, the emergency bylaws will cease to be operative.

607.0304 Ultra vires.—

(1) Except as provided in subsection (2), the validity of corporate action, including, but not limited to, any conveyance, transfer, or encumbrance of real or personal property to or by a corporation, may not be challenged on the ground that the corporation lacks or lacked power to act.

(2) A corporation's power to act may be challenged:

(a) In a proceeding by a shareholder against the corporation to enjoin the act;

(b) In a proceeding by the corporation, directly, derivatively, or through a receiver, trustee, or other legal representative, or through shareholders in a representative suit, against an incumbent or former officer, employee, or agent of the corporation; or

(c) In a proceeding by the Attorney General, as provided in this act, to dissolve the corporation or in a proceeding by the Attorney General to enjoin the corporation from the transaction of unauthorized business.

(3) In a shareholder's proceeding under paragraph (2)(a) to enjoin an unauthorized corporate act, the court may enjoin or set aside the act, if equitable and if all affected persons are parties to the proceeding, and may award damages for loss (other than anticipated profits) suffered by the corporation or another party because of enjoining the unauthorized act.

607.0401 Corporate name.—A corporate name:

(1) Must contain the word "corporation," "company," or "incorporated" or the abbreviation "corp.," "Inc.," or "Co.," or the designation "Corp," "Inc," or "Co," as will clearly indicate that it is a corporation instead of a natural person, partnership, or other business entity;

(2) May not contain language stating or implying that the corporation is organized for a purpose other than that permitted in this act and its articles of incorporation;

(3) May not contain language stating or implying that the corporation is connected with a state or federal government agency or a corporation chartered under the laws of the United States; and

(4) Must be distinguishable from the names of all other entities or filings, except fictitious name registrations pursuant to s. 865.09, organized, registered, or reserved under the laws of this state, which names are on file with the Division of Corporations.

(5) The name of the corporation as filed with the Department of State shall be for public notice only and shall not alone create any presumption of ownership beyond that which is created under the common law.

607.0403 Registered name; application; renewal; revocation.—

(1) A foreign corporation may register its corporate name, or its corporate name with any addition required by s. 607.1506, if the name is distinguishable upon the records of the Department of State from the corporate names that are not available under s. 607.0401(4).

(2) A foreign corporation registers its corporate name, or its corporate name with any addition required by s. 607.1506, by delivering to the Department of State for filing an application:

(a) Setting forth its corporate name, or its corporate name with any addition required by s. 607.1506, the state or country and date of its incorporation, and a brief description of the nature of the business in which it is engaged; and

(b) Accompanied by a certificate of existence, or a certificate setting forth that such corporation is in good standing under the laws of the state or country wherein it is organized (or a document of similar import), from the state or country of incorporation.

(3) The name is registered for the applicant's exclusive use upon the effective date of the application and shall be effective until the close of the calendar year in which the application for registration is filed.

(4) A foreign corporation the registration of which is effective may renew it from year to year by annually filing a renewal application which complies with the requirements of subsection (2) between October 1 and December 31 of the preceding year. The renewal application when filed renews the registration for the following calendar year.

(5) A foreign corporation the registration of which is effective may thereafter qualify as a foreign corporation under the registered name or consent in writing to the use of that name by a corporation thereafter incorporated under this act or by another foreign corporation thereafter authorized to transact business in this state. The registration terminates when the domestic corporation is incorporated or the foreign corporation qualifies or consents to the qualification of another foreign corporation under the registered name.

(6) The Department of State may revoke any registration if, after a hearing, it finds that the application therefor or any renewal thereof was not made in good faith.

607.0501 Registered office and registered agent.—

(1) Each corporation shall have and continuously maintain in this state:

(a) A registered office which may be the same as its place of business; and

(b) A registered agent, who may be either:

1. An individual who resides in this state whose business office is identical with such registered office;

2. Another corporation or not-for-profit corporation as defined in chapter 617, authorized to transact business or conduct its affairs in this state, having a business office identical with the registered office; or

3. A foreign corporation or not-for-profit foreign corporation authorized pursuant to this chapter or chapter 617 to transact business or conduct its affairs in this state, having a business office identical with the registered office.

(2) This section does not apply to corporations which are required by law to designate the Insurance Commissioner and Treasurer as their attorney for the service of process, associations subject to the provisions of chapter 665, and banks and trust companies subject to the provisions of the financial institutions codes.

(3) A registered agent appointed pursuant to this section or a successor registered agent appointed pursuant to s. 607.0502 on whom process may be served shall each file a statement in writing

with the Department of State, in such form and manner as shall be prescribed by the department, accepting the appointment as a registered agent simultaneously with his or her being designated. Such statement of acceptance shall state that the registered agent is familiar with, and accepts, the obligations of that position.

(4) The Department of State shall maintain an accurate record of the registered agents and registered offices for the service of process and shall furnish any information disclosed thereby promptly upon request and payment of the required fee. There shall be no charge for telephone requests for general corporate information, including the corporation's status, names of officers and directors, address of principal place of business, and name and address of registered agent.

(5) A corporation may not maintain any action in a court in this state until the corporation complies with the provisions of this section or s. 607.1507, as applicable, and pays to the Department of State a penalty of $5 for each day it has failed to so comply or $500, whichever is less.

607.0502 Change of registered office or registered agent; resignation of registered agent.—

(1) A corporation may change its registered office or its registered agent upon filing with the Department of State a statement of change setting forth:

(a) The name of the corporation;

(b) The street address of its current registered office;

(c) If the current registered office is to be changed, the street address of the new registered office;

(d) The name of its current registered agent;

(e) If its current registered agent is to be changed, the name of the new registered agent and the new agent's written consent (either on the statement or attached to it) to the appointment;

(f) That the street address of its registered office and the street address of the business office of its registered agent, as changed, will be identical;

(g) That such change was authorized by resolution duly adopted by its board of directors or by an officer of the corporation so authorized by the board of directors.

(2) Any registered agent may resign his or her agency appointment by signing and delivering for filing with the Department of State a statement of resignation and mailing a copy of such statement to the corporation at its principal office address shown in its most recent annual report or, if none, filed in the articles of incorporation or other most recently filed document. The statement of resignation shall state that a copy of such statement has been mailed to the corporation at the address so stated. The agency is terminated as of the 31st day after the date on which the statement was filed and unless otherwise provided in the statement, termination of the agency acts as a termination of the registered office.

(3) If a registered agent changes his or her business name or business address, he or she may change such name or address and the address of the registered office of any corporation for which he or she is the registered agent by:

(a) Notifying all such corporations in writing of the change,

(b) Signing (either manually or in facsimile) and delivering to the Department of State for filing a statement that substantially complies with the requirements of paragraphs (1)(a)-(f), setting forth the names of all such corporations represented by the registered agent, and

(c) Reciting that each corporation has been notified of the change.

(4) Changes of the registered office or registered agent may be made by a change on the corporation's annual report form filed with the Department of State.

(5) The Department of State shall collect a fee pursuant to s. 15.09(2) for the filings authorized under this section.
6-212; s. 1714, ch. 97-102.

607.0504 Service of process, notice, or demand on a corporation.—

(1) Process against any corporation may be served in accordance with chapter 48 or chapter 49.

(2) Any notice to or demand on a corporation under this act may be made to the chair of the board, the president, any vice president, the secretary, or the treasurer; to the registered agent of the corporation at the registered office of the corporation in this state; or to any other address in this state that is in fact the principal office of the corporation in this state.

(3) This section does not prescribe the only means, or necessarily the required means, of serving notice or demand on a corporation.

607.0505 Registered agent; duties.—

(1)(a) Each corporation, foreign corporation, or alien business organization that owns real property located in this state, that owns a mortgage on real property located in this state, or that transacts business in this state shall have and continuously maintain in this state a registered office and a registered agent and shall file with the Department of State notice of the registered office and registered agent as provided in ss. 607.0501 and 607.0502. The appointment of a registered agent in compliance with s. 607.0501 or s. 607.1507 is sufficient for purposes of this section provided the registered agent so appointed files, in such form and manner as prescribed by the Department of State, an acceptance of the obligations provided for in this section.

(b) Each such corporation, foreign corporation, or alien business organization which fails to have and continuously maintain a registered office and a registered agent as required in this section will be liable to this state for $500 for each year, or part of a year, during which the corporation, foreign corporation, or alien business organization fails to comply with these requirements; but such liability will be forgiven in full upon the compliance by the corporation, foreign corporation, or alien business organization with the requirements of this subsection, even if such compliance occurs after an action to collect such liability is instituted. The Department of Legal Affairs may file an action in the circuit court for the judicial circuit in which the corporation, foreign corporation, or alien business organization is found or transacts business, or in which real property belonging to the corporation, foreign corporation, or alien business organization is located, to petition the court for an order directing that a registered agent be appointed and that a registered office be designated, and to obtain judgment for the amount owed under this subsection. In connection with such proceeding, the department may, without prior approval by the court, file a lis pendens against real property owned by the corporation, foreign corporation, or alien business organization, which lis pendens shall set forth the legal description of the real property and shall be filed in the public records of the county where the real property is located. If the lis pendens is filed in any county other than the county in which the action is pending, the lis pendens which is filed must be a certified copy of the original lis pendens. The failure to comply timely or fully with an order directing that a registered agent be appointed and that a registered office be designated will result in a civil penalty of not more than $1,000 for each day of noncompliance. A judgment or an order of payment entered pursuant to this subsection will become a judgment lien against any real property owned by the corporation, foreign corporation, or alien business organization when a certified copy of the judgment or order is recorded as required by s. 55.10. The department will be able to avail itself of, and is entitled to use, any provision of law or of the Florida Rules of Civil Procedure to further the collecting or obtaining of payment pursuant to a judgment or order of payment. The state, through the Attorney General, may bid, at any judicial sale to enforce its judgment lien, any amount up to the amount of the judgment or lien obtained pursuant to this subsection. All moneys recovered under this subsection shall be treated as forfeitures under ss. 895.01-895.09 and used or distributed in accordance with the procedure set forth in s. 895.09. A corporation, foreign corporation, or alien business organization which fails to have and continuously maintain a registered office and a registered agent as required in this section may not defend itself against any action instituted by the Department of Legal Affairs or by any other agency of this state until the requirements of this subsection have been met.

(2) Each corporation, foreign corporation, or alien business organization that owns real property located in this state, that owns a mortgage on real property located in this state, or that transacts business in this state shall, pursuant to subpoena served upon the registered agent of the corporation, foreign corporation, or alien business organization issued by the Department of Legal Affairs, produce, through its registered agent or through a designated representative within 30 days after service of the subpoena, testimony and records reflecting the following:

(a) True copies of documents evidencing the legal existence of the entity, including the articles of incorporation and any amendments to the articles of incorporation or the legal equivalent of the articles of incorporation and such amendments.

(b) The names and addresses of each current officer and director of the entity or persons holding equivalent positions.

(c) The names and addresses of all prior officers and directors of the entity or persons holding equivalent positions, for a period not to exceed the 5 years previous to the date of issuance of the subpoena.

(d) The names and addresses of each current shareholder, equivalent equitable owner, and ultimate equitable owner of the entity, the number of which names is limited to the names of the 100 shareholders, equivalent equitable owners, and ultimate equitable owners that, in comparison to all other shareholders, equivalent equitable owners, or ultimate equitable owners, respectively, own the largest number of shares of stock of the corporation, foreign corporation, or alien business organization or the largest percentage of an equivalent form of equitable ownership of the corporation, foreign corporation, or alien business organization.

(e) The names and addresses of all prior shareholders, equivalent equitable owners, and ultimate equitable owners of the entity for the 12-month period preceding the date of issuance of the subpoena, the number of which names is limited to the 100 shareholders, equivalent equitable owners, and ultimate equitable owners that, in comparison to all other shareholders, equivalent equitable owners, or ultimate equitable owners, respectively, own the largest number of shares of stock of the corporation, foreign corporation, or alien business organization or the largest percentage of an equivalent form of equitable ownership of the corporation, foreign corporation, or alien business organization.

(f) The names and addresses of the person or persons who provided the records and information to the registered agent or designated representative of the entity.

(g) The requirements of paragraphs (d) and (e) do not apply to:

1. A financial institution;

2. A corporation, foreign corporation, or alien business organization the securities of which are registered pursuant to s. 12 of the Securities Exchange Act of 1934, 15 U.S.C. ss. 78a-78kk, if such corporation, foreign corporation, or alien business organization files with the United States Securities and Exchange Commission the reports required by s. 13 of that act; or

3. A corporation, foreign corporation, or alien business organization, the securities of which are regularly traded on an established securities market located in the United States or on an established securities market located outside the United States, if such non-United States securities market is designated by rule adopted by the Department of Legal Affairs; upon a showing by the corporation, foreign corporation, or alien business organization that the exception in subparagraph 1., subparagraph 2., or subparagraph 3. applies to the corporation, foreign corporation, or alien business organization. Such exception in subparagraph 1., subparagraph 2., or subparagraph 3. does not, however, exempt the corporation, foreign corporation, or alien business organization from the requirements for producing records, information, or testimony otherwise imposed under this section for any period of time when the requisite conditions for the exception did not exist.

(3) The time limit for producing records and testimony may be extended for good cause shown by the corporation, foreign corporation, or alien business organization.

(4) A person, corporation, foreign corporation, or alien business organization designating an attorney, accountant, or spouse as a registered agent or designated representative shall, with respect to this state or any agency or subdivision of this state, be deemed to have waived any privilege that might otherwise attach to communications with respect to the information required to be produced pursuant to subsection (2), which communications are among such corporation, foreign corporation, or alien business organization; the registered agent or designated representative of such corporation, foreign corporation, or alien business organization; and the beneficial owners of such corporation, foreign corporation, or alien business organization. The duty to comply with the provisions of this section will not be excused by virtue of any privilege or provision of law of this state or any other state or country, which privilege or provision authorizes or directs that the testimony or records required to be produced under subsection (2) are privileged or confidential or otherwise may not be disclosed.

(5) If a corporation, foreign corporation, or alien business organization fails without lawful excuse to comply timely or fully with a subpoena issued pursuant to subsection (2), the Department of Legal Affairs may file an action in the circuit court for the judicial circuit in which the corporation, foreign corporation, or alien business organization is found or transacts business or in which real property belonging to the corporation, foreign corporation, or alien business organization is located, for an order compelling compliance with the subpoena. The failure without a lawful excuse to comply timely or fully with an order compelling compliance with the subpoena will result in a civil penalty of not more than $1,000 for each day of noncompliance with the order. In connection with such proceeding, the department may, without prior approval by the court, file a lis pendens against real property owned by the corporation, foreign corporation, or alien business organization, which lis pendens shall set forth the legal description of the real property and shall be filed in the public records of the county where the real property is located. If the lis pendens is filed in any county other than the county in which the action is pending, the lis pendens which is filed must be a certified copy of the original lis pendens. A judgment or an order of payment entered pursuant to this subsection will become a judgment lien against any real property owned by the corporation, foreign corporation, or alien business organization when a certified copy of the judgment or order is recorded as required by s. 55.10. The department will be able to avail itself of, and is entitled to use, any provision of law or of the Florida Rules of Civil Procedure to further the collecting or obtaining of payment pursuant to a judgment or order of payment. The state, through the Attorney General, may bid, at any judicial sale to enforce its judgment lien, an amount up to the amount of the judgment or lien obtained pursuant to this subsection. All moneys recovered under this subsection shall be treated as forfeitures under ss. 895.01-895.09 and used or distributed in accordance with the procedure set forth in s. 895.09.

(6) Information provided to, and records and transcriptions of testimony obtained by, the Department of Legal Affairs pursuant to this section are confidential and exempt from the provisions of s. 119.07(1) while the investigation is active. For purposes of this section, an investigation shall be considered "active" while such investigation is being conducted with a reasonable, good faith belief that it may lead to the filing of an administrative, civil, or criminal proceeding. An investigation does not cease to be active so long as the department is proceeding with reasonable dispatch and there is a good faith belief that action may be initiated by the department or other administrative or law enforcement agency. Except for active criminal intelligence or criminal investigative information, as defined in s. 119.011, and information which, if disclosed, would reveal a trade secret, as defined in s. 688.002, or would jeopardize the safety of an individual, all information, records, and transcriptions become public record when the investigation is completed or ceases to be active. The department shall not disclose confidential information, records, or transcriptions of testimony except pursuant to the authorization by the Attorney General in any of the following circumstances:

(a) To a law enforcement agency participating in or conducting a civil investigation under chapter 895, or participating in or conducting a criminal investigation.

(b) In the course of filing, participating in, or conducting a judicial proceeding instituted pursuant to this section or chapter 895.

(c) In the course of filing, participating in, or conducting a judicial proceeding to enforce an order or judgment entered pursuant to this section or chapter 895.

(d) In the course of a criminal or civil proceeding.

A person or law enforcement agency which receives any information, record, or transcription of testimony that has been made confidential by this subsection shall maintain the confidentiality of such material and shall not disclose such information, record, or transcription of testimony except as provided for herein. Any person who willfully discloses any information, record, or transcription of testimony that has been made confidential by this subsection, except as provided for herein, is guilty of a misdemeanor of the first degree, punishable as provided in s. 775.082 or s. 775.083. If any information, record, or testimony obtained pursuant to subsection (2) is offered in evidence in any judicial proceeding, the court may, in its discretion, seal that portion of the record to further the policies of confidentiality set forth herein.

(7) This section is supplemental and shall not be construed to preclude or limit the scope of evidence gathering or other permissible discovery pursuant to any other subpoena or discovery method authorized by law or rule of procedure.

(8) It is unlawful for any person, with respect to any record or testimony produced pursuant to a subpoena issued by the Department of Legal Affairs under subsection (2), to knowingly and willfully falsify, conceal, or cover up a material fact by a trick, scheme, or device; make any false, fictitious, or fraudulent statement or representation; or make or use any false writing or document knowing the writing or document to contain any false, fictitious, or fraudulent statement or entry. A person who violates this provision is guilty of a felony of the third degree, punishable as provided in s. 775.082, s. 775.083, or s. 775.084.

(9) In the absence of a written agreement to the contrary, a registered agent is not liable for the failure to give notice of the receipt of a subpoena under subsection (2) to the corporation, foreign corporation, or alien business organization which appointed such registered agent if such registered agent timely sends written notice of the receipt of such subpoena by first-class mail or domestic or international air mail, postage fees prepaid, to the last address that has been designated in writing to the registered agent by such appointing corporation, foreign corporation, or alien business organization.

(10) The designation of a registered agent and a registered office as required by subsection (1) for a corporation, foreign corporation, or alien business organization which owns real property in this state or a mortgage on real property in this state is solely for the purposes of this act; and, notwithstanding s. 48.181, s. 607.1502, s. 607.1503, or any other relevant section of the Florida Statutes, such designation shall not be used in determining whether the corporation, foreign corporation, or alien business organization is actually doing business in this state.

(11) As used in this section, the term:

(a) "Alien business organization" means:

1. Any corporation, association, partnership, trust, joint stock company, or other entity organized under any laws other than the laws of the United States, of any United States territory or possession, or of any state of the United States; or

2. Any corporation, association, partnership, trust, joint stock company, or other entity or device 10 percent or more of which is owned or controlled, directly or indirectly, by an entity described in subparagraph 1. or by a foreign natural person.

(b) "Financial institution" means:

1. A bank, banking organization, or savings association, as defined in s. 220.62;

2. An insurance company, trust company, credit union, or industrial savings bank, any of which is licensed or regulated by an agency of the United States or any state of the United States; or

3. Any person licensed under the provisions of ss. 494.006-494.0077.

(c) "Mortgage" means a mortgage on real property situated in this state, except a mortgage owned by a financial institution.

(d) "Real property" means any real property situated in this state or any interest in such real property.

(e) "Ultimate equitable owner" means a natural person who, directly or indirectly, owns or controls an ownership interest in a corporation, foreign corporation, or alien business organization, regardless of whether such natural person owns or controls such ownership interest through one or other natural persons or one or more proxies, powers of attorney, nominees, corporations, associations, partnerships, trusts, joint stock companies, or other entities or devices, or any combination thereof.

(12) Any alien business organization may withdraw its registered agent designation by delivering an application for certificate of withdrawal to the Department of State for filing.

Such application shall set forth:

(a) The name of the alien business organization and the jurisdiction under the law of which it is incorporated or organized.

(b) That it is no longer required to maintain a registered agent in this state.

607.0601 Authorized shares.—

(1) The articles of incorporation must prescribe the classes of shares and the number of shares of each class that the corporation is authorized to issue. If more than one class of shares is authorized, the articles of incorporation must prescribe a distinguishing designation for each class, and prior to the issuance of shares of a class the preferences, limitations, and relative rights of that class must be described in the articles of incorporation. All shares of a class must have preferences, limitations, and relative rights identical with those of other shares of the same class except to the extent otherwise permitted by s. 607.0602 or s. 607.0624.

(2) The articles of incorporation must authorize:

(a) One or more classes of shares that together have unlimited voting rights, and

(b) One or more classes of shares (which may be the same class or classes as those with voting rights) that together are entitled to receive the net assets of the corporation upon dissolution.

(3) The articles of incorporation may authorize one or more classes of shares that:

(a) Have special, conditional, or limited voting rights, or no right to vote, except to the extent prohibited by this act;

(b) Are redeemable or convertible as specified in the articles of incorporation:

1. At the option of the corporation, the shareholder, or another person or upon the occurrence of a designated event;

2. For cash, indebtedness, securities, or other property; or

3. In a designated amount or in an amount determined in accordance with a designated formula or by reference to extrinsic data or events;

(c) Entitle the holders to distributions calculated in any manner, including dividends that may be cumulative, noncumulative, or partially cumulative;

(d) Have preference over any other class of shares with respect to distributions, including dividends and distributions upon the dissolution of the corporation.

(4) The description of the designations, preferences, limitations, and relative rights of share classes in subsection (3) is not exhaustive.

(5) Shares which are entitled to preference in the distribution of dividends or assets shall not be designated as common shares. Shares which are not entitled to preference in the distribution of dividends or assets shall be common shares and shall not be designated as preferred shares.

607.0602 Terms of class or series determined by board of directors.—

(1) If the articles of incorporation so provide, the board of directors may determine, in whole or part, the preferences, limitations, and relative rights (within the limits set forth in s. 607.0601) of:

(a) Any class of shares before the issuance of any shares of that class, or

(b) One or more series within a class before the issuance of any shares of that series.

(2) Each series of a class must be given a distinguishing designation.

(3) All shares of a series must have preferences, limitations, and relative rights identical with those of other shares of the same series and, except to the extent otherwise provided in the description of the series, of those of other series of the same class.

(4) Before issuing any shares of a class or series created under this section, the corporation must deliver to the Department of State for filing articles of amendment, which are effective without shareholder action, that set forth:

(a) The name of the corporation;

(b) The text of the amendment determining the terms of the class or series of shares;

(c) The date the amendment was adopted; and

(d) A statement that the amendment was duly adopted by the board of directors.

607.0603 Issued and outstanding shares.—

(1) A corporation may issue the number of shares of each class or series authorized by the articles of incorporation. Shares that are issued are outstanding shares until they are reacquired, redeemed, converted, or canceled, except as provided in s. 607.0631.

(2) The reacquisition, redemption, or conversion of outstanding shares is subject to the limitations of subsection (3) and to s. 607.06401.

(3) At all times that shares of the corporation are outstanding, one or more shares that together have unlimited voting rights and one or more shares that together are entitled to receive the net assets of the corporation upon dissolution must be outstanding.

607.0604 Fractional shares.—

(1) A corporation may:

(a) Issue fractions of a share or pay in money the fair value of fractions of a share;

(b) Make arrangements, or provide reasonable opportunity, for any person entitled to or holding a fractional interest in a share to sell such fractional interest or to purchase such additional fractional interests as may be necessary to acquire a full share;

(c) Issue scrip in registered or bearer form, over the manual or facsimile signature of an officer of the corporation or its agent, entitling the holder to receive a full share upon surrendering enough scrip to equal a full share.

(2) The board of directors may authorize the issuance of scrip subject to any condition considered desirable, including:

(a) That the scrip will become void if not exchanged for full shares before a specified date; and

(b) That the shares for which the scrip is exchangeable may be sold and the proceeds paid to the scripholders.

(3) Each certificate representing scrip must be conspicuously labeled "scrip" and must contain the information required by s. 607.0625.

(4) The holder of a fractional share is entitled to exercise the rights of a shareholder, including the right to vote, to receive dividends, and to participate in the assets of the corporation upon liquidation. The holder of scrip is not entitled to any of these rights unless the scrip provides for them.

(5) When a corporation is to pay in money the value of fractions of a share, the good faith judgment of the board of directors as to the fair value shall be conclusive.

607.0620 Subscriptions for shares.—

(1) A subscription for shares entered into before incorporation is irrevocable for 6 months unless the subscription agreement provides a longer or shorter period or all the subscribers agree to revocation.

(2) A subscription for shares, whether made before or after incorporation, is not enforceable unless in writing and signed by the subscriber.

(3) The board of directors may determine the payment terms of subscriptions for shares that were entered into before incorporation, unless the subscription agreement specifies them. A call for payment by the board of directors must be uniform as to all shares of the same class or series, unless the subscription agreement specifies otherwise.

(4) Shares issued pursuant to subscriptions entered into before incorporation are fully paid and nonassessable when the corporation receives the consideration specified in the subscription agreement.

(5) If a subscriber defaults in payment of money or property under a subscription agreement entered into before incorporation, the corporation may collect the amount owed as any other debt. Alternatively, unless the subscription agreement provides otherwise, the corporation may rescind the agreement and may sell the shares if the debt remains unpaid more than 20 days after the corporation sends written demand for payment to the subscriber. If mailed, such written demand shall be deemed to be made when deposited in the United States mail in a sealed envelope addressed to the subscriber at his or her last post office address known to the corporation, with first-class postage thereon prepaid. The defaulting subscriber or his or her legal representative shall be entitled to be paid the excess of the sale proceeds over the sum of the amount due and unpaid on the subscription and the reasonable expenses incurred in selling the shares, but in no event shall the defaulting subscriber or his or her legal representative be entitled to be paid an amount greater than the amount paid by the subscriber on the subscription.

607.0621 Issuance of shares.—

(1) The powers granted in this section to the board of directors may be reserved to the shareholders by the articles of incorporation.

(2) The board of directors may authorize shares to be issued for consideration consisting of any tangible or intangible property or benefit to the corporation, including cash, promissory notes, services performed, promises to perform services evidenced by a written contract, or other securities of the corporation.

(3) Before the corporation issues shares, the board of directors must determine that the consideration received or to be received for shares to be issued is adequate. That determination by the board of directors is conclusive insofar as the adequacy of consideration for the issuance of shares relates to whether the shares are validly issued, fully paid, and nonassessable. When it cannot be determined that outstanding shares are fully paid and nonassessable, there shall be a conclusive presumption that such shares are fully paid and nonassessable if the board of directors makes a good faith determination that there is no substantial evidence that the full consideration for such shares has not been paid.

(4) When the corporation receives the consideration for which the board of directors authorized the issuance of shares, the shares issued therefor are fully paid and nonassessable. Consideration in the form of a promise to pay money or a promise to perform services is received by the corporation at the time of the making of the promise, unless the agreement specifically provides otherwise.

(5) The corporation may place in escrow shares issued for a contract for future services or benefits or a promissory note, or make other arrangements to restrict the transfer of the shares, and may credit distributions in respect of the shares against their purchase price, until the services are performed, the note is paid, or the benefits received. If the services are not performed, the shares escrowed or restricted and the distributions credited may be canceled in whole or part.

607.0622 Liability for shares issued before payment.—

(1) A holder of, or subscriber to, shares of a corporation shall be under no obligation to the corporation or its creditors with respect to such shares other than the obligation to pay to the corporation the full consideration for which such shares were issued or to be issued. Such an obligation may be enforced by the corporation and its successors or assigns; by a shareholder suing derivatively on behalf of the corporation; by a receiver, liquidator, or trustee in bankruptcy of the corporation; or by another person having the legal right to marshal the assets of such corporation.

(2) Any person becoming an assignee or transferee of shares, or of a subscription for shares, in good faith and without knowledge or notice that the full consideration therefor has not been paid shall not be personally liable to the corporation or its creditors for any unpaid portion of such consideration, but the assignor or transferor shall continue to be liable therefor.

(3) No pledgee or other holder of shares as collateral security shall be personally liable as a shareholder, but the pledgor or other person transferring such shares as collateral shall be considered the holder thereof for purposes of liability under this section.

(4) An executor, administrator, conservator, guardian, trustee, assignee for the benefit of creditors, receiver, or other fiduciary shall not be personally liable to the corporation as a holder of, or subscriber to, shares of a corporation, but the estate and funds in her or his hands shall be so liable.

(5) No liability under this section may be asserted more than 5 years after the earlier of:

(a) The issuance of the stock, or

(b) The date of the subscription upon which the assessment is sought.

607.0623 Share dividends.—

(1) Unless the articles of incorporation provide otherwise, shares may be issued pro rata and without consideration to the corporation's shareholders or to the shareholders of one or more classes or series. An issuance of shares under this subsection is a share dividend.

(2) Shares of one class or series may not be issued as a share dividend in respect of shares of another class or series unless:

(a) The articles of incorporation so authorize,

(b) A majority of the votes entitled to be cast by the class or series to be issued approves the issue, or,

(c) There are no outstanding shares of the class or series to be issued.

(3) If the board of directors does not fix the record date for determining shareholders entitled to a share dividend, it is the date the board of directors authorizes the share dividend.

607.0624 Share options.—

(1) Unless the articles of incorporation provide otherwise, a corporation may issue rights, options, or warrants for the purchase of shares of the corporation. The board of directors shall determine the terms upon which the rights, options, or warrants are issued, their form and content, and the consideration for which the shares are to be issued.

(2) The terms and conditions of stock rights and options which are created and issued by a corporation formed under this chapter, or its successor, and which entitle the holders thereof to purchase from the corporation shares of any class or classes, whether authorized but unissued shares, treasury shares, or shares to be purchased or acquired by the corporation, may include, without limitation, restrictions, or conditions that preclude or limit the exercise, transfer, receipt, or holding of such rights or options by any person or persons, including any person or persons owning or offering to acquire a specified number or percentage of the outstanding common shares or other securities of the corporation, or any transferee or transferees of any such person or persons, or that invalidate or void such rights or options held by any such person or persons or any such transferee or transferees.

607.0625 Form and content of certificates.—

(1) Shares may but need not be represented by certificates. Unless this act or another statute expressly provides otherwise, the rights and obligations of shareholders are identical whether or not their shares are represented by certificates.

(2) At a minimum, each share certificate must state on its face:

(a) The name of the issuing corporation and that the corporation is organized under the laws of this state;

(b) The name of the person to whom issued; and

(c) The number and class of shares and the designation of the series, if any, the certificate represents.

(3) If the issuing corporation is authorized to issue different classes of shares or different series within a class, the designations, relative rights, preferences, and limitations applicable to each class and the variations in rights, preferences, and limitations determined for each series (and the authority of the board of directors to determine variations for future series) must be summarized on the front or back of each certificate. Alternatively, each certificate may state conspicuously on its front or back that the corporation will furnish the shareholder a full statement of this information on request and without charge.

(4) Each share certificate:

(a) Must be signed (either manually or in facsimile) by an officer or officers designated in the bylaws or designated by the board of directors, and

(b) May bear the corporate seal or its facsimile.

(5) If the person who signed (either manually or in facsimile) a share certificate no longer holds office when the certificate is issued, the certificate is nevertheless valid.

(6) Nothing in this section may be construed to invalidate any share certificate validly issued and outstanding under the general corporation law on July 1, 1990.

607.0626 Shares without certificates.—

(1) Unless the articles of incorporation or bylaws provide otherwise, the board of directors of a corporation may authorize the issue of some or all of the shares of any or all of its classes or series without certificates. The authorization does not affect shares already represented by certificates until they are surrendered to the corporation.

(2) Within a reasonable time after the issue or transfer of shares without certificates, the corporation shall send the shareholder a written statement of the information required on certificates by s. 607.0625(2) and (3), and, if applicable, s. 607.0627.

607.0627 Restriction on transfer of shares and other securities.—

(1) The articles of incorporation, the bylaws, an agreement among shareholders, or an agreement between shareholders and the corporation may impose restrictions on the transfer or registration of transfer of shares of the corporation. A restriction does not affect shares issued before the restriction was adopted unless the holders of such shares are parties to the restriction agreement or voted in favor of the restriction.

(2) A restriction on the transfer or registration of transfer of shares is valid and enforceable against the holder or a transferee of the holder if the restriction is authorized by this section and its existence is noted conspicuously on the front or back of the certificate or is contained in the information statement required by s. 607.0626(2). Unless so noted, a restriction is not enforceable against a person without knowledge of the restriction.

(3) A restriction on the transfer or registration of transfer of shares is authorized:

(a) To maintain the corporation's status when it is dependent on the number or identity of its shareholders;

(b) To preserve exemptions under federal or state securities law; or

(c) For any other reasonable purpose.

(4) A restriction on the transfer or registration of transfer of shares may:

(a) Obligate the shareholder first to offer the corporation or other persons (separately, consecutively, or simultaneously) an opportunity to acquire the restricted shares;

(b) Obligate the corporation or other persons (separately, consecutively, or simultaneously) to acquire the restricted shares;

(c) Require the corporation, the holders of any class of its shares, or another person to approve the transfer of the restricted shares, if the requirement is not manifestly unreasonable; or

(d) Prohibit the transfer of the restricted shares to designated persons or classes of persons, if the prohibition is not manifestly unreasonable.

(5) For purposes of this section, "shares" includes a security convertible into or carrying a right to subscribe for or acquire shares.

607.0628 Expenses of issue.—A corporation may pay the expenses of selling or underwriting its shares and of organizing or reorganizing the corporation from the consideration received for shares.

607.0630 Shareholders' preemptive rights.—

(1) The shareholders of a corporation do not have a preemptive right to acquire the corporation's unissued shares or the corporation's treasury shares, except in each case to the extent the articles of incorporation so provide.

(2) A statement included in the articles of incorporation that "the corporation elects to have preemptive rights" (or words of similar import) means that the following principles apply except to the extent the articles of incorporation expressly provide otherwise:

(a) The shareholders of the corporation have a preemptive right, granted on uniform terms and conditions prescribed by the board of directors to provide a fair and reasonable opportunity to exercise the right, to acquire proportional amounts of the corporation's unissued shares and treasury shares upon the decision of the board of directors to issue them.

(b) A shareholder may waive his or her preemptive right. A waiver evidenced by a writing is irrevocable even though it is not supported by consideration.

(c) There is no preemptive right with respect to:

1. Shares issued as compensation to directors, officers, agents, or employees of the corporation or its subsidiaries or affiliates;

2. Shares issued to satisfy conversion or option rights created to provide compensation to directors, officers, agents, or employees of the corporation or its subsidiaries or affiliates;

3. Shares authorized in articles of incorporation that are issued within 6 months from the effective date of incorporation;

4. Shares issued pursuant to a plan of reorganization approved by a court of competent jurisdiction pursuant to a law of this state or of the United States; or

5. Shares issued for consideration other than money.

(d) Holders of shares of any class or series without general voting rights but with preferential rights to distributions or net assets upon dissolution and liquidation have no preemptive rights with respect to shares of any class.

(e) Holders of shares of any class or series with general voting rights but without preferential rights to distributions or net assets upon dissolution and liquidation have no preemptive rights with respect to shares of any class with preferential rights to distributions or assets unless the shares with preferential rights are convertible into or carry a right to subscribe for or acquire shares without preferential rights.

(f) Shares subject to preemptive rights that are not acquired by shareholders may be issued to any person for a period of 1 year after being offered to shareholders at a consideration set by the board of directors that is not lower than the consideration set for the exercise of preemptive rights. An offer at a lower consideration or after the expiration of 1 year is subject to the shareholders' preemptive rights.

(3) For purposes of this section, "shares" includes a security convertible into or carrying a right to subscribe for or acquire shares.

(4) In the case of any corporation in existence prior to January 1, 1976, shareholders of such corporation shall continue to have the preemptive rights in such corporation which they had immediately prior to that date, unless and until the articles of incorporation are amended to alter or terminate shareholders' preemptive rights.

607.0631 Corporation's acquisition of its own shares.—

(1) A corporation may acquire its own shares, and, unless otherwise provided in the articles of incorporation or except as provided in subsection (4) or subsection (5), shares so acquired constitute authorized but unissued shares of the same class but undesignated as to series.

(2) If the articles of incorporation prohibit the reissue of acquired shares, the number of authorized shares is reduced by the number of shares acquired, effective upon amendment of the articles of incorporation.

(3) Articles of amendment may be adopted by the board of directors without shareholder action, shall be delivered to the Department of State for filing, and shall set forth:

(a) The name of the corporation;

(b) The reduction in the number of authorized shares, itemized by class and series; and

(c) The total number of authorized shares, itemized by class and series, remaining after reduction of the shares.

(4) Shares of a corporation in existence on June 30, 1990, which are treasury shares under s. 607.004(18), Florida Statutes (1987), shall be issued, but not outstanding, until canceled or disposed of by the corporation.

(5) A corporation that has shares of any class or series which are either registered on a national securities exchange or designated as a national market system security on an interdealer quotation system by the National Association of Securities Dealers, Inc., may acquire such shares and designate, either in the bylaws or in the resolutions of its board, that shares so acquired by the corporation shall constitute treasury shares.

607.06401 Distributions to shareholders.—

(1) A board of directors may authorize and the corporation may make distributions to its shareholders subject to restriction by the articles of incorporation and the limitations in subsection (3).

(2) If the board of directors does not fix the record date for determining shareholders entitled to a distribution (other than one involving a purchase, redemption, or other acquisition of the corporation's shares), it is the date the board of directors authorizes the distribution.

(3) No distribution may be made if, after giving it effect:

(a) The corporation would not be able to pay its debts as they become due in the usual course of business; or

(b) The corporation's total assets would be less than the sum of its total liabilities plus (unless the articles of incorporation permit otherwise) the amount that would be needed, if the corporation were to be dissolved at the time of the distribution, to satisfy the preferential rights upon dissolution of shareholders whose preferential rights are superior to those receiving the distribution.

(4) The board of directors may base a determination that a distribution is not prohibited under subsection (3) either on financial statements prepared on the basis of accounting practices and principles that are reasonable in the circumstances or on a fair valuation or other method that is reasonable in the circumstances. In the case of any distribution based upon such a valuation, each such distribution shall be identified as a distribution based upon a current valuation of assets, and the amount per share paid on the basis of such valuation shall be disclosed to the shareholders concurrent with their receipt of the distribution.

(5) If the articles of incorporation of a corporation engaged in the business of exploiting natural resources or other wasting assets so provide, distributions may be paid in cash out of depletion or similar reserves; and each such distribution shall be identified as a distribution based upon such reserves, and the amount per share paid on the basis of such reserves shall be disclosed to the shareholders concurrent with their receipt of the distribution.

(6) Except as provided in subsection (8), the effect of a distribution under subsection (3) is measured:

(a) In the case of distribution by purchase, redemption, or other acquisition of the corporation's shares, as of the earlier of:

1. The date money or other property is transferred or debt incurred by the corporation, or

2. The date the shareholder ceases to be a shareholder with respect to the acquired shares;

(b) In the case of any other distribution of indebtedness, as of the date the indebtedness is distributed;

(c) In all other cases, as of:

1. The date the distribution is authorized if the payment occurs within 120 days after the date of authorization, or

2. The date the payment is made if it occurs more than 120 days after the date of authorization.

(7) A corporation's indebtedness to a shareholder incurred by reason of a distribution made in accordance with this section is at parity with the corporation's indebtedness to its general, unsecured creditors except to the extent subordinated by agreement.

(8) Indebtedness of a corporation, including indebtedness issued as a distribution, is not considered a liability for purposes of determinations under subsection (3) if its terms provide that payment of principal and interest are made only if and to the extent that payment of a distribution to shareholders could then be made under this section. If the indebtedness is issued as a distribution, each payment of principal or interest is treated as a distribution, the effect of which is measured on the date the payment is actually made.

607.0640.

607.0701 Annual meeting.—

(1) A corporation shall hold a meeting of shareholders annually, for the election of directors and for the transaction of any proper business, at a time stated in or fixed in accordance with the bylaws.

(2) Annual shareholders' meetings may be held in or out of this state at a place stated in or fixed in accordance with the bylaws or, when not inconsistent with the bylaws, stated in the notice of the annual meeting. If no place is stated in or fixed in accordance with the bylaws, or stated in the notice of the annual meeting, annual meetings shall be held at the corporation's principal office.

(3) The failure to hold the annual meeting at the time stated in or fixed in accordance with a corporation's bylaws or pursuant to this act does not affect the validity of any corporate action and shall not work a forfeiture of or dissolution of the corporation.

(4) If authorized by the board of directors, and subject to such guidelines and procedures as the board of directors may adopt, shareholders and proxyholders not physically present at an annual meeting of shareholders may, by means of remote communication:

(a) Participate in an annual meeting of shareholders.

(b) Be deemed present in person and vote at an annual

meeting of shareholders, whether such meeting is to be held at a designated place or solely by means of remote communication, provided that:

1. The corporation shall implement reasonable measures to verify that each person deemed present and permitted to vote at the annual meeting by means of remote communication is a shareholder or proxyholder;

2. The corporation shall implement reasonable measures to provide such shareholders or proxyholders a reasonable opportunity to participate in the annual meeting and to vote on matters submitted to the shareholders, including, without limitation, an opportunity to communicate and to read or hear the proceedings of the annual meeting substantially concurrently with such proceedings; and

3. If any shareholder or proxyholder votes or takes other action at the annual meeting by means of remote communication, a record of such vote or other action shall be maintained by the corporation.

607.0702 Special meeting.—

(1) A corporation shall hold a special meeting of shareholders:

(a) On call of its board of directors or the person or persons authorized to do so by the articles of incorporation or bylaws; or

(b) If the holders of not less than 10 percent, unless a greater percentage not to exceed 50 percent is required by the articles of incorporation, of all the votes entitled to be cast on any issue proposed to be considered at the proposed special meeting sign, date, and deliver to the corporation's secretary one or more written demands for the meeting describing the purpose or purposes for which it is to be held.

(2) Special shareholders' meetings may be held in or out of the state at a place stated in or fixed in accordance with the bylaws or, when not inconsistent with the bylaws, in the notice of the special meeting. If no place is stated in or fixed in accordance with the bylaws or in the notice of the special meeting, special meetings shall be held at the corporation's principal office.

(3) Only business within the purpose or purposes described in the special meeting notice required by s. 607.0705 may be conducted at a special shareholders' meeting.

(4) If authorized by the board of directors, and subject to such guidelines and procedures as the board of directors may adopt, shareholders and proxyholders not physically present at a special meeting of shareholders may, by means of remote communication:

(a) Participate in a special meeting of shareholders.

(b) Be deemed present in person and vote at a special meeting of shareholders, whether such meeting is to be held at a designated place or solely by means of remote communication, provided that:

1. The corporation shall implement reasonable measures to verify that each person deemed present and permitted to vote at the special meeting by means of remote communication is a shareholder or proxyholder;

2. The corporation shall implement reasonable measures to provide such shareholders or proxyholders a reasonable opportunity to participate in the special meeting and to vote on matters submitted to the shareholders, including, without limitation, an opportunity to communicate and to read or hear the proceedings of the special meeting substantially concurrently with such proceedings; and

3. If any shareholder or proxyholder votes or takes other action at the special meeting by means of remote communication, a record of such vote or other action shall be maintained by the corporation.

607.0703 Court-ordered meeting.—

(1) The circuit court of the county where a corporation's principal office is located, if located in this state, or where a corporation's registered office is located if its principal office is not located in this state, may, after notice to the corporation, order a meeting to be held:

(a) On application of any shareholder of the corporation entitled to vote in an annual meeting if an annual meeting has not been held within any 13-month period; or

(b) On application of a shareholder who signed a demand for a special meeting valid under s. 607.0702, if:

1. Notice of the special meeting was not given within 60 days after the date the demand was delivered to the corporation's secretary; or

2. The special meeting was not held in accordance with the notice.

(2) The court may fix the time and place of the meeting, determine the shares entitled to participate in the meeting, specify a record date for determining shareholders entitled to notice of and to vote at the meeting, prescribe the form and content of the meeting notice, and enter other orders as may be appropriate.

607.0704 Action by shareholders without a meeting.—

(1) Unless otherwise provided in the articles of incorporation, action required or permitted by this act to be taken at an annual or special meeting of shareholders may be taken without a meeting, without prior notice, and without a vote if the action is taken by the holders of outstanding stock of each voting group entitled to vote thereon having not less than the minimum number of votes with respect to each voting group that would be necessary to

authorize or take such action at a meeting at which all voting groups and shares entitled to vote thereon were present and voted. In order to be effective the action must be evidenced by one or more written consents describing the action taken, dated and signed by approving shareholders having the requisite number of votes of each voting group entitled to vote thereon, and delivered to the corporation by delivery to its principal office in this state, its principal place of business, the corporate secretary, or another officer or agent of the corporation having custody of the book in which proceedings of meetings of shareholders are recorded. No written consent shall be effective to take the corporate action referred to therein unless, within 60 days of the date of the earliest dated consent delivered in the manner required by this section, written consents signed by the number of holders required to take action are delivered to the corporation by delivery as set forth in this section.

(2) Any written consent may be revoked prior to the date that the corporation receives the required number of consents to authorize the proposed action. No revocation is effective unless in writing and until received by the corporation at its principal office or received by the corporate secretary or other officer or agent of the corporation having custody of the book in which proceedings of meetings of shareholders are recorded.

(3) Within 10 days after obtaining such authorization by written consent, notice must be given to those shareholders who have not consented in writing or who are not entitled to vote on the action. The notice shall fairly summarize the material features of the authorized action and, if the action be such for which dissenters' rights are provided under this act, the notice shall contain a clear statement of the right of shareholders dissenting therefrom to be paid the fair value of their shares upon compliance with further provisions of this act regarding the rights of dissenting shareholders.

(4) A consent signed under this section has the effect of a meeting vote and may be described as such in any document.

(5) In the event that the action to which the shareholders consent is such as would have required the filing of a certificate under any other section of this act if such action had been voted on by shareholders at a meeting thereof, the certificate filed under such other section shall state that written consent has been given in accordance with the provisions of this section.

(6) Whenever action is taken pursuant to this section, the written consent of the shareholders consenting thereto or the written reports of inspectors appointed to tabulate such consents shall be filed with the minutes of proceedings of shareholders.

607.0705 Notice of meeting.—

(1) A corporation shall notify shareholders of the date, time, and place of each annual and special shareholders' meeting no fewer than 10 or more than 60 days before the meeting date. Unless this act or the articles of incorporation require otherwise, the corporation is required to give notice only to shareholders entitled to vote at the meeting. Notice shall be given in the manner provided in s. 607.0141, by or at the direction of the president, the secretary, or the officer or persons calling the meeting. If the notice is mailed at least 30 days before the date of the meeting, it may be done by a class of United States mail other than first class. Notwithstanding s. 607.0141, if mailed, such notice shall be deemed to be delivered when deposited in the United States mail addressed to the shareholder at her or his address as it appears on the stock transfer books of the corporation, with postage thereon prepaid.

(2) Unless this act or the articles of incorporation require otherwise, notice of an annual meeting need not include a description of the purpose or purposes for which the meeting is called.

(3) Notice of a special meeting must include a description of the purpose or purposes for which the meeting is called.

(4) Unless the bylaws require otherwise, if an annual or special shareholders' meeting is adjourned to a different date, time, or place, notice need not be given of the new date, time, or place if the new date, time, or place is announced at the meeting before an adjournment is taken, and any business may be transacted at the adjourned meeting that might have been transacted on the original date of the meeting. If a new record date for the adjourned meeting is or must be fixed under s. 607.0707, however, notice of the adjourned meeting must be given under this section to persons who are shareholders as of the new record date who are entitled to notice of the meeting.

(5) Notwithstanding the foregoing, no notice of a shareholders' meeting need be given to a shareholder if:

(a) An annual report and proxy statements for two consecutive annual meetings of shareholders or

(b) All, and at least two checks in payment of dividends or interest on securities during a 12-month period, have been sent by first-class United States mail, addressed to the shareholder at her or his address as it appears on the share transfer books of the corporation, and returned undeliverable. The obligation of the corporation to give notice of a shareholders' meeting to any such shareholder shall be reinstated once the corporation has received a new address for such shareholder for entry on its share transfer books.

607.0706 Waiver of notice.—

(1) A shareholder may waive any notice required by this act, the articles of incorporation, or bylaws before or after the date and time stated in the notice. The waiver must be in writing, be signed by the shareholder entitled to the notice, and be delivered to the corporation for inclusion in the minutes or filing with the corporate records. Neither the business to be transacted at nor the purpose of any regular or special meeting of the shareholders need be specified in any written waiver of notice unless so required by the articles of incorporation or the bylaws.

(2) A shareholder's attendance at a meeting:

(a) Waives objection to lack of notice or defective notice of the meeting, unless the shareholder at the beginning of the meeting objects to holding the meeting or transacting business at the meeting; or

(b) Waives objection to consideration of a particular matter at the meeting that is not within the purpose or purposes described in the meeting notice, unless the shareholder objects to considering the matter when it is presented.

607.0707 Record date.—

(1) The bylaws may fix or provide the manner of fixing the record date for one or more voting groups in order to determine the shareholders entitled to notice of a shareholders' meeting, to demand a special meeting, to vote, or to take any other action. If the bylaws do not fix or provide for fixing such a record date, the board of directors of the corporation may fix the record date. In no event may a record date fixed by the board of directors be a date preceding the date upon which the resolution fixing the record date is adopted.

(2) If not otherwise provided by or pursuant to the bylaws, the record date for determining shareholders entitled to demand a special meeting is the date the first shareholder delivers his or her demand to the corporation.

(3) If not otherwise provided by or pursuant to the bylaws and no prior action is required by the board of directors pursuant to this act, the record date for determining shareholders entitled to take action without a meeting is the date the first signed written consent is delivered to the corporation under s. 607.0704. If not otherwise fixed, and prior action is required by the board of directors pursuant to this chapter, the record date for determining shareholders entitled to take action without a meeting is at the close of business on the day on which the board of directors adopts the resolution taking such prior action.

(4) If not otherwise provided by or pursuant to the bylaws, the record date for determining shareholders entitled to notice of and to vote at an annual or special shareholders' meeting is the close of business on the day before the first notice is delivered to shareholders.

(5) A record date for purposes of this section may not be more than 70 days before the meeting or action requiring a determination of shareholders.

(6) A determination of shareholders entitled to notice of or to vote at a shareholders' meeting is effective for any adjournment of the meeting unless the board of directors fixes a new record date, which it must do if the meeting is adjourned to a date more than 120 days after the date fixed for the original meeting.

(7) If a court orders a meeting adjourned to a date more than 120 days after the date fixed for the original meeting, it may provide that the original record date continues in effect or it may fix a new record date.

607.0720 Shareholders' list for meeting.—

(1) After fixing a record date for a meeting, a corporation shall prepare an alphabetical list of the names of all its shareholders who are entitled to notice of a shareholders' meeting, arranged by voting group with the address of, and the number and class and series, if any, of shares held by, each.

(2) The shareholders' list must be available for inspection by any shareholder for a period of 10 days prior to the meeting or such shorter time as exists between the record date and the meeting and continuing through the meeting at the corporation's principal office, at a place identified in the meeting notice in the city where the meeting will be held, or at the office of the corporation's transfer agent or registrar. A shareholder or the shareholder's agent or attorney is entitled on written demand to inspect the list (subject to the requirements of s. 607.1602(3)), during regular business hours and at his or her expense, during the period it is available for inspection.

(3) The corporation shall make the shareholders' list available at the meeting, and any shareholder or the shareholder's agent or attorney is entitled to inspect the list at any time during the meeting or any adjournment.

(4) The shareholders' list is prima facie evidence of the identity of shareholders entitled to examine the shareholders' list or to vote at a meeting of shareholders.

(5) If the requirements of this section have not been substantially complied with or if the corporation refuses to allow a shareholder or the shareholder's agent or attorney to inspect the shareholders' list before or at the meeting, the meeting shall be adjourned until such requirements are complied with on the demand of any shareholder in person or by proxy who failed to get such access, or, if not adjourned upon such demand and such requirements are not complied with, the circuit court of the county where a corporation's principal office (or, if none in this state, its registered office) is located, on application of the shareholder, may summarily order the inspection or copying at the corporation's expense and may postpone the meeting for which the list was prepared until the inspection or copying is complete.

(6) Refusal or failure to comply with the requirements of this section shall not affect the validity of any action taken at such meeting.

(7) A shareholder may not sell or otherwise distribute any information or records inspected under this section, except to the extent that such use is for a proper purpose as defined in s. 607.1602(3). Any person who violates this provision shall be subject to a civil penalty of $5,000.

607.0721 Voting entitlement of shares.—

(1) Except as provided in subsections (2), (3), and (4) or unless the articles of incorporation or this act provides otherwise, each outstanding share, regardless of class, is entitled to one vote on each matter submitted to a vote at a meeting of shareholders. Only shares are entitled to vote. If the articles of incorporation provide for more or less than one vote for any share on any matter, every reference in this act to a majority or other proportion of shares shall refer to such a majority or other proportion of votes entitled to be cast.

(2) The shares of a corporation are not entitled to vote if they are owned, directly or indirectly, by a second corporation, domestic or foreign, and the first corporation owns, directly or indirectly, a majority of the shares entitled to vote for directors of the second corporation.

(3) Subsection (2) does not limit the power of a corporation to vote any shares, including its own shares, held by it in a fiduciary capacity.

(4) Redeemable shares are not entitled to vote on any matter, and shall not be deemed to be outstanding, after notice of redemption is mailed to the holders thereof and a sum sufficient to redeem such shares has been deposited with a bank, trust company, or other financial institution upon an irrevocable obligation to pay the holders the redemption price upon surrender of the shares.

(5) Shares standing in the name of another corporation, domestic or foreign, may be voted by such officer, agent, or proxy as the bylaws of the corporate shareholder may prescribe or, in the absence of any applicable provision, by such person as the board of directors of the corporate shareholder may designate. In the absence of any such designation or in case of conflicting designation by the corporate shareholder, the chair of the board, the president, any vice president, the secretary, and the treasurer of the corporate shareholder, in that order, shall be presumed to be fully authorized to vote such shares.

(6) Shares held by an administrator, executor, guardian, personal representative, or conservator may be voted by him or her, either in person or by proxy, without a transfer of such shares into his or her name. Shares standing in the name of a trustee may be voted by him or her, either in person or by proxy, but no trustee shall be entitled to vote shares held by him or her without a transfer of such shares into his or her name or the name of his or her nominee.

(7) Shares held by or under the control of a receiver, a trustee in bankruptcy proceedings, or an assignee for the benefit of creditors may be voted by him or her without the transfer thereof into his or her name.

(8) If a share or shares stand of record in the names of two or more persons, whether fiduciaries, members of a partnership, joint tenants, tenants in common, tenants by the entirety, or otherwise, or if two or more persons have the same fiduciary relationship respecting the same shares, unless the secretary of the corporation is given notice to the contrary and is furnished with a copy of the instrument or order appointing them or creating the relationship wherein it is so provided, then acts with respect to voting have the following effect:

(a) If only one votes, in person or by proxy, his or her act binds all;

(b) If more than one vote, in person or by proxy, the act of the majority so voting binds all;

(c) If more than one vote, in person or by proxy, but the vote is evenly split on any particular matter, each faction is entitled to vote the share or shares in question proportionally;

(d) If the instrument or order so filed shows that any such tenancy is held in unequal interest, a majority or a vote evenly split for purposes of this subsection shall be a majority or a vote evenly split in interest;

(e) The principles of this subsection shall apply, insofar as possible, to execution of proxies, waivers, consents, or objections and for the purpose of ascertaining the presence of a quorum.

(9) Subject to s. 607.0723, nothing herein contained shall prevent trustees or other fiduciaries holding shares registered in the name of a nominee from causing such shares to be voted by such nominee as the trustee or other fiduciary may direct. Such nominee may vote shares as directed by a trustee or other fiduciary without the necessity of transferring the shares to the name of the trustee or other fiduciary.

607.0722 Proxies.—

(1) A shareholder, other person entitled to vote on behalf of a shareholder pursuant to s. 607.0721, or attorney in fact for a shareholder may vote the shareholder's shares in person or by proxy.

(2)(a) A shareholder, other person entitled to vote on behalf of a shareholder pursuant to s. 607.0721, or attorney in fact for a shareholder may appoint a proxy to vote or otherwise act for the shareholder by signing an appointment form or by electronic transmission. Any type of electronic transmission appearing to have been, or containing or accompanied by such information or obtained under such procedures to reasonably ensure that the electronic transmission was, transmitted by such person is a sufficient appointment, subject to the verification requested by the corporation under s. 607.0724.

(b) Without limiting the manner in which a shareholder, other person entitled to vote on behalf of a shareholder pursuant to s. 607.0721, or attorney in fact for a shareholder may appoint a proxy to vote or otherwise act for the shareholder pursuant to paragraph (a), a shareholder, other person entitled to vote on behalf of a shareholder pursuant to s. 607.0721, or attorney in fact for a shareholder may make such an appointment by:

1. Signing an appointment form, with the signature affixed, by any reasonable means including, but not limited to, facsimile or electronic signature.

2. Transmitting or authorizing the transmission of an electronic transmission to the person who will be appointed as the proxy or to a proxy solicitation firm, proxy support service organization, registrar, or agent authorized by the person who will be designated as the proxy to receive such transmission. However, any electronic transmission must set forth or be submitted with information from which it can be determined that the electronic transmission was authorized by the shareholder, other person entitled to vote on behalf of a shareholder pursuant to s. 607.0721, or attorney in fact for a shareholder. If it is determined that the electronic transmission is valid, the inspectors of election or, if there are no inspectors, such other persons making that determination shall specify the information upon which they relied.

(3) An appointment of a proxy is effective when received by the secretary or other officer or agent authorized to tabulate votes. An appointment is valid for up to 11 months unless a longer period is expressly provided in the appointment.

(4) The death or incapacity of the shareholder appointing a proxy does not affect the right of the corporation to accept the proxy's authority unless notice of the death or incapacity is received by the secretary or other officer or agent authorized to tabulate votes before the proxy exercises his or her authority under the appointment.

(5) An appointment of a proxy is revocable by the shareholder unless the appointment form or electronic transmission conspicuously states that it is irrevocable and the appointment is coupled with an interest. Appointments coupled with an interest include the appointment of:

(a) A pledgee;

(b) A person who purchased or agreed to purchase the shares;

(c) A creditor of the corporation who extended credit to the corporation under terms requiring the appointment;

(d) An employee of the corporation whose employment contract requires the appointment; or

(e) A party to a voting agreement created under s. 607.0731.

(6) An appointment made irrevocable under subsection (5) becomes revocable when the interest with which it is coupled is extinguished.

(7) A transferee for value of shares subject to an irrevocable appointment may revoke the appointment if the transferee did not know of its existence when he or she acquired the shares and the existence of the irrevocable appointment was not noted conspicuously on the certificate representing the shares or on the information statement for shares without certificates.

(8) Subject to s. 607.0724 and to any express limitation on the proxy's authority appearing on the face of the appointment form or in the electronic transmission, a corporation is entitled to accept the proxy's vote or other action as that of the shareholder making the appointment.

(9) If an appointment form expressly provides, any proxy holder may appoint, in writing, a substitute to act in his or her place.

(10) Any copy, facsimile transmission, or other reliable reproduction of the writing or electronic transmission created under subsection (2) may be substituted or used in lieu of the original writing or electronic transmission for any purpose for which the original writing or electronic transmission could be used if the copy, facsimile transmission, or other reproduction is a complete reproduction of the entire original writing or electronic transmission.

(11) A corporation may adopt bylaws authorizing additional means or procedures for shareholders to use in exercising rights granted by this section.

607.0723 Shares held by nominees.—

(1) A corporation may establish a procedure by which the beneficial owner of shares that are registered in the name of a nominee is recognized by the corporation as the shareholder. The extent of this recognition may be determined in the procedure.

(2) The procedure may set forth:

(a) The types of nominees to which it applies;

(b) The rights or privileges that the corporation recognizes in a beneficial owner;

(c) The manner in which the procedure is selected by the nominee;

(d) The information that must be provided when the procedure is selected;

(e) The period for which selection of the procedure is effective; and

(f) Other aspects of the rights and duties created.

607.0724 Corporation's acceptance of votes.—

(1) If the name signed on a vote, consent, waiver, or proxy appointment corresponds to the name of a shareholder, the corporation if acting in good faith is entitled to accept the vote, consent, waiver, or proxy appointment and give it effect as the act of the shareholder.

(2) If the name signed on a vote, consent, waiver, or proxy appointment does not correspond to the name of its shareholder, the corporation if acting in good faith is nevertheless entitled to accept the vote, consent, waiver, or proxy appointment and give it effect as the act of the shareholder if:

(a) The shareholder is an entity and the name signed purports to be that of an officer or agent of the entity;

(b) The name signed purports to be that of an administrator, executor, guardian, personal representative, or conservator representing the shareholder and, if the corporation requests, evidence

of fiduciary status acceptable to the corporation has been presented with respect to the vote, consent, waiver, or proxy appointment;

(c) The name signed purports to be that of a receiver, trustee in bankruptcy, or assignee for the benefit of creditors of the shareholder and, if the corporation requests, evidence of this status acceptable to the corporation has been presented with respect to the vote, consent, waiver, or proxy appointment;

(d) The name signed purports to be that of a pledgee, beneficial owner, or attorney in fact of the shareholder and, if the corporation requests, evidence acceptable to the corporation of the signatory's authority to sign for the shareholder has been presented with respect to the vote, consent, waiver, or proxy appointment; or

(e) Two or more persons are the shareholder as cotenants or fiduciaries and the name signed purports to be the name of at least one of the coowners and the person signing appears to be acting on behalf of all the coowners.

(3) The corporation is entitled to reject a vote, consent, waiver, or proxy appointment if the secretary or other officer or agent authorized to tabulate votes, acting in good faith, has reasonable basis for doubt about the validity of the signature on it or about the signatory's authority to sign for the shareholder.

(4) The corporation and its officer or agent who accepts or rejects a vote, consent, waiver, or proxy appointment in good faith and in accordance with the standards of this section are not liable in damages to the shareholder for the consequences of the acceptance or rejection.

(5) Corporate action based on the acceptance or rejection of a vote, consent, waiver, or proxy appointment under this section is valid unless a court of competent jurisdiction determines otherwise.

60, ch. 89-154.

607.0725 Quorum and voting requirements for voting groups.—

(1) Shares entitled to vote as a separate voting group may take action on a matter at a meeting only if a quorum of those shares exists with respect to that matter. Unless the articles of incorporation or this act provides otherwise, a majority of the votes entitled to be cast on the matter by the voting group constitutes a quorum of that voting group for action on that matter.

(2) Once a share is represented for any purpose at a meeting, it is deemed present for quorum purposes for the remainder of the meeting and for any adjournment of that meeting unless a new record date is or must be set for that adjourned meeting.

(3) If a quorum exists, action on a matter (other than the election of directors) by a voting group is approved if the votes cast within the voting group favoring the action exceed the votes cast opposing the action, unless the articles of incorporation or this act requires a greater number of affirmative votes.

(4) The holders of a majority of the shares represented, and who would be entitled to vote at a meeting if a quorum were present, where a quorum is not present, may adjourn such meeting from time to time.

(5) The articles of incorporation may provide for a greater voting requirement or a greater or lesser quorum requirement for shareholders, or voting groups of shareholders, than is provided by this act, but in no event shall a quorum consist of less than one-third of the shares entitled to vote.

(6) An amendment to the articles of incorporation that adds, changes, or deletes a greater or lesser quorum or voting requirement shall meet the same quorum requirement and be adopted by the same vote and voting groups required to take action under the quorum and voting requirements then in effect or proposed to be adopted, whichever is greater.

(7) The election of directors is governed by s. 607.0728.

607.0726 Action by single and multiple voting groups.—

(1) If the articles of incorporation or this act provides for voting by a single voting group on a matter, action on that matter is taken when voted upon by that voting group as provided in s. 607.0725.

(2) If the articles of incorporation or this act provides for voting by two or more voting groups on a matter, action on that matter is taken only when voted upon by each of those voting groups counted separately as provided in s. 607.0725. Action may be taken by one voting group on a matter even though no action is taken by another voting group entitled to vote on the matter.

607.0728 Voting for directors; cumulative voting.—

(1) Unless otherwise provided in the articles of incorporation, directors are elected by a plurality of the votes cast by the shares entitled to vote in the election at a meeting at which a quorum is present.

(2) Each shareholder who is entitled to vote at an election of directors has the right to vote the number of shares owned by him or her for as many persons as there are directors to be elected and for whose election the shareholder has a right to vote. Shareholders do not have a right to cumulate their votes for directors unless the articles of incorporation so provide.

(3) A statement included in the articles of incorporation that "all or a designated voting group of shareholders are entitled to cumulate their votes for directors," or words of similar import, means that the shareholders designated are entitled to multiply the number of votes they are entitled to cast by the number of directors for whom they are entitled to vote and cast the product for a single candidate or distribute the product among two or more candidates.

607.0730 Voting trusts.—

(1) One or more shareholders may create a voting trust, conferring on a trustee the right to vote or otherwise act for him or her or for them, by signing an agreement setting out the provisions of the trust (which may include anything consistent with its purpose) and transferring their shares to the trustee. When a voting trust agreement is signed, the trustee shall prepare a list of the names and addresses of all owners of beneficial interests in the trust, together with the number and class of shares each transferred to the trust, and deliver copies of the list and agreement to the corporation's principal office. After filing a copy of the list and agreement in the corporation's principal office, such copy shall be open to inspection by any shareholder of the corporation (subject to the requirements of s. 607.1602(3)) or any beneficiary of the trust under the agreement during business hours.

(2) A voting trust becomes effective on the date the first shares subject to the trust are registered in the trustee's name.

607.0731 Shareholders' agreements.—

(1) Two or more shareholders may provide for the manner in which they will vote their shares by signing an agreement for that purpose. A shareholders' agreement created under this section is not subject to the provisions of s. 607.0730.

(2) A shareholders' agreement created under this section is specifically enforceable.

(3) A transferee of shares in a corporation the shareholders of which have entered into an agreement authorized by subsection (1) shall be bound by such agreement if the transferee takes shares subject to such agreement with notice thereof. A transferee shall be deemed to have notice of any such agreement or any such renewal if the existence thereof is noted on the face or back of the certificate or certificates representing such shares.

607.0732 Shareholder agreements.—

(1) An agreement among the shareholders of a corporation with 100 or fewer shareholders at the time of the agreement, that complies with this section, is effective among the shareholders and the corporation, even though it is inconsistent with one or more other provisions of this chapter, if it:

(a) Eliminates the board of directors or restricts the discretion or powers of the board of directors;

(b) Governs the authorization or making of distributions whether or not in proportion to ownership of shares, subject to the limitations in s. 607.06401;

(c) Establishes who shall be directors or officers of the corporation, or their terms of office or manner of selection or removal;

(d) Governs, in general or in regard to specific matters, the exercise or division of voting power by the shareholders and directors, including use of weighted voting rights or director proxies;

(e) Establishes the terms and conditions of any agreement for the transfer or use of property or the provision of services between the corporation and any shareholder, director, officer, or employee of the corporation;

(f) Transfers to any shareholder or other person any authority to exercise the corporate powers or to manage the business and affairs of the corporation, including the resolution of any issue about which there exists a deadlock among directors or shareholders; or

(g) Requires dissolution of the corporation at the request of one or more of the shareholders or upon the occurrence of a specified event or contingency.

(h) Otherwise governs the exercise of the corporate powers or the management of the business and affairs of the corporation or the relationship between the shareholders, the directors, or the corporation, and is not contrary to public policy. For purposes of this paragraph, agreements contrary to public policy include, but are not limited to, agreements that reduce the duties of care and loyalty to the corporation as required by ss. 607.0830 and 607.0832, exculpate directors from liability that may be imposed under s. 607.0831, adversely affect shareholders' rights to bring derivative actions under s. 607.07401, or abrogate dissenters' rights under ss. 607.1301-607.1320.

(2) An agreement authorized by this section shall be:

(a)1. Set forth in the articles of incorporation or bylaws and approved by all persons who are shareholders at the time the agreement; or

2. Set forth in a written agreement that is signed by all persons who are shareholders at the time of the agreement and such written agreement is made known to the corporation.

(b) Subject to termination or amendment only by all persons who are shareholders at the time of the termination or amendment, unless the agreement provides otherwise with respect to termination and with respect to amendments that do not change the designation, rights, preferences, or limitations of any of the shares of a class or series.

(3) The existence of an agreement authorized by this section shall be noted conspicuously on the front or back of each certificate for outstanding shares or on the information statement required by s. 607.0626(2). If at the time of the agreement the corporation has shares outstanding which are represented by certificates, the corporation shall recall such certificates and issue substitute certificates that comply with this subsection. The failure to note the existence of the agreement on the certificate or information statement shall not affect the validity of the agreement or any action taken pursuant to it. Any purchaser of shares who, at the time of purchase, did not have knowledge of the existence of the agreement shall be entitled to rescission of the purchase. A purchaser shall be deemed to have knowledge of the existence of the agreement if its existence is noted on the certificate or information statement for the shares in compliance with this subsection and, if the shares are not represented by a certificate, the information statement is delivered to the purchaser at or prior to the time of the purchase of the shares. An action to enforce the right

of rescission authorized by this subsection must be commenced within earlier of 90 days after discovery of the existence of the agreement or 2 years after the time of purchase of the shares.

(4) An agreement authorized by this section shall cease to be effective when shares of the corporation are listed on a national securities exchange or regularly quoted in a market maintained by one or more members of a national or affiliated securities association. If the agreement ceases to be effective for any reason, the board of directors may, if the agreement is contained or referred to in the corporation's articles of incorporation or bylaws, adopt an amendment to the articles of incorporation or bylaws, without shareholder action, to delete the agreement and any references to it.

(5) An agreement authorized by this section that limits the discretion or powers of the board of directors shall relieve the directors of, and impose upon the person or persons in whom such discretion or powers are vested, liability for acts or omissions imposed by law on directors to the extent that the discretion or powers of the directors are limited by the agreement.

(6) The existence or performance of an agreement authorized by this section shall not be a ground for imposing personal liability on any shareholder for the acts or debts of the corporation even if the agreement or its performance treats the corporation as if it were a partnership or results in failure to observe the corporate formalities otherwise applicable to the matters governed by the agreement.

(7) Incorporators or subscribers for shares may act as shareholders with respect to an agreement authorized by this section if no shares have been issued when the agreement is made.

607.07401 Shareholders' derivative actions.—

(1) A person may not commence a proceeding in the right of a domestic or foreign corporation unless the person was a shareholder of the corporation when the transaction complained of occurred or unless the person became a shareholder through transfer by operation of law from one who was a shareholder at that time.

(2) A complaint in a proceeding brought in the right of a corporation must be verified and allege with particularity the demand made to obtain action by the board of directors and that the demand was refused or ignored by the board of directors for a period of at least 90 days from the first demand unless, prior to the expiration of the 90 days, the person was notified in writing that the corporation rejected the demand, or unless irreparable injury to the corporation would result by waiting for the expiration of the 90-day period. . If the corporation commences an investigation of the charges made in the demand or complaint, the court may stay any proceeding until the investigation is completed.

(3) The court may dismiss a derivative proceeding if, on motion by the corporation, the court finds that one of the groups specified below has made a determination in good faith after conducting a reasonable investigation upon which its conclusions are based that the maintenance of the derivative suit is not in the best interests of the corporation. The corporation shall have the burden of proving the independence and good faith of the group making the determination and the reasonableness of the investigation. The determination shall be made by:

(a) A majority vote of independent directors present at a meeting of the board of directors, if the independent directors constitute a quorum;

(b) A majority vote of a committee consisting of two or more independent directors appointed by a majority vote of independent directors present at a meeting of the board of directors, whether or not such independent directors constitute a quorum; or

(c) A panel of one or more independent persons appointed by the court upon motion by the corporation.

(4) A proceeding commenced under this section may not be discontinued or settled without the court's approval. If the court determines that a proposed discontinuance or settlement will substantially affect the interest of the corporation's shareholders or a class, series, or voting group of shareholders, the court shall direct that notice be given to the shareholders affected. The court may determine which party or parties to the proceeding shall bear the expense of giving the notice.

(5) On termination of the proceeding, the court may require the plaintiff to pay any defendant's reasonable expenses, including reasonable attorney's fees, incurred in defending the proceeding if it finds that the proceeding was commenced without reasonable cause.

(6) The court may award reasonable expenses for maintaining the proceeding, including reasonable attorney's fees, to a successful plaintiff or to the person commencing the proceeding who receives any relief, whether by judgment, compromise, or settlement, and require that the person account for the remainder of any proceeds to the corporation; however, this subsection does not apply to any relief rendered for the benefit of injured shareholders only and limited to a recovery of the loss or damage of the injured shareholders.

(7) For purposes of this section, "shareholder" includes a beneficial owner whose shares are held in a voting trust or held by a nominee on his or her behalf.

607.0740.

607.0801 Requirement for and duties of board of directors.—

(1) Except as provided in s. 607.0732(1), each corporation must have a board of directors.

(2) All corporate powers shall be exercised by or under the authority of, and the business and affairs of the corporation managed under the direction of, its board of directors, subject to any limitation set forth in the articles of incorporation or in an agreement authorized under s. 607.0732.

607.0802 Qualifications of directors.—

(1) Directors must be natural persons who are 18 years of age or older but need not be residents of this state or shareholders of the corporation unless the articles of incorporation or bylaws so require. The articles of incorporation or bylaws may prescribe additional qualifications for directors.

(2) In the event that the eligibility to serve as a member of the board of directors of a condominium association, cooperative association, homeowners' association, or mobile home owners' association is restricted to membership in such association and membership is appurtenant to ownership of a unit, parcel, or mobile home, a grantor of a trust described in s. 733.707(3), or a beneficiary as defined in s. 737.303(4)(b) of a trust which owns a unit, parcel, or mobile home shall be deemed a member of the association and eligible to serve as a director of the condominium association, cooperative association, homeowners' association, or mobile home owners' association, provided that said beneficiary occupies the unit, parcel, or mobile home.

607.0803 Number of directors.—

(1) A board of directors must consist of one or more individuals, with the number specified in or fixed in accordance with the articles of incorporation or bylaws.

(2) The number of directors may be increased or decreased from time to time by amendment to, or in the manner provided in, the articles of incorporation or the bylaws.

(3) Directors are elected at the first annual shareholders' meeting and at each annual meeting thereafter unless their terms are staggered under s. 607.0806.

607.0804 Election of directors by certain voting groups.—The articles of incorporation may confer upon holders of any voting group the right to elect one or more directors who shall serve for such term and have such voting powers as are stated in the articles of incorporation. The terms of office and voting powers of the directors elected in the manner provided in the articles of incorporation may be greater than or less than those of any other director or class of directors. If the articles of incorporation provide that directors elected by the holders of a voting group shall have more or less than one vote per director on any matter, every reference in this act to a majority or other proportion of directors shall refer to a majority or other proportion of the votes of such directors.

607.0805 Terms of directors generally.—

(1) The terms of the initial directors of a corporation expire at the first shareholders' meeting at which directors are elected.

(2) The terms of all other directors expire at the next annual shareholders' meeting following their election unless their terms are staggered under s. 607.0806.

(3) A decrease in the number of directors does not shorten an incumbent director's term.

(4) The term of a director elected to fill a vacancy expires at the next shareholders' meeting at which directors are elected.

(5) Despite the expiration of a director's term, the director continues to serve until his or her successor is elected and qualifies or until there is a decrease in the number of directors.

607.0806 Staggered terms for directors.—

(1) The directors of any corporation organized under this act may, by the articles of incorporation or by an initial bylaw, or by a bylaw adopted by a vote of the shareholders, be divided into one, two, or three classes with the number of directors in each class being as nearly equal as possible; the term of office of those of the first class to expire at the annual meeting next ensuing; of the second class 1 year thereafter; of the third class 2 years thereafter; and at each annual election held after such classification and election, directors shall be chosen for a full term, as the case may be, to succeed those whose terms expire. If the directors have staggered terms, then any increase or decrease in the number of directors shall be so apportioned among the classes as to make all classes as nearly equal in number as possible.

(2) In the case of any Florida corporation in existence prior to July 1, 1990, directors of such corporation divided into four classes may continue to serve staggered terms as the articles of incorporation or bylaws of such corporation provided immediately prior to the effective date of this act, unless and until the articles of incorporation or bylaws are amended to alter or terminate such classes.

607.0807 Resignation of directors.—

(1) A director may resign at any time by delivering written notice to the board of directors or its chair or to the corporation.

(2) A resignation is effective when the notice is delivered unless the notice specifies a later effective date. If a resignation is made effective at a later date, the board of directors may fill the pending vacancy before the effective date if the board of directors provides that the successor does not take office until the effective date.

607.0808 Removal of directors by shareholders.—

(1) The shareholders may remove one or more directors with or without cause unless the articles of incorporation provide that directors may be removed only for cause.

(2) If a director is elected by a voting group of shareholders, only the shareholders of that voting group may participate in the vote to remove him or her.

(3) If cumulative voting is authorized, a director may not be removed if the number of votes sufficient to elect the director under cumulative voting is voted against his or her removal. If cumulate voting is not authorized, a director may be removed only if the number of votes cast to remove the director exceeds the number of votes cast not to remove him or her.

(4) A director may be removed by the shareholders at a meeting of shareholders, provided the notice of the meeting states that the purpose, or one of the purposes, of the meeting is removal of the director.

607.0809 Vacancy on board.—

(1) Whenever a vacancy occurs on a board of directors, including a vacancy resulting from an increase in the number of directors, it may be filled by the affirmative vote of a majority of the remaining directors, though less than a quorum of the board of directors, or by the shareholders, unless the articles of incorporation provide otherwise.

(2) Whenever the holders of shares of any voting group are entitled to elect a class of one or more directors by the provisions of the articles of incorporation, vacancies in such class may be filled by holders of shares of that voting group or by a majority of the directors then in office elected by such voting group or by a sole remaining director so elected. If no director elected by such voting group remains in office, unless the articles of incorporation provide otherwise, directors not elected by such voting group may fill vacancies as provided in subsection (1).

(3) A vacancy that will occur at a specific later date (by reason of a resignation effective at a later date under s. 607.0807(2) or otherwise) may be filled before the vacancy occurs but the new director may not take office until the vacancy occurs.

607.08101 Compensation of directors.—Unless the articles of incorporation or bylaws provide otherwise, the board of directors may fix the compensation of directors.

607.0810.

607.0820 Meetings.—

(1) The board of directors may hold regular or special meetings in or out of this state.

(2) A majority of the directors present, whether or not a quorum exists, may adjourn any meeting of the board of directors to another time and place. Unless the bylaws otherwise provide, notice of any such adjourned meeting shall be given to the directors who were not present at the time of the adjournment and, unless the time and place of the adjourned meeting are announced at the time of the adjournment, to the other directors.

(3) Meetings of the board of directors may be called by the chair of the board or by the president unless otherwise provided in the articles of incorporation or the bylaws.

(4) Unless the articles of incorporation or bylaws provide otherwise, the board of directors may permit any or all directors to participate in a regular or special meeting by, or conduct the meeting through the use of, any means of communication by which all directors participating may simultaneously hear each other during the meeting. A director participating in a meeting by this means is deemed to be present in person at the meeting.

607.0821 Action by directors without a meeting.—

(1) Unless the articles of incorporation or bylaws provide otherwise, action required or permitted by this act to be taken at a board of directors' meeting or committee meeting may be taken without a meeting if the action is taken by all members of the board or of the committee. The action must be evidenced by one or more written consents describing the action taken and signed by each director or committee member.

(2) Action taken under this section is effective when the last director signs the consent, unless the consent specifies a different effective date.

(3) A consent signed under this section has the effect of a meeting vote and may be described as such in any document.

607.0822 Notice of meetings.—

(1) Unless the articles of incorporation or bylaws provide otherwise, regular meetings of the board of directors may be held without notice of the date, time, place, or purpose of the meeting.

(2) Unless the articles of incorporation or bylaws provide for a longer or shorter period, special meetings of the board of directors must be preceded by at least 2 days' notice of the date, time, and place of the meeting. The notice need not describe the purpose of the special meeting unless required by the articles of incorporation or bylaws.

607.0823 Waiver of notice.—Notice of a meeting of the board of directors need not be given to any director who signs a waiver of notice either before or after the meeting. Attendance of a director at a meeting shall constitute a waiver of notice of such meeting and a waiver of any and all objections to the place of the meeting, the time of the meeting, or the manner in which it has been called or convened, except when a director states, at the beginning of the meeting or promptly upon arrival at the meeting, any objection to the transaction of business because the meeting is not lawfully called or convened.

607.0824 Quorum and voting.—

(1) Unless the articles of incorporation or bylaws require a different number, a quorum of a board of directors consists of a majority of the number of directors prescribed by the articles of incorporation or the bylaws.

(2) The articles of incorporation may authorize a quorum of a board of directors to consist of less than a majority but no fewer than one-third of the prescribed number of directors determined under the articles of incorporation or the bylaws.

(3) If a quorum is present when a vote is taken, the affirmative vote of a majority of directors present is the act of the board of directors unless the articles of incorporation or bylaws require the vote of a greater number of directors.

(4) A director of a corporation who is present at a meeting of the board of directors or a committee of the board of directors when corporate action is taken is deemed to have assented to the action taken unless the director:

(a) Objects at the beginning of the meeting (or promptly upon his or her arrival) to holding it or transacting specified business at the meeting; or

(b) Votes against or abstains from the action taken.

607.0825 Committees.—

(1) Unless the articles of incorporation or the bylaws otherwise provide, the board of directors, by resolution adopted by a majority of the full board of directors, may designate from among its members an executive committee and one or more other committees each of which, to the extent provided in such resolution or in the articles of incorporation or the bylaws of the corporation, shall have and may exercise all the authority of the board of directors, except that no such committee shall have the authority to:

(a) Approve or recommend to shareholders actions or proposals required by this act to be approved by shareholders.

(b) Fill vacancies on the board of directors or any committee thereof.

(c) Adopt, amend, or repeal the bylaws.

(d) Authorize or approve the reacquisition of shares unless pursuant to a general formula or method specified by the board of directors.

(e) Authorize or approve the issuance or sale or contract for the sale of shares, or determine the designation and relative rights, preferences, and limitations of a voting group except that the board of directors may authorize a committee (or a senior executive officer of the corporation) to do so within limits specifically prescribed by the board of directors.

(2) Unless the articles of incorporation or bylaws provide otherwise, ss. 607.0820, 607.0822, 607.0823, and 607.0824 which govern meetings, notice and waiver of notice, and quorum and voting requirements of the board of directors apply to committees and their members as well.

(3) Each committee must have two or more members who serve at the pleasure of the board of directors. The board, by resolution adopted in accordance with subsection (1), may designate one or more directors as alternate members of any such committee who may act in the place and stead of any absent member or members at any meeting of such committee.

(4) Neither the designation of any such committee, the delegation thereto of authority, nor action by such committee pursuant to such authority shall alone constitute compliance by any member of the board of directors not a member of the committee in question with his or her responsibility to act in good faith, in a manner he or she reasonably believes to be in the best interests of the corporation, and with such care as an ordinarily prudent person in a like position would use under similar circumstances.

607.0830 General standards for directors.—

(1) A director shall discharge his or her duties as a director, including his or her duties as a member of a committee:

(a) In good faith;

(b) With the care an ordinarily prudent person in a like position would exercise under similar circumstances; and

(c) In a manner he or she reasonably believes to be in the best interests of the corporation.

(2) In discharging his or her duties, a director is entitled to rely on information, opinions, reports, or statements, including financial statements and other financial data, if prepared or presented by:

(a) One or more officers or employees of the corporation whom the director reasonably believes to be reliable and competent in the matters presented;

(b) Legal counsel, public accountants, or other persons as to matters the director reasonably believes are within the persons' professional or expert competence; or

(c) A committee of the board of directors of which he or she is not a member if the director reasonably believes the committee merits confidence.

(3) In discharging his or her duties, a director may consider such factors as the director deems relevant, including the long-term prospects and interests of the corporation and its shareholders, and the social, economic, legal, or other effects of any action on the employees, suppliers, customers of the corporation or its subsidiaries, the communities and society in which the corporation or its subsidiaries operate, and the economy of the state and the nation.

(4) A director is not acting in good faith if he or she has knowledge concerning the matter in question that makes reliance otherwise permitted by subsection (2) unwarranted.

(5) A director is not liable for any action taken as a director, or any failure to take any action, if he or she performed the duties of his or her office in compliance with this section.

607.0831 Liability of directors.—

(1) A director is not personally liable for monetary damages to the corporation or any other person for any statement, vote, decision, or failure to act, regarding corporate management or policy, by a director, unless:

(a) The director breached or failed to perform his or her duties as a director; and

(b) The director's breach of, or failure to perform, those duties constitutes:

1. A violation of the criminal law, unless the director had reasonable cause to believe his or her conduct was lawful or had no reasonable cause to believe his or her conduct was unlawful. A judgment or other final adjudication against a director in any criminal proceeding for a violation of the criminal law estops that director from contesting the fact that his or her breach, or failure to perform, constitutes a violation of the criminal law; but does not estop the director from establishing that he or she had reasonable cause to believe that his or her conduct was lawful or had no reasonable cause to believe that his or her conduct was unlawful;

2. A transaction from which the director derived an improper personal benefit, either directly or indirectly;

3. A circumstance under which the liability provisions of s. 607.0834 are applicable;

4. In a proceeding by or in the right of the corporation to procure a judgment in its favor or by or in the right of a shareholder, conscious disregard for the best interest of the corporation, or willful misconduct; or

5. In a proceeding by or in the right of someone other than the corporation or a shareholder, recklessness or an act or omission which was committed in bad faith or with malicious purpose or in a manner exhibiting wanton and willful disregard of human rights, safety, or property.

(2) For the purposes of this section, the term "recklessness" means the action, or omission to act, in conscious disregard of a risk:

(a) Known, or so obvious that it should have been known, to the director; and

(b) Known to the director, or so obvious that it should have been known, to be so great as to make it highly probable that harm would follow from such action or omission.

(3) A director is deemed not to have derived an improper personal benefit from any transaction if the transaction and the nature of any personal benefit derived by the director are not prohibited by state or federal law or regulation and, without further limitation:

(a) In an action other than a derivative suit regarding a decision by the director to approve, reject, or otherwise affect the outcome of an offer to purchase the stock of, or to effect a merger of, the corporation, the transaction and the nature of any personal benefits derived by a director are disclosed or known to all directors voting on the matter, and the transaction was authorized, approved, or ratified by at least two directors who comprise a majority of the disinterested directors (whether or not such disinterested directors constitute a quorum);

(b) The transaction and the nature of any personal benefits derived by a director are disclosed or known to the shareholders entitled to vote, and the transaction was authorized, approved, or ratified by the affirmative vote or written consent of such shareholders who hold a majority of the shares, the voting of which is not controlled by directors who derived a personal benefit from or otherwise had a personal interest in the transaction; or

(c) The transaction was fair and reasonable to the corporation at the time it was authorized by the board, a committee, or the shareholders, notwithstanding that a director received a personal benefit.

(4) The circumstances set forth in subsection (3) are not exclusive and do not preclude the existence of other circumstances under which a director will be deemed not to have derived an improper benefit.

607.0832 Director conflicts of interest.—

(1) No contract or other transaction between a corporation and one or more of its directors or any other corporation, firm, association, or entity in which one or more of its directors are directors or officers or are financially interested shall be either void or voidable because of such relationship or interest, because such director or directors are present at the meeting of the board of directors or a committee thereof which authorizes, approves, or ratifies such contract or transaction, or because his or her or their votes are counted for such purpose, if:

(a) The fact of such relationship or interest is disclosed or known to the board of directors or committee which authorizes, approves, or ratifies the contract or transaction by a vote or consent sufficient for the purpose without counting the votes or consents of such interested directors;

(b) The fact of such relationship or interest is disclosed or known to the shareholders entitled to vote and they authorize, approve, or ratify such contract or transaction by vote or written consent; or

(c) The contract or transaction is fair and reasonable as to the corporation at the time it is authorized by the board, a committee, or the shareholders.

(2) For purposes of paragraph (1)(a) only, a conflict of interest transaction is authorized, approved, or ratified if it receives the affirmative vote of a majority of the directors on the board of directors, or on the committee, who have no relationship or interest in the transaction described in subsection (1), but a transaction may not be authorized, approved, or ratified under this section by a single director. If a majority of the directors who have no such relationship or interest in the transaction vote to authorize, approve, or ratify the transaction, a quorum is present for the purpose of taking action under this section. The presence of, or a vote cast by, a director with such relationship or interest in the transaction does not affect the validity of any action taken under paragraph (1)(a) if the transaction is otherwise authorized, approved, or ratified as provided in that subsection, but such presence or vote of those directors may be counted for purposes of determining whether the transaction is approved under other sections of this act.

(3) For purposes of paragraph (1)(b), a conflict of interest transaction is authorized, approved, or ratified if it receives the vote of a majority of the shares entitled to be counted under this subsection. Shares owned by or voted under the control of a director who has a relationship or interest in the transaction described in subsection (1) may not be counted in a vote of shareholders to determine whether to authorize, approve, or ratify a conflict of interest transaction under paragraph (1)(b). The vote of those shares, however, is counted in determining whether the transaction is approved under other sections of this act. A majority of the shares, whether or not present, that are entitled to be counted in a vote on the transaction under this subsection constitutes a quorum for the purpose of taking action under this section.

607.0833 Loans to officers, directors, and employees; guaranty of obligations.—Any corporation may lend money to, guarantee any obligation of, or otherwise assist any officer, director, or employee of the corporation or of a subsidiary, whenever, in the judgment of the board of directors, such loan, guaranty, or assistance may reasonably be expected to benefit the corporation. The loan, guaranty, or other assistance may be with or without interest and may be unsecured or secured in such manner as the board of directors shall approve, including, without limitation, a pledge of shares of stock of the corporation. Nothing in this section shall be deemed to deny, limit, or restrict the powers of guaranty or warranty of any corporation at common law or under any statute. Loans, guarantees, or other types of assistance are subject to s. 607.0832.

607.0834 Liability for unlawful distributions.—

(1) A director who votes for or assents to a distribution made in violation of s. 607.06401 or the articles of incorporation is personally liable to the corporation for the amount of the distribution that exceeds what could have been distributed without violating s. 607.06401 or the articles of incorporation if it is

established that the director did not perform his or her duties in compliance with s. 607.0830. In any proceeding commenced under this section, a director has all of the defenses ordinarily available to a director.

(2) A director held liable under subsection (1) for an unlawful distribution is entitled to contribution:

(a) From every other director who could be liable under subsection (1) for the unlawful distribution; and

(b) From each shareholder for the amount the shareholder accepted knowing the distribution was made in violation of s. 607.06401 or the articles of incorporation.

(3) A proceeding under this section is barred unless it is commenced within 2 years after the date on which the effect of the distribution was measured under s. 607.06401(6) or (8).

607.08401 Required officers.—

(1) A corporation shall have the officers described in its bylaws or appointed by the board of directors in accordance with the bylaws.

(2) A duly appointed officer may appoint one or more officers or assistant officers if authorized by the bylaws or the board of directors.

(3) The bylaws or the board of directors shall delegate to one of the officers responsibility for preparing minutes of the directors' and shareholders' meetings and for authenticating records of the corporation.

(4) The same individual may simultaneously hold more than one office in a corporation.

607.0840.

607.0841 Duties of officers.—Each officer has the authority and shall perform the duties set forth in the bylaws or, to the extent consistent with the bylaws, the duties prescribed by the board of directors or by direction of any officer authorized by the bylaws or the board of directors to prescribe the duties of other officers.

607.0842 Resignation and removal of officers.—

(1) An officer may resign at any time by delivering notice to the corporation. A resignation is effective when the notice is delivered unless the notice specifies a later effective date. If a resignation is made effective at a later date and the corporation accepts the future effective date, its board of directors may fill the pending vacancy before the effective date if the board of directors provides that the successor does not take office until the effective date.

(2) A board of directors may remove any officer at any time with or without cause. Any officer or assistant officer, if appointed by another officer, may likewise be removed by such officer.

607.0843 Contract rights of officers.—

(1) The appointment of an officer does not itself create contract rights.

(2) An officer's removal does not affect the officer's contract rights, if any, with the corporation. An officer's resignation does not affect the corporation's contract rights, if any, with the officer.

607.0850 Indemnification of officers, directors, employees, and agents.—

(1) A corporation shall have power to indemnify any person who was or is a party to any proceeding (other than an action by, or in the right of, the corporation), by reason of the fact that he or she is or was a director, officer, employee, or agent of the corporation or is or was serving at the request of the corporation as a director, officer, employee, or agent of another corporation, partnership, joint venture, trust, or other enterprise against liability incurred in connection with such proceeding, including any appeal thereof, if he or she acted in good faith and in a manner he or she reasonably believed to be in, or not opposed to, the best interests of the corporation and, with respect to any criminal action or proceeding, had no reasonable cause to believe his or her conduct was

unlawful. The termination of any proceeding by judgment, order, settlement, or conviction or upon a plea of nolo contendere or its equivalent shall not, of itself, create a presumption that the person did not act in good faith and in a manner which he or she reasonably believed to be in, or not opposed to, the best interests of the corporation or, with respect to any criminal action or proceeding, had reasonable cause to believe that his or her conduct was unlawful.

(2) A corporation shall have power to indemnify any person, who was or is a party to any proceeding by or in the right of the corporation to procure a judgment in its favor by reason of the fact that the person is or was a director, officer, employee, or agent of the corporation or is or was serving at the request of the corporation as a director, officer, employee, or agent of another corporation, partnership, joint venture, trust, or other enterprise, against expenses and amounts paid in settlement not exceeding, in the judgment of the board of directors, the estimated expense of litigating the proceeding to conclusion, actually and reasonably incurred in connection with the defense or settlement of such proceeding, including any appeal thereof. Such indemnification shall be authorized if such person acted in good faith and in a manner he or she reasonably believed to be in, or not opposed to, the best interests of the corporation, except that no indemnification shall be made under this subsection in respect of any claim, issue, or matter as to which such person shall have been adjudged to be liable unless, and only to the extent that, the court in which such proceeding was brought, or any other court of competent jurisdiction, shall determine upon application that, despite the adjudication of liability but in view of all circumstances of the case, such person is fairly and reasonably entitled to indemnity for such expenses which such court shall deem proper.

(3) To the extent that a director, officer, employee, or agent of a corporation has been successful on the merits or otherwise in defense of any proceeding referred to in subsection (1) or subsection (2), or in defense of any claim, issue, or matter therein, he or she shall be indemnified against expenses actually and reasonably incurred by him or her in connection therewith.

(4) Any indemnification under subsection (1) or subsection (2), unless pursuant to a determination by a court, shall be made by the corporation only as authorized in the specific case upon a determination that indemnification of the director, officer, employee, or agent is proper in the circumstances because he or she has met the applicable standard of conduct set forth in subsection (1) or subsection (2). Such determination shall be made:

(a) By the board of directors by a majority vote of a quorum consisting of directors who were not parties to such proceeding;

(b) If such a quorum is not obtainable or, even if obtainable, by majority vote of a committee duly designated by the board of directors (in which directors who are parties may participate) consisting solely of two or more directors not at the time parties to the proceeding;

(c) By independent legal counsel:

1. Selected by the board of directors prescribed in paragraph (a) or the committee prescribed in paragraph (b); or

2. If a quorum of the directors cannot be obtained for paragraph (a) and the committee cannot be designated under paragraph (b), selected by majority vote of the full board of directors (in which directors who are parties may participate); or

(d) By the shareholders by a majority vote of a quorum consisting of shareholders who were not parties to such proceeding or, if no such quorum is obtainable, by a majority vote of shareholders who were not parties to such proceeding.

(5) Evaluation of the reasonableness of expenses and authorization of indemnification shall be made in the same manner as the determination that indemnification is permissible. However, if the determination of permissibility is made by independent legal

counsel, persons specified by paragraph (4)(c) shall evaluate the reasonableness of expenses and may authorize indemnification.

(6) Expenses incurred by an officer or director in defending a civil or criminal proceeding may be paid by the corporation in advance of the final disposition of such proceeding upon receipt of an undertaking by or on behalf of such director or officer to repay such amount if he or she is ultimately found not to be entitled to indemnification by the corporation pursuant to this section. Expenses incurred by other employees and agents may be paid in advance upon such terms or conditions that the board of directors deems appropriate.

(7) The indemnification and advancement of expenses provided pursuant to this section are not exclusive, and a corporation may make any other or further indemnification or advancement of expenses of any of its directors, officers, employees, or agents, under any bylaw, agreement, vote of shareholders or disinterested directors, or otherwise, both as to action in his or her official capacity and as to action in another capacity while holding such office. However, indemnification or advancement of expenses shall not be made to or on behalf of any director, officer, employee, or agent if a judgment or other final adjudication establishes that his or her actions, or omissions to act, were material to the cause of action so adjudicated and constitute:

(a) A violation of the criminal law, unless the director, officer, employee, or agent had reasonable cause to believe his or her conduct was lawful or had no reasonable cause to believe his or her conduct was unlawful;

(b) A transaction from which the director, officer, employee, or agent derived an improper personal benefit;

(c) In the case of a director, a circumstance under which the liability provisions of s. 607.0834 are applicable; or

(d) Willful misconduct or a conscious disregard for the best interests of the corporation in a proceeding by or in the right of the corporation to procure a judgment in its favor or in a proceeding by or in the right of a shareholder.

(8) Indemnification and advancement of expenses as provided in this section shall continue as, unless otherwise provided when authorized or ratified, to a person who has ceased to be a director, officer, employee, or agent and shall inure to the benefit of the heirs, executors, and administrators of such a person, unless otherwise provided when authorized or ratified.

(9) Unless the corporation's articles of incorporation provide otherwise, notwithstanding the failure of a corporation to provide indemnification, and despite any contrary determination of the board or of the shareholders in the specific case, a director, officer, employee, or agent of the corporation who is or was a party to a proceeding may apply for indemnification or advancement of expenses, or both, to the court conducting the proceeding, to the circuit court, or to another court of competent jurisdiction. On receipt of an application, the court, after giving any notice that it considers necessary, may order indemnification and advancement of expenses, including expenses incurred in seeking court-ordered indemnification or advancement of expenses, if it determines that:

(a) The director, officer, employee, or agent is entitled to mandatory indemnification under subsection (3), in which case the court shall also order the corporation to pay the director reasonable expenses incurred in obtaining court-ordered indemnification or advancement of expenses;

(b) The director, officer, employee, or agent is entitled to indemnification or advancement of expenses, or both, by virtue of the exercise by the corporation of its power pursuant to subsection (7); or

(c) The director, officer, employee, or agent is fairly and reasonably entitled to indemnification or advancement of expenses, or both, in view of all the relevant circumstances, regardless of whether such person met the standard of conduct set forth in subsection (1), subsection (2), or subsection (7).

(10) For purposes of this section, the term "corporation" includes, in addition to the resulting corporation, any constituent corporation (including any constituent of a constituent) absorbed in a consolidation or merger, so that any person who is or was a director, officer, employee, or agent of a constituent corporation, or is or was serving at the request of a constituent corporation as a director, officer, employee, or agent of another corporation, partnership, joint venture, trust, or other enterprise, is in the same position under this section with respect to the resulting or surviving corporation as he or she would have with respect to such constituent corporation if its separate existence had continued.

(11) For purposes of this section:

(a) The term "other enterprises" includes employee benefit plans;

(b) The term "expenses" includes counsel fees, including those for appeal;

(c) The term "liability" includes obligations to pay a judgment, settlement, penalty, fine (including an excise tax assessed with respect to any employee benefit plan), and expenses actually and reasonably incurred with respect to a proceeding;

(d) The term "proceeding" includes any threatened, pending, or completed action, suit, or other type of proceeding, whether civil, criminal, administrative, or investigative and whether formal or informal;

(e) The term "agent" includes a volunteer;

(f) The term "serving at the request of the corporation" includes any service as a director, officer, employee, or agent of the corporation that imposes duties on such persons, including duties relating to an employee benefit plan and its participants or beneficiaries; and

(g) The term "not opposed to the best interest of the corporation" describes the actions of a person who acts in good faith and in a manner he or she reasonably believes to be in the best interests of the participants and beneficiaries of an employee benefit plan.

(12) A corporation shall have power to purchase and maintain insurance on behalf of any person who is or was a director, officer, employee, or agent of the corporation or is or was serving at the request of the corporation as a director, officer, employee, or agent of another corporation, partnership, joint venture, trust, or other enterprise against any liability asserted against the person and incurred by him or her in any such capacity or arising out of his or her status as such, whether or not the corporation would have the power to indemnify the person against such liability under the provisions of this section.

607.0901 Affiliated transactions.—

(1) For purposes of this section:

(a) "Affiliate" means a person who directly, or indirectly through one or more intermediaries, controls or is controlled by, or is under common control with, a specified person.

(b) "Affiliated transaction," when used in reference to the corporation and any interested shareholder, means:

1. Any merger or consolidation of the corporation or any subsidiary of the corporation with:

a. The interested shareholder; or

b. Any other corporation (whether or not itself an interested shareholder) which is, or after such merger or consolidation would be, an affiliate or associate of the interested shareholder;

2. Any sale, lease, exchange, mortgage, pledge, transfer, or other disposition (in one transaction or a series of transactions) to or with the interested shareholder or any affiliate or associate of the interested shareholder of assets of the corporation or any subsidiary of the corporation:

a. Having an aggregate fair market value equal to 5 percent or more of the aggregate fair market value of all the assets, determined on a consolidated basis, of the corporation;

b. Having an aggregate fair market value equal to 5 percent or more of the aggregate fair market value of all the outstanding shares of the corporation; or

c. Representing 5 percent or more of the earning power or net income, determined on a consolidated basis, of the corporation;

3. The issuance or transfer by the corporation or any subsidiary of the corporation (in one transaction or a series of transactions) of any shares of the corporation or any subsidiary of the corporation which have an aggregate fair market value equal to 5 percent or more of the aggregate fair market value of all the outstanding shares of the corporation to the interested shareholder or any affiliate or associate of the interested shareholder except pursuant to the exercise of warrants or rights to purchase stock offered, or a dividend or distribution paid or made, pro rata to all shareholders of the corporation;

4. The adoption of any plan or proposal for the liquidation or dissolution of the corporation proposed by, or pursuant to any agreement, arrangement, or understanding (whether or not in writing) with, the interested shareholder or any affiliate or associate of the interested shareholder;

5. Any reclassification of securities (including, without limitation, any stock split, stock dividend, or other distribution of shares in respect of shares, or any reverse stock split) or recapitalization of the corporation, or any merger or consolidation of the corporation with any subsidiary of the corporation, or any other transaction (whether or not with or into or otherwise involving the interested shareholder), with the interested shareholder or any affiliate or associate of the interested shareholder, which has the effect, directly or indirectly (in one transaction or a series of transactions during any 12-month period), of increasing by more than 5 percent the percentage of the outstanding voting shares of the corporation or any subsidiary of the corporation beneficially owned by the interested shareholder; or

6. Any receipt by the interested shareholder or any affiliate or associate of the interested shareholder of the benefit, directly or indirectly (except proportionately as a shareholder of the corporation), of any loans, advances, guaranties, pledges, or other financial assistance or any tax credits or other tax advantages provided by or through the corporation.

(c) "Announcement date," when used in reference to any affiliated transaction, means the date of the first general public announcement of the proposed affiliated transaction or of the intention to propose an affiliated transaction, or the date on which the proposed affiliated transaction or the intention to propose an affiliated transaction is first communicated generally to the shareholders of the corporation, whichever is earlier.

(d) "Associate," when used to indicate a relationship with any person, means any entity, other than the corporation or any of its subsidiaries, of which such person is an officer, director, or partner or is, directly or indirectly, the beneficial owner of 10 percent or more of any class of voting shares; any trust or other estate in which such person has a substantial beneficial interest or as to which such person serves as trustee or in a similar fiduciary capacity; and any relative or spouse of such person, or any relative of such spouse, who has the same home as such person or who is an officer or director of the corporation or any of its affiliates.

(e) A person is deemed to be a "beneficial owner" of voting shares as to which such person and such person's affiliates and associates, individually or in the aggregate, have or share directly, or indirectly through any contract, arrangement, understanding, relationship, or otherwise:

1. Voting power, which includes the power to vote or to direct the voting of the voting shares;

2. Investment power, which includes the power to dispose of or to direct the disposition of the voting shares; or

3. The right to acquire the voting power or investment power, whether such right is exercisable immediately or only after the passage of time, pursuant to any contract, arrangement, or understanding, upon the exercise of conversion rights, exchange rights, warrants, or options, or otherwise; however, in no case shall a director of the corporation be deemed to be the beneficial owner of voting shares beneficially owned by another director of the corporation solely by reason of actions undertaken by such persons in their capacity as directors of the corporation.

(f) "Control" means the possession, directly or indirectly, through the ownership of voting shares, by contract, arrangement, understanding, relationship, or otherwise, of the power to direct or cause the direction of the management and policies of a person. Notwithstanding the foregoing, a person shall not be deemed to have control of a corporation if such person holds voting shares, in good faith and not for the purpose of circumventing this section, as an agent, bank, broker, nominee, custodian, or trustee for one or more beneficial owners who do not individually or as a group have control of such corporation.

(g) "Determination date" means the date on which an interested shareholder became an interested shareholder.

(h) Unless otherwise specified in the articles of incorporation initially filed with the Department of State, a "disinterested director" means as to any particular interested shareholder:

1. Any member of the board of directors of the corporation who was a member of the board of directors before the later of January 1, 1987, or the determination date; and

2. Any member of the board of directors of the corporation who was recommended for election by, or was elected to fill a vacancy and received the affirmative vote of, a majority of the disinterested directors then on the board.

(i) "Exchange Act" means the Act of Congress known as the Securities Exchange Act of 1934, as the same has been or hereafter may be amended from time to time.

(j) "Fair market value" means:

1. In the case of shares, the highest closing sale price of a share quoted during the 30-day period immediately preceding the date in question on the composite tape for shares listed on the New York Stock Exchange; or, if such shares are not quoted on the composite tape on the New York Stock Exchange or if such shares are not listed on such exchange, the highest closing sale price quoted during such period on the principal United States securities exchange registered under the Exchange Act on which such shares are listed; or, if such shares are not listed on any such exchange, the highest closing bid quotation with respect to a share during the 30-day period preceding the date in question on the National Association of Securities Dealers, Inc., automated quotations system or any similar system then in general use; or, if no such quotations are available, the fair market value of a share on the date in question as determined by a majority of disinterested directors; and

2. In the case of property other than cash or shares, the fair market value of such property on the date in question as determined by a majority of the disinterested directors.

(k) "Interested shareholder" means any person who is the beneficial owner of more than 10 percent of the outstanding voting shares of the corporation. However, the term "interested shareholder" shall not include the corporation or any of its subsidiaries; any savings, employee stock ownership, or other employee benefit plan of the corporation or any of its subsidiaries; or any fiduciary with respect to any such plan when acting in such capacity. For the purpose of determining whether a person is an interested shareholder, the number of voting shares deemed to be outstanding shall include shares deemed owned by the interested shareholder through application of subparagraph (e)3. but shall not include any other voting shares that may be issuable pursuant to any contract, arrangement, or understanding, upon the exercise of conversion rights, exchange rights, warrants, or options, or otherwise.

(l) "Shares" means the units into which the proprietary interests in an entity are divided and includes:

1. Any stock or similar security, any certificate of interest, any participation in any profit-sharing agreement, any voting trust certificate, or any certificate of deposit for shares; and

2. Any security convertible, with or without consideration, into shares; or any warrant, call, or other option or privilege of buying shares without being bound to do so; or any other security carrying any right to acquire, subscribe to, or purchase shares.

(m) "Subsidiary" means, as to any corporation, any other corporation of which it owns, directly or indirectly through one or more subsidiaries, a majority of the voting shares.

(n) "Valuation date" means, if the affiliated transaction is voted upon by shareholders, the day before the date of the vote of shareholders or, if the affiliated transaction is not voted upon by shareholders, the date of the consummation of the affiliated transaction.

(o) "Voting shares" means the outstanding shares of all classes or series of the corporation entitled to vote generally in the election of directors.

(2) Except as provided in subsection (4), in addition to any affirmative vote required by any other section of this act or by the articles of incorporation, an affiliated transaction shall be approved by the affirmative vote of the holders of two-thirds of the voting shares other than the shares beneficially owned by the interested shareholder.

(3) A majority of the disinterested directors shall have the power to determine for the purposes of this section:

(a) Whether a person is an interested shareholder;

(b) The number of voting shares beneficially owned by any person;

(c) Whether a person is an affiliate or associate of another; and

(d) Whether the securities to be issued or transferred by the corporation or any of its subsidiaries to any interested shareholder or any affiliate or associate of the interested shareholder have an aggregate fair market value equal to or greater than 5 percent of the aggregate fair market value of all of the outstanding voting shares of the corporation or any of its subsidiaries.

(4) The voting requirements set forth in subsection (2) do not apply to a particular affiliated transaction if all of the conditions specified in any one of the following paragraphs are met:

(a) The affiliated transaction has been approved by a majority of the disinterested directors;

(b) The corporation has not had more than 300 shareholders of record at any time during the 3 years preceding the announcement date;

(c) The interested shareholder has been the beneficial owner of at least 80 percent of the corporation's outstanding voting shares for at least 5 years preceding the announcement date;

(d) The interested shareholder is the beneficial owner of at least 90 percent of the outstanding voting shares of the corporation, exclusive of shares acquired directly from the corporation in a transaction not approved by a majority of the disinterested directors;

(e) The corporation is an investment company registered under the Investment Company Act of 1940; or

(f) In the affiliated transaction, consideration shall be paid to the holders of each class or series of voting shares and all of the following conditions shall be met:

1. The aggregate amount of the cash and the fair market value as of the valuation date of consideration other than cash to be received per share by holders of each class or series of voting shares in such affiliated transaction are at least equal to the highest of the following:

a. If applicable, the highest per share price, including any brokerage commissions, transfer taxes, and soliciting dealers' fees, paid by the interested shareholder for any shares of such class or series acquired by it within the 2-year period immediately preceding the announcement date or in the transaction in which it became an interested shareholder, whichever is higher;

b. The fair market value per share of such class or series on the announcement date or on the determination date, whichever is higher;

c. If applicable, the price per share equal to the fair market value per share of such class or series determined pursuant to sub-sub-paragraph b., multiplied by the ratio of the highest per share price, including any brokerage commissions, transfer taxes, and soliciting dealers' fees, paid by the interested shareholder for any shares of such class or series acquired by it within the 2-year period immediately preceding the announcement date, to the fair market value per share of such class or series on the first day in such 2-year period on which the interested shareholder acquired any shares of such class or series; and

d. If applicable, the highest preferential amount, if any, per share to which the holders of such class or series are entitled in the event of any voluntary or involuntary dissolution of the corporation.

2. The consideration to be received by holders of outstanding shares shall be in cash or in the same form as the interested shareholder has previously paid for shares of the same class or series, and if the interested shareholder has paid for shares with varying forms of consideration, the form of the consideration shall be either cash or the form used to acquire the largest number of shares of such class or series previously acquired by the interested shareholder.

3. During such portion of the 3-year period preceding the announcement date that such interested shareholder has been an interested shareholder, except as approved by a majority of the disinterested directors:

a. There shall have been no failure to declare and pay at the regular date therefor any full periodic dividends, whether or not cumulative, on any outstanding shares of the corporation;

b. There shall have been:

(I) No reduction in the annual rate of dividends paid on any class or series of voting shares, except as necessary to reflect any subdivision of the class or series; and

(II) An increase in such annual rate of dividends as necessary to reflect any reclassification, including any reverse stock split, recapitalization, reorganization, or similar transaction which has the effect of reducing the number of outstanding shares of the class or series; and

c. Such interested shareholder shall not have become the beneficial owner of any additional voting shares except as part of the transaction which results in such interested shareholder becoming an interested shareholder.

4. During such portion of the 3-year period preceding the announcement date that such interested shareholder has been an interested shareholder, except as approved by a majority of the disinterested directors, such interested shareholder shall not have received the benefit, directly or indirectly (except proportionately as a shareholder), of any loans, advances, guaranties, pledges, or other financial assistance or any tax credits or other tax advantages provided by the corporation, whether in anticipation of or in connection with such affiliated transaction or otherwise.

5. Except as otherwise approved by a majority of the disinterested directors, a proxy or information statement describing the affili-

ated transaction and complying with the requirements of the Exchange Act and the rules and regulations thereunder has been mailed to holders of voting shares of the corporation at least 25 days before the consummation of such affiliated transaction, whether or not such proxy or information statement is required to be mailed pursuant to the Exchange Act or such rules or regulations.

(5) The provisions of this section do not apply:

(a) To any corporation the original articles of incorporation of which contain a provision expressly electing not to be governed by this section;

(b) To any corporation which adopted an amendment to its articles of incorporation prior to January 1, 1989, expressly electing not to be governed by this section, provided that such amendment does not apply to any affiliated transaction of the corporation with an interested shareholder whose determination date is on or prior to the effective date of such amendment;

(c) To any corporation which adopts an amendment to its articles of incorporation or bylaws, approved by the affirmative vote of the holders, other than interested shareholders and their affiliates and associates, of a majority of the outstanding voting shares of the corporation, excluding the voting shares of interested shareholders and their affiliates and associates, expressly electing not to be governed by this section, provided that such amendment to the articles of incorporation or bylaws shall not be effective until 18 months after such vote of the corporation's shareholders and shall not apply to any affiliated transaction of the corporation with an interested shareholder whose determination date is on or prior to the effective date of such amendment; or

(d) To any affiliated transaction of the corporation with an interested shareholder of the corporation which became an interested shareholder inadvertently, if such interested shareholder, as soon as practicable, divests itself of a sufficient amount of the voting shares of the corporation so that it no longer is the beneficial owner, directly or indirectly, of 10 percent or more of the outstanding voting shares of the corporation, and would not at any time within the 5-year period preceding the announcement date with respect to such affiliated transaction have been an interested shareholder but for such inadvertent acquisition.

(6) Any corporation that elected not to be governed by this section, either through a provision in its original articles of incorporation or through an amendment to its articles of incorporation or bylaws may elect to be bound by the provisions of this section by adopting an amendment to its articles of incorporation or bylaws that repeals the original article or the amendment. In addition to any requirements of this act, or the articles of incorporation or bylaws of the corporation, any such amendment shall be approved by the affirmative vote of the holders of two-thirds of the voting shares other than shares beneficially owned by any interested shareholder.

607.0902 Control-share acquisitions.—

(1) "CONTROL SHARES."—As used in this section, "control shares" means shares that, except for this section, would have voting power with respect to shares of an issuing public corporation that, when added to all other shares of the issuing public corporation owned by a person or in respect to which that person may exercise or direct the exercise of voting power, would entitle that person, immediately after acquisition of the shares, directly or indirectly, alone or as a part of a group, to exercise or direct the exercise of the voting power of the issuing public corporation in the election of directors within any of the following ranges of voting power:

(a) One-fifth or more but less than one-third of all voting power.

(b) One-third or more but less than a majority of all voting power.

(c) A majority or more of all voting power.

(2) "CONTROL-SHARE ACQUISITION."—

(a) As used in this section, "control-share acquisition" means the acquisition, directly or indirectly, by any person of ownership of, or the power to direct the exercise of voting power with respect to, issued and outstanding control shares.

(b) For purposes of this section, all shares, the beneficial ownership of which is acquired within 90 days before or after the date of the acquisition of the beneficial ownership of shares which result in a control share acquisition, and all shares the beneficial ownership of which is acquired pursuant to a plan to make a control-share acquisition shall be deemed to have been acquired in the same acquisition.

(c) For purposes of this section, a person who acquires shares in the ordinary course of business for the benefit of others in good faith and not for the purpose of circumventing this section has voting power only of shares in respect of which that person would be able to exercise or direct the exercise of votes without further instruction from others.

(d) The acquisition of any shares of an issuing public corporation does not constitute a control-share acquisition if the acquisition is consummated in any of the following circumstances:

1. Before July 2, 1987.

2. Pursuant to a contract existing before July 2, 1987.

3. Pursuant to the laws of intestate succession or pursuant to a gift or testamentary transfer.

4. Pursuant to the satisfaction of a pledge or other security interest created in good faith and not for the purpose of circumventing this section.

5. Pursuant to a merger or share exchange effected in compliance with s. 607.1101, s. 607.1102, s. 607.1103, s. 607.1104, or s. 607.1107, if the issuing public corporation is a party to the agreement of merger or plan of share exchange.

6. Pursuant to any savings, employee stock ownership, or other employee benefit plan of the issuing public corporation or any of its subsidiaries or any fiduciary with respect to any such plan when acting in such fiduciary capacity.

7. Pursuant to an acquisition of shares of an issuing public corporation if the acquisition has been approved by the board of directors of such issuing public corporation before acquisition.

(e) The acquisition of shares of an issuing public corporation in good faith and not for the purpose of circumventing this section by or from:

1. Any person whose voting rights had previously been authorized by shareholders in compliance with this section; or

2. Any person whose previous acquisition of shares of an issuing public corporation would have constituted a control-share acquisition but for paragraph (d), does not constitute a control-share acquisition, unless the acquisition entitles any person, directly or indirectly, alone or as a part of a group, to exercise or direct the exercise of voting power of the corporation in the election of directors in excess of the range of the voting power otherwise authorized.

(f) For the purpose of this section, persons shall not be deemed to be part of a "group" if such persons join together to exercise or direct the exercise of the voting power of an issuing public corporation (whether through a voting trust, a shareholder agreement, or through other arrangements), and the voting trustee of any voting trust shall not be deemed to be an "acquiring person" if such persons or all the parties to the voting trust:

1. Are related by blood or marriage or are the personal representatives or trustees of such persons; and

2. Such persons were shareholders (or the beneficial owners of shares) of the issuing public corporation (or were trustees, personal representatives, or heirs of such shareholders or beneficial owners) on July 1, 1987, and have continued to be shareholders

(or the beneficial owners of shares) of the issuing public corporation (or have been trustees, personal representatives, or heirs of such shareholders or beneficial owners) since that time.

(3) "INTERESTED SHARES."—As used in this section, "interested shares" means the shares of an issuing public corporation in respect of which any of the following persons may exercise or direct the exercise of the voting power of the corporation in the election of directors:

(a) An acquiring person or member of a group with respect to a control-share acquisition.

(b) Any officer of the issuing public corporation.

(c) Any employee of the issuing public corporation who is also a director of the corporation.

(4) "ISSUING PUBLIC CORPORATION."—

(a) As used in this section, "issuing public corporation" means a corporation that has:

1. One hundred or more shareholders;

2. Its principal place of business, its principal office, or substantial assets within this state; and

3. Either:

a. More than 10 percent of its shareholders resident in this state;

b. More than 10 percent of its shares owned by residents of this state; or

c. One thousand shareholders resident in this state.

(b) The residence of a shareholder is presumed to be the address appearing in the records of the corporation.

(c) Shares held by banks (except as trustee or guardian), brokers, or nominees shall be disregarded for purposes of calculating the percentages or numbers described in this subsection.

(5) LAW APPLICABLE TO CONTROL-SHARE VOTING RIGHTS.—Unless the corporation's articles of incorporation or bylaws provide that this section does not apply to control-share acquisitions of shares of the corporation before the control-share acquisition, control shares of an issuing public corporation acquired in a control-share acquisition have only such voting rights as are conferred by subsection (9).

(6) NOTICE OF CONTROL-SHARE ACQUISITION.—Any person who proposes to make or has made a control-share acquisition may at the person's election deliver an acquiring person statement to the issuing public corporation at the issuing public corporation's principal office. The acquiring person statement must set forth all of the following:

(a) The identity of the acquiring person and each other member of any group of which the person is a part for purposes of determining control shares.

(b) A statement that the acquiring person statement is given pursuant to this section.

(c) The number of shares of the issuing public corporation owned, directly or indirectly, by the acquiring person and each other member of the group.

(d) The range of voting power under which the control-share acquisition falls or would, if consummated, fall.

(e) If the control-share acquisition has not taken place:

1. A description in reasonable detail of the terms of the proposed control-share acquisition; and

2. Representations of the acquiring person, together with a statement, in reasonable detail of the facts upon which they are based, that the proposed control-share acquisition, if consummated, will not be contrary to law and that the acquiring person has the financial capacity to make the proposed control-share acquisition.

(7) SHAREHOLDER MEETING TO DETERMINE CONTROL-SHARE VOTING RIGHTS.—

(a) If the acquiring person so requests at the time of delivery of an acquiring person statement and gives an undertaking to pay the corporation's expenses of a special meeting, within 10 days thereafter, the directors of the issuing public corporation or others authorized to call such a meeting under the issuing public corporation's articles of incorporation or bylaws shall call a special meeting of shareholders of the issuing public corporation for the purpose of considering the voting rights to be accorded the shares acquired or to be acquired in the control-share acquisition.

(b) Unless the acquiring person agrees in writing to another date, the special meeting of shareholders shall be held within 50 days after receipt by the issuing public corporation of the request.

(c) If the acquiring person so requests in writing at the time of delivery of the acquiring person statement, the special meeting must not be held sooner than 30 days after receipt by the issuing public corporation of the acquiring person statement.

(d) If no request is made, the voting rights to be accorded the shares acquired in the control-share acquisition shall be presented to the next special or annual meeting of the shareholders.

(8) NOTICE OF SHAREHOLDER MEETING.—

(a) If a special meeting is requested, notice of the special meeting of shareholders shall be given as promptly as reasonably practicable by the issuing public corporation to all shareholders of record as of the record date set for the meeting, whether or not entitled to vote at the meeting.

(b) Notice of the special or annual shareholder meeting at which the voting rights are to be considered must include or be accompanied by each of the following:

1. A copy of the acquiring person statement delivered to the issuing public corporation pursuant to this section.

2. A statement by the board of directors of the corporation, authorized by its directors, of its position or recommendation, or that it is taking no position or making no recommendation, with respect to the proposed control-share acquisition.

(9) RESOLUTION GRANTING CONTROL-SHARE VOTING RIGHTS.—

(a) Control shares acquired in a control-share acquisition have the same voting rights as were accorded the shares before the control-share acquisition only to the extent granted by resolution approved by the shareholders of the issuing public corporation.

(b) To be approved under this subsection, the resolution must be approved by:

1. Each class or series entitled to vote separately on the proposal by a majority of all the votes entitled to be cast by the class or series, with the holders of the outstanding shares of a class or series being entitled to vote as a separate class if the proposed control-share acquisition would, if fully carried out, result in any of the changes described in s. 607.1004; and

2. Each class or series entitled to vote separately on the proposal by a majority of all the votes entitled to be cast by that group, excluding all interested shares.

(c) Any control shares that do not have voting rights because such rights were not accorded to such shares by approval of a resolution by the shareholders pursuant to paragraph (b) shall regain voting rights and shall no longer be deemed control shares upon a transfer to a person other than the acquiring person or associate or affiliate, as defined in s. 607.0901, of the acquiring person unless the acquisition of the shares by the other person constitutes a control-share acquisition, in which case the voting rights of the shares remain subject to the provisions of this section.

(10) REDEMPTION OF CONTROL SHARES.—

(a) If authorized in a corporation's articles of incorporation or bylaws before a control-share acquisition has occurred, control shares acquired in a control-share acquisition with respect to which no acquiring person statement has been filed with the issuing public corporation may, at any time during the period ending 60 days after the last acquisition of control shares by the acquiring person, be subject to redemption by the corporation at the fair value thereof pursuant to the procedures adopted by the corporation.

(b) Control shares acquired in a control-share acquisition are not subject to redemption after an acquiring person statement has been filed unless the shares are not accorded full voting rights by the shareholders as provided in subsection (9).

607.0903 Application of ss. 607.0901 and 607.0902 to certain foreign corporations.—

(1) The provisions of s. 607.0901 also apply to a foreign corporation that has:

(a) Been granted authority pursuant to this act to conduct business in this state;

(b) One hundred or more shareholders;

(c) Its principal place of business, its principal office, or substantial assets within this state;

(d) More than 500 residents of this state as employees, including employees of an entity as to which the foreign corporation owns, directly or indirectly, shares or other interests of such entity having a majority of the unlimited voting rights in matters as to which shareholders or interestholders of such entity are accorded voting rights;

(e) Gross annual payroll, including the payroll of an entity as to which the foreign corporation owns, directly or indirectly, shares or other interests of such entity having a majority of the unlimited voting rights in matters as to which shareholders or interestholders of such entity are accorded voting rights, of more than $5 million to residents of this state; and

(f) Either:

1. More than 10 percent of its shareholders resident in this state;

2. More than 10 percent of its shares owned by residents of this state; or

3. More than 1,000 shareholders resident in this state.

For purposes of paragraph (f), the residence of a shareholder is presumed to be the address appearing in the records of the corporation, and shares held by banks (except as trustee or guardian), brokers, or nominees shall be disregarded for purposes of calculating the percentages or numbers described.

(2) Except as provided in subsection (3), the provisions of s. 607.0902 apply to a foreign corporation which meets the requirements of an "issuing public corporation" in s. 607.0902(4) and, in addition, has:

(a) Authority pursuant to this act to conduct business in this state;

(b) More than 500 residents of this state as employees, including employees of an entity as to which the foreign corporation owns, directly or indirectly, shares or other interests of such entity having a majority of the unlimited voting rights in matters as to which shareholders or interestholders of such entity are accorded voting rights; and

(c) Gross annual payroll, including the payroll of an entity as to which the foreign corporation owns, directly or indirectly, shares or other interests of such entity having a majority of the unlimited voting rights in matters as to which shareholders or interestholders of such entity are accorded voting rights, of more than $5 million to residents of this state.

(3) The acquisition of any shares of any foreign corporation which is subject to subsection (2) does not constitute a control-share acquisition if the acquisition is consummated pursuant to a merger or share exchange effected in compliance with s. 607.1107 and such foreign corporation is a party to the agreement of merger or plan of share exchange.

(4) The merger, consolidation, or share exchange of two foreign corporations does not constitute a control-share acquisition if the merger, consolidation, or share exchange is effected in compliance with the laws of the jurisdictions under which such corporations are organized and with the approval of the board of directors of the foreign corporation subject to subsection (2).

(5) If the laws of any jurisdiction under the laws of which a foreign corporation is organized contain provisions that are expressly inconsistent with the provisions of this section as applicable to such foreign corporation, the provisions of this section shall be inapplicable to such foreign corporation to the extent necessary to resolve such inconsistency.

607.1001 Authority to amend the articles of incorporation.—

(1) A corporation may amend its articles of incorporation at any time to add or change a provision that is required or permitted in the articles of incorporation or to delete a provision not required in the articles of incorporation. Whether a provision is required or permitted in the articles of incorporation is determined as of the effective date of the amendment.

(2) A shareholder of the corporation does not have a vested property right resulting from any provision in the articles of incorporation, including provisions relating to management, control, capital structure, dividend entitlement, or purpose or duration of the corporation.

607.1002 Amendment by board of directors.—Unless the articles of incorporation provide otherwise, a corporation's board of directors may adopt one or more amendments to the corporation's articles of incorporation without shareholder action:

(1) To extend the duration of the corporation if it was incorporated at a time when limited duration was required by law;

(2) To delete the names and addresses of the initial directors;

(3) To delete the name and address of the initial registered agent or registered office, if a statement of change is on file with the Department of State;

(4) To delete any other information contained in the articles of incorporation that is solely of historical interest;

(5) To delete the authorization for a class or series of shares authorized pursuant to s. 607.0602, if no shares of such class or series are issued;

(6) To change the corporate name by substituting the word "corporation," "incorporated," or "company," or the abbreviation "corp.," "Inc.," or "Co.," for a similar word or abbreviation in the name, or by adding, deleting, or changing a geographical attribution for the name;

(7) To change the par value for a class or series of shares;

(8) To provide that if the corporation acquires its own shares, such shares belong to the corporation and constitute treasury shares until disposed of or canceled by the corporation; or

(9) To make any other change expressly permitted by this act to be made without shareholder action.

607.10025 Shares; combination or division.—

(1) A corporation may effect a division or combination of its shares in the manner as provided in this section. For purposes of this section, the terms "division" and "combination" mean dividing or combining shares of any issued and outstanding class or series into a greater or lesser number of shares of the same class or series.

(2) Unless the articles of incorporation provide otherwise, a division or combination may be effected solely by the action of the board of directors. In effecting a share combination or division, the board shall have authority to amend the articles to:

(a) Increase or decrease the par value of shares;

(b) Increase or decrease the number of authorized shares; or

(c) Make any other changes necessary or appropriate to assure that the rights or preferences of each holder of outstanding shares of all classes and series will not be adversely affected by the combination or division.

The board shall not have the authority to amend the articles, and shareholder approval of any amendment shall be required pursuant to s. 607.1003, if, as a result of the amendment, the rights or preferences of the holders of any outstanding class or series will be adversely affected, or the percentage of authorized shares remaining unissued after the share division or combination will exceed the percentage of authorized shares that was unissued before the division or combination.

(3) Fractional shares created by a division or combination effected under this section may not be redeemed for cash under s. 607.0604.

(4) If a division or combination is effected by a board action without shareholder approval and includes an amendment to the articles of incorporation, there shall be executed in accordance with s. 607.0120 on behalf of the corporation and filed in the office of the Department of State articles of amendment which shall set forth:

(a) The name of the corporation.

(b) The date of adoption by the board of directors of the resolution approving the division or combination.

(c) That the amendment to the articles of incorporation does not adversely affect the rights or preferences of the holders of outstanding shares of any class or series and does not result in the percentage of authorized shares that remain unissued after the division or combination exceeding the percentage of authorized shares that were unissued before the division or combination.

(d) The class or series and number of shares subject to the division or combination and the number of shares into which the shares are to be divided or combined.

(e) The amendment of the articles of incorporation made in connection with the division or combination.

(f) If the division or combination is to become effective at a time subsequent to the time of filing, the date, which may not exceed 90 days after the date of filing, when the division or combination becomes effective.

(5) Within 30 days after effecting a division or combination without shareholder approval, the corporation shall give written notice to its shareholders setting forth the material terms of the division or combination.

(6) If a division or combination is effected by action of the board and of the shareholders, there shall be executed on behalf of the corporation and filed with the Department of State articles of amendment as provided in s. 607.1003, which articles shall set forth, in addition to the information required by s. 607.1003, the information required in subsection (4).

(7) Upon the effectiveness of a combination, the authorized shares of the classes or series affected by the combination shall be reduced by the same percentage by which the issued shares of such class or series were reduced as a result of the combination, unless the articles of incorporation otherwise provide or the combination was approved by the shareholders pursuant to s. 607.1003.

(8) This section applies only to corporations with more than 35 shareholders of record.

607.1003 Amendment by board of directors and shareholders.—

(1) A corporation's board of directors may propose one or more amendments to the articles of incorporation for submission to the shareholders.

(2) For the amendment to be adopted:

(a) The board of directors must recommend the amendment to the shareholders, unless the board of directors determines that because of conflict of interest or other special circumstances it

should make no recommendation and communicates the basis for its determination to the shareholders with the amendment; and

(b) The shareholders entitled to vote on the amendment must approve the amendment as provided in subsection (5).

(3) The board of directors may condition its submission of the proposed amendment on any basis.

(4) The corporation shall notify each shareholder, whether or not entitled to vote, of the proposed shareholders' meeting in accordance with s. 607.0705. The notice of meeting must also state that the purpose, or one of the purposes, of the meeting is to consider the proposed amendment and contain or be accompanied by a copy or summary of the amendment.

(5) Unless this act, the articles of incorporation, or the board of directors (acting pursuant to subsection (3)) requires a greater vote or a vote by voting groups, the amendment to be adopted must be approved by:

(a) A majority of the votes entitled to be cast on the amendment by any voting group with respect to which the amendment would create dissenters' rights; and

(b) The votes required by ss. 607.0725 and 607.0726 by every other voting group entitled to vote on the amendment.

(6) Unless otherwise provided in the articles of incorporation, the shareholders of a corporation having 35 or fewer shareholders may amend the articles of incorporation without an act of the directors at a meeting for which notice of the changes to be made is given.

607.1004 Voting on amendments by voting groups.—

(1) The holders of the outstanding shares of a class are entitled to vote as a class (if shareholder voting is otherwise required by this act) upon a proposed amendment, if the amendment would:

(a) Effect an exchange or reclassification of all or part of the shares of the class into shares of another class.

(b) Effect an exchange or reclassification, or create a right of exchange, of all or part of the shares of another class into the shares of the class.

(c) Change the designation, rights, preferences, or limitations of all or part of the shares of the class.

(d) Change the shares of all or part of the class into a different number of shares of the same class.

(e) Create a new class of shares having rights or preferences with respect to distributions or to dissolution that are prior or superior to the shares of the class.

(f) Increase the rights, preferences, or number of authorized shares of any class that, after giving effect to the amendment, have rights or preferences with respect to distributions or to dissolution that are prior or superior to the shares of the class.

(g) Limit or deny an existing preemptive right of all or part of the shares of the class.

(h) Cancel or otherwise affect rights to distributions or dividends that have accumulated but not yet been declared on all or part of the shares of the class.

(2) If a proposed amendment would affect a series of a class of shares in one or more of the ways described in subsection (1), the shares of that series are entitled to vote as a separate class on the proposed amendment.

(3) If a proposed amendment that entitles the holders of two or more classes or series of shares to vote as separate voting groups under this section would affect those two or more classes or series in the same or substantially similar way, the holders of the shares of all the classes or series so affected must vote together as a single voting group on the proposed amendment, unless otherwise provided in the articles of incorporation.

(4) A class or series of shares is entitled to the voting rights granted by this section although the articles of incorporation provide that the shares are nonvoting shares.

607.1005 Amendment before issuance of shares.—If a corporation has not yet issued shares, a majority of its incorporators or board of directors may adopt one or more amendments to the corporation's articles of incorporation.

607.1006 Articles of amendment.—

A corporation amending its articles of incorporation shall deliver to the Department of State for filing articles of amendment which shall be executed in accordance with s. 607.0120 and which shall set forth:

(1) The name of the corporation;

(2) The text of each amendment adopted;

(3) If an amendment provides for an exchange, reclassification, or cancellation of issued shares, provisions for implementing the amendment if not contained in the amendment itself;

(4) The date of each amendment's adoption;

(5) If an amendment was adopted by the incorporators or board of directors without shareholder action, a statement to that effect and that shareholder action was not required;

(6) If an amendment was approved by the shareholders, a statement that the number of votes cast for the amendment by the shareholders was sufficient for approval and if more than one voting group was entitled to vote on the amendment, a statement designating each voting group entitled to vote separately on the amendment, and a statement that the number of votes cast for the amendment by the shareholders in each voting group was sufficient for approval by that voting group.

607.1007 Restated articles of incorporation.—

(1) A corporation's board of directors may restate its articles of incorporation at any time with or without shareholder action.

(2) The restatement may include one or more amendments to the articles. If the restatement includes an amendment requiring shareholder approval, it must be adopted as provided in s. 607.1003.

(3) If the board of directors submits a restatement for shareholder action, the corporation shall notify each shareholder, whether or not entitled to vote, of the proposed shareholders' meeting in accordance with s. 607.0705. The notice must also state that the purpose, or one of the purposes, of the meeting is to consider the proposed restatement and contain or be accompanied by a copy of the restatement that identifies any amendment or other change it would make in the articles.

(4) A corporation restating its articles of incorporation shall execute and deliver to the Department of State for filing articles of restatement, that comply with the provisions of s. 607.0120, and to the extent applicable, s. 607.0202, setting forth the name of the corporation and the text of the restated articles of incorporation together with a certificate setting forth:

(a) Whether the restatement contains an amendment to the articles requiring shareholder approval and, if it does not, that the board of directors adopted the restatement; or

(b) If the restatement contains an amendment to the articles requiring shareholder approval, the information required by s. 607.1006.

(5) Duly adopted restated articles of incorporation supersede the original articles of incorporation and all amendments to them.

(6) The Department of State may certify restated articles of incorporation, as the articles of incorporation currently in effect, without including the certificate information required by subsection (4).

607.1008 Amendment pursuant to reorganization.—

(1) A corporation's articles of incorporation may be amended without action by the board of directors or shareholders to carry out a plan of reorganization ordered or decreed by a court of competent jurisdiction under any federal or Florida statute if the articles of incorporation after amendment contain only provisions required or permitted by s. 607.0202.

(2) The individual or individuals designated by the court shall deliver to the Department of State for filing articles of amendment setting forth:

(a) The name of the corporation;

(b) The text of each amendment approved by the court;

(c) The date of the court's order or decree approving the articles of amendment;

(d) The title of the reorganization proceeding in which the order or decree was entered; and

(e) A statement that the court had jurisdiction of the proceeding under a federal or Florida statute.

(3) Shareholders of a corporation undergoing reorganization do not have dissenters' rights except as and to the extent provided in the reorganization plan.

(4) This section does not apply after entry of a final decree in the reorganization proceeding even though the court retains jurisdiction of the proceeding for limited purposes unrelated to consummation of the reorganization plan.

607.1009 Effect of amendment.—An amendment to articles of incorporation does not affect a cause of action existing against or in favor of the corporation, a proceeding to which the corporation is a party, or the existing rights of persons other than shareholders of the corporation. An amendment changing a corporation's name does not abate a proceeding brought by or against the corporation in its former name.

607.1020 Amendment of bylaws by board of directors or shareholders.—

(1) A corporation's board of directors may amend or repeal the corporation's bylaws unless:

(a) The articles of incorporation or this act reserves the power to amend the bylaws generally or a particular bylaw provision exclusively to the shareholders; or

(b) The shareholders, in amending or repealing the bylaws generally or a particular bylaw provision, provide expressly that the board of directors may not amend or repeal the bylaws or that bylaw provision.

(2) A corporation's shareholders may amend or repeal the corporation's bylaws even though the bylaws may also be amended or repealed by its board of directors.

607.1021 Bylaw increasing quorum or voting requirements for shareholders.—

(1) If authorized by the articles of incorporation, the shareholders may adopt or amend a bylaw that fixes a greater quorum or voting requirement for shareholders (or voting groups of shareholders) than is required by this act. The adoption or amendment of a bylaw that adds, changes, or deletes a greater quorum or voting requirement for shareholders must meet the same quorum requirement and be adopted by the same vote and voting groups required to take action under the quorum and voting requirement then in effect or proposed to be adopted, whichever is greater.

(2) A bylaw that fixes a greater quorum or voting requirement for shareholders under subsection (1) may not be adopted, amended, or repealed by the board of directors.

607.1022 Bylaw increasing quorum or voting requirements for directors.—

(1) A bylaw that fixes a greater quorum or voting requirement for the board of directors may be amended or repealed:

(a) If originally adopted by the shareholders, only by the shareholders;

(b) If originally adopted by the board of directors, either by the shareholders or by the board of directors.

(2) A bylaw adopted or amended by the shareholders that fixes a greater quorum or voting requirement for the board of directors may provide that it may be amended or repealed only by a specified vote of either the shareholders or the board of directors.

(3) Action by the board of directors under paragraph (1)(b) to adopt or amend a bylaw that changes the quorum or voting requirement for the board of directors must meet the same quorum requirement and be adopted by the same vote required to take action under the quorum and voting requirement then in effect or proposed to be adopted, whichever is greater.

607.1101 Merger.—

(1) One or more corporations may merge into another corporation if the board of directors of each corporation adopts and its shareholders (if required by s. 607.1103) approve a plan of merger.

(2) The plan of merger shall set forth:

(a) The name of each corporation planning to merge and the name of the surviving corporation into which each other corporation plans to merge, which is hereinafter designated as the surviving corporation;

(b) The terms and conditions of the proposed merger; and

(c) The manner and basis of converting the shares of each corporation into shares, obligations, or other securities of the surviving corporation or any other corporation or, in whole or in part, into cash or other property and the manner and basis of converting rights to acquire shares of each corporation into rights to acquire shares, obligations, or other securities of the surviving or any other corporation or, in whole or in part, into cash or other property.

(3) The plan of merger may set forth:

(a) Amendments to, or a restatement of, the articles of incorporation of the surviving corporation;

(b) The effective date of the merger, which may be on or after the date of filing the certificate; and

(c) Other provisions relating to the merger.

607.1102 Share exchange.—

(1) A corporation may acquire all of the outstanding shares of one or more classes or series of another corporation if the board of directors of each corporation adopts and its shareholders (if required by s. 607.1103) approve a plan of share exchange.

(2) The plan of share exchange shall set forth:

(a) The name of the corporation the shares of which will be acquired and the name of the acquiring corporation;

(b) The terms and conditions of the exchange;

(c) The manner and basis of exchanging the shares to be acquired for shares, obligations, or other securities of the acquiring or any other corporation or, in whole or in part, for cash or other property, and the manner and basis of exchanging rights to acquire shares of the corporation to be acquired for rights to acquire shares, obligations, or, in whole or in part, other securities of the acquiring or any other corporation or, in whole or in part, for cash or other property.

(3) The plan of share exchange may set forth other provisions relating to the exchange.

(4) This section does not limit the power of a corporation to acquire all or part of the shares of one or more classes or series of another corporation through a voluntary exchange or otherwise.

607.1103 Action on plan.—

(1) After adopting a plan of merger or share exchange, the board of directors of each corporation party to the merger, and the board of directors of the corporation the shares of which will be acquired in the share exchange, shall submit the plan of merger (except as provided in subsection (7)) or the plan of share exchange for approval by its shareholders.

(2) For a plan of merger or share exchange to be approved:

(a) The board of directors must recommend the plan of merger or share exchange to the shareholders, unless the board of directors determines that it should make no recommendation because of conflict of interest or other special circumstances and communicates the basis for its determination to the shareholders with the plan; and

(b) The shareholders entitled to vote must approve the plan as provided in subsection (5).

(3) The board of directors may condition its submission of the proposed merger or share exchange on any basis.

(4) The corporation the shareholders of which are entitled to vote on the matter shall notify each shareholder, whether or not entitled to vote, of the proposed shareholders' meeting in accordance with s. 607.0705. The notice shall also state that the purpose, or one of the purposes, of the meeting is to consider the plan of merger or share exchange, regardless of whether or not the meeting is an annual or a special meeting, and contain or be accompanied by a copy or summary of the plan. Furthermore, the notice shall contain a clear and concise statement that, if the plan of merger or share exchange is effected, shareholders dissenting therefrom may be entitled, if they comply with the provisions of this act regarding appraisal rights, to be paid the fair value of their shares, and shall be accompanied by a copy of ss. 607.1301-607.1333.

(5) Unless this act, the articles of incorporation, or the board of directors (acting pursuant to subsection (3)) requires a greater vote or a vote by classes, the plan of merger or share exchange to be authorized shall be approved by each class entitled to vote on the plan by a majority of all the votes entitled to be cast on the plan by that class.

(6) Voting by a class or series as a separate voting group is required:

(a) On a plan of merger if the plan contains a provision which, if contained in a proposed amendment to articles of incorporation, would entitle the class or series to vote as a separate voting group on the proposed amendment under s. 607.1004; or

(b) On a plan of share exchange if the shares of such class or series of shares are to be converted or exchanged under such plan or if the plan contains any provisions which, if contained in a proposed amendment to articles of incorporation, would entitle the class or series to vote as a separate voting group on the proposed amendment under s. 607.1004.

(7) Notwithstanding the requirements of this section, unless required by its articles of incorporation, action by the shareholders of the surviving corporation on a plan of merger is not required if:

(a) The articles of incorporation of the surviving corporation will not differ (except for amendments enumerated in s. 607.1002) from its articles before the merger; and

(b) Each shareholder of the surviving corporation whose shares were outstanding immediately prior to the effective date of the merger will hold the same number of shares, with identical designations, preferences, limitations, and relative rights, immediately after the merger.

(8) Any plan of merger or share exchange may authorize the board of directors of each corporation party to the merger or share exchange to amend the plan at any time prior to the filing of the articles of merger or share exchange. An amendment made subse-

quent to the approval of the plan by the shareholders of any corporation party to the merger or share exchange may not:

(a) Change the amount or kind of shares, securities, cash, property, or rights to be received in exchange for or on conversion of any or all of the shares of any class or series of such corporation;

(b) Change any other terms and conditions of the plan if such change would materially and adversely affect such corporation or the holders of the shares of any class or series of such corporation; or

(c) Except as specified in s. 607.1002 or without the vote of shareholders entitled to vote on the matter, change any term of the articles of incorporation of any corporation the shareholders of which must approve the plan of merger or share exchange.

If articles of merger or share exchange already have been filed with the Department of State, amended articles of merger or share exchange shall be filed with the Department of State prior to the effective date of the merger or share exchange.

(9) Unless a plan of merger or share exchange prohibits abandonment of the merger or share exchange without shareholder approval after a merger or share exchange has been authorized, the planned merger or share exchange may be abandoned (subject to any contractual rights) at any time prior to the filing of articles of merger or share exchange by any corporation party to the merger or share exchange, without further shareholder action, in accordance with the procedure set forth in the plan of merger or share exchange or, if none is set forth, in the manner determined by the board of directors of such corporation.

607.1104 Merger of subsidiary corporation.—

(1)(a) A parent corporation owning at least 80 percent of the outstanding shares of each class of a subsidiary corporation may merge the subsidiary into itself, may merge itself into the subsidiary, or may merge the subsidiary into and with another subsidiary in which the parent corporation owns at least 80 percent of the outstanding shares of each class of the subsidiary without the approval of the shareholders of the parent or subsidiary. In a merger of a parent corporation into its subsidiary corporation, the approval of the shareholders of the parent corporation shall be required if the articles of incorporation of the surviving corporation will differ, except for amendments enumerated in s. 607.1002, from the articles of incorporation of the parent corporation before the merger, and the required vote shall be the greater of the vote required to approve the merger and the vote required to adopt each change to the articles of incorporation as if each change had been presented as an amendment to the articles of incorporation of the parent corporation.

(b) The board of directors of the parent shall adopt a plan of merger that sets forth:

1. The names of the parent and subsidiary corporations;

2. The manner and basis of converting the shares of the subsidiary or parent into shares, obligations, or other securities of the parent or any other corporation or, in whole or in part, into cash or other property, and the manner and basis of converting rights to acquire shares of each corporation into rights to acquire shares, obligations, and other securities of the surviving or any other corporation or, in whole or in part, into cash or other property;

3. If the merger is between the parent and a subsidiary corporation and the parent is not the surviving corporation, a provision for the pro rata issuance of shares of the subsidiary to the holders of the shares of the parent corporation upon surrender of any certificates therefor; and

4. A clear and concise statement that shareholders of the subsidiary who, except for the applicability of this section, would be entitled to vote and who dissent from the merger pursuant to s. 607.1, may be entitled, if they comply with the provisions of this act regarding appraisal rights, to be paid the fair value of their shares.

(2) The parent shall mail a copy or summary of the plan of merger to each shareholder of the subsidiary who does not waive the mailing requirement in writing.

(3) The parent may not deliver articles of merger to the Department of State for filing until at least 30 days after the date it mailed a copy of the plan of merger to each shareholder of the subsidiary who did not waive the mailing requirement, or, if earlier, upon the waiver thereof by the holders of all of the outstanding shares of the subsidiary.

(4) Articles of merger under this section may not contain amendments to the articles of incorporation of the parent corporation (except for amendments enumerated in s. 607.1002).

(5) Two or more subsidiaries may be merged into the parent pursuant to this section.

607.11045 Holding company formation by merger by certain corporations.—

(1) This section applies only to a corporation that has shares of any class or series which are either registered on a national securities exchange or designated as a national market system security on an interdealer quotation system by the National Association of Securities Dealers, Inc., or held of record by not fewer than 2,000 shareholders.

(2) As used in this section, the term:

(a) "Constituent corporation" means a corporation that is a party to a merger governed by this section.

(b) "Holding company" means a corporation that, from the date it first issued shares until consummation of a merger governed by this section, was at all times a wholly owned subsidiary of a constituent corporation, and whose shares are issued in such merger.

(c) "Wholly owned subsidiary" means, as to a corporation, any other corporation of which it owns, directly or indirectly through one or more subsidiaries, all of the issued and outstanding shares.

(3) Notwithstanding the requirements of s. 607.1103, unless expressly required by its articles of incorporation, no vote of shareholders of a corporation is necessary to authorize a merger of the corporation with or into a wholly owned subsidiary of such corporation if:

(a) Such corporation and wholly owned subsidiary are the only constituent corporations to the merger;

(b) Each share or fraction of a share of the constituent corporation whose shares are being converted pursuant to the merger which are outstanding immediately prior to the effective date of the merger is converted in the merger into a share or equal fraction of share of a holding company having the same designations, rights, powers and preferences, and qualifications, limitations and restrictions thereof as the share of the constituent corporation being converted in the merger;

(c) The holding company and each of the constituent corporations to the merger are domestic corporations;

(d) The articles of incorporation and bylaws of the holding company immediately following the effective date of the merger contain provisions identical to the articles of incorporation and bylaws of the constituent corporation whose shares are being converted pursuant to the merger immediately prior to the effective date of the merger, except provisions regarding the incorporators, the corporate name, the registered office and agent, the initial board of directors, the initial subscribers for shares and matters solely of historical significance, and such provisions contained in any amendment to the articles of incorporation as were necessary to effect a change, exchange, reclassification, or cancellation of shares, if such change, exchange, reclassification, or cancellation has become effective;

(e) As a result of the merger, the constituent corporation whose shares are being converted pursuant to the merger or its successor corporation becomes or remains a direct or indirect wholly owned subsidiary of the holding company;

(f) The directors of the constituent corporation become or remain the directors of the holding company upon the effective date of the merger;

(g) The articles of incorporation of the surviving corporation immediately following the effective date of the merger are identical to the articles of incorporation of the constituent corporation whose shares are being converted pursuant to the merger immediately prior to the effective date of the merger, except provisions regarding the incorporators, the corporate name, the registered office and agent, the initial board of directors, the initial subscribers for shares and matters solely of historical significance, and such provisions contained in any amendment to the articles of incorporation as were necessary to effect a change, exchange, reclassification, or cancellation of shares, if such change, exchange, reclassification, or cancellation has become effective. The articles of incorporation of the surviving corporation must be amended in the merger to contain a provision requiring, by specific reference to this section, that any act or transaction by or involving the surviving corporation which requires for its adoption under this act or its articles of incorporation the approval of the shareholders of the surviving corporation also be approved by the shareholders of the holding company, or any successor by merger, by the same vote as is required by this act or the articles of incorporation of the surviving corporation. The articles of incorporation of the surviving corporation may be amended in the merger to reduce the number of classes and shares which the surviving corporation is authorized to issue;

(h) The board of directors of the constituent corporation determines that the shareholders of the constituent corporation will not recognize gain or loss for United States federal income tax purposes; and

(i) The board of directors of such corporation adopts a plan of merger that sets forth:

1. The names of the constituent corporations;

2. The manner and basis of converting the shares of the corporation into shares of the holding company and the manner and basis of converting rights to acquire shares of such corporation into rights to acquire shares of the holding company; and

3. A provision for the pro rata issuance of shares of the holding company to the holders of shares of the corporation upon surrender of any certificates therefor.

(4) From and after the effective time of a merger adopted by a constituent corporation by action of its board of directors and without any vote of shareholders pursuant to this section:

(a) To the extent the restrictions of ss. 607.0901 and 607.0902 applied to the constituent corporation and its shareholders at the effective time of the merger, such restrictions also apply to the holding company and its shareholders immediately after the effective time of the merger as though it were the constituent corporation, and all shares of the holding company acquired in the merger shall, for purposes of ss. 607.0901 and 607.0902, be deemed to have been acquired at the time that the shares of the constituent corporation converted in the merger were acquired, and provided further that any shareholder who immediately prior to the effective time of the merger was not an interested shareholder within the meaning of s. 607.0901 shall not, solely by reason of the merger, become an interested shareholder of the holding company; and

(b) If the corporate name of the holding company immediately following the effective time of the merger is the same as the corporate name of the constituent corporation immediately prior to the effective time of the merger, the shares of the holding company into which the shares of the constituent corporation are converted in the merger shall be represented by the share certifi-

cates that previously represented shares of the constituent corporation.

(5) If a plan of merger is adopted by a constituent corporation by selection of its board of directors without any vote of shareholders pursuant to this section, the secretary or assistant secretary of the constituent corporation shall certify in the articles of merger that the plan of merger has been adopted pursuant to this section and that the conditions specified in subsection (3) have been satisfied. The articles of merger so certified shall then be filed and become effective in accordance with s. 607.1106.

607.1105 Articles of merger or share exchange.—

(1) After a plan of merger or share exchange is approved by the shareholders, or adopted by the board of directors if shareholder approval is not required, the surviving or acquiring corporation shall deliver to the Department of State for filing articles of merger or share exchange which shall be executed by each corporation as required by s. 607.0120 and which shall set forth:

(a) The plan of merger or share exchange;

(b) The effective date of the merger or share exchange, which may be on or after the date of filing the articles of merger or share exchange; if the articles of merger or share exchange do not provide for an effective date of the merger or share exchange, then the effective date shall be the date on which the articles of merger or share exchange are filed;

(c) If shareholder approval was not required, a statement to that effect; and

(d) As to each corporation, to the extent applicable, the date of adoption of the plan of merger or share exchange by the shareholders or by the board of directors when no vote of the shareholders is required.

(2) A copy of the articles of merger or share exchange, certified by the Department of State, may be filed in the office of the official who is the recording officer of each county in this state in which real property of a constituent corporation other than the surviving corporation is situated.

607.1106 Effect of merger or share exchange.—

(1) When a merger becomes effective:

(a) Every other corporation party to the merger merges into the surviving corporation and the separate existence of every corporation except the surviving corporation ceases;

(b) The title to all real estate and other property, or any interest therein, owned by each corporation party to the merger is vested in the surviving corporation without reversion or impairment;

(c) The surviving corporation shall thenceforth be responsible and liable for all the liabilities and obligations of each corporation party to the merger;

(d) Any claim existing or action or proceeding pending by or against any corporation party to the merger may be continued as if the merger did not occur or the surviving corporation may be substituted in the proceeding for the corporation which ceased existence;

(e) Neither the rights of creditors nor any liens upon the property of any corporation party to the merger shall be impaired by such merger;

(f) The articles of incorporation of the surviving corporation are amended to the extent provided in the plan of merger; and

(g) The shares (and the rights to acquire shares, obligations, or other securities) of each corporation party to the merger that are to be converted into shares, rights, obligations, or other securities of the surviving or any other corporation or into cash or other property are converted, and the former holders of the shares are entitled only to the rights provided in the articles of merger or to their rights under s. 607.1302.

(2) When a share exchange becomes effective, the shares of each acquired corporation are exchanged as provided in the plan of

exchange, and the former holders of the shares are entitled only to the exchange rights provided in the articles of share exchange or to their rights under s. 607.1302.

607.1107 Merger or share exchange with foreign corporations.—

(1) One or more foreign corporations may merge or enter into a share exchange with one or more domestic corporations if:

(a) In a merger, the merger is permitted by the law of the state or country under the law of which each foreign corporation is incorporated and each foreign corporation complies with that law in effecting the merger;

(b) In a share exchange, the corporation the shares of which will be acquired is a domestic corporation, whether or not a share exchange is permitted by law of the state or country under the law of which the acquiring corporation is incorporated;

(c) The foreign corporation complies with s. 607.1105 if it is the surviving corporation of the merger or acquiring corporation of the share exchange; and

(d) Each domestic corporation complies with the applicable provisions of ss. 607.1101-607.1104 and, if it is the surviving corporation of the merger or acquiring corporation of the share exchange, with s. 607.1105.

(2) Upon the merger becoming effective, the surviving foreign corporation of a merger, and the acquiring foreign corporation in a share exchange, is deemed:

(a) To appoint the Secretary of State as its agent for service of process in a proceeding to enforce any obligation or the rights of dissenting shareholders of each domestic corporation party to the merger or share exchange; and

(b) To agree that it will promptly pay to the dissenting shareholders of each domestic corporation party to the merger or share exchange the amount, if any, to which they are entitled under s. 607.1302.

(3) This section does not limit the power of a foreign corporation to acquire all or part of the shares of one or more classes or series of a domestic corporation through a voluntary exchange or otherwise.

(4) The effect of such merger shall be the same as in the case of the merger of domestic corporations if the surviving corporation is to be governed by the laws of this state. If the surviving corporation is to be governed by the laws of any state other than this state, the effect of such merger shall be the same as in the case of the merger of domestic corporations except insofar as the laws of such other state provide otherwise.

(5) The redomestication of a foreign insurer to this state under s. 628.520 shall be deemed a merger of a foreign corporation and a domestic corporation, and the surviving corporation shall be deemed to be a domestic corporation incorporated under the laws of this state. The redomestication of a Florida corporation to a foreign jurisdiction under s. 628.525 shall be deemed a merger of a domestic corporation and a foreign corporation, and the surviving corporation shall be deemed to be a foreign corporation.

607.1108 Merger of domestic corporation and other business entity.—

(1) As used in this section and ss. 607.1109 and 607.11101, the term "other business entity" means a limited liability company, a foreign corporation, a not-for-profit corporation, a business trust or association, a real estate investment trust, a common law trust, an unincorporated business, a general partnership, a limited partnership, or any other entity that is formed pursuant to the requirements of applicable law. Notwithstanding the provisions of chapter 617, a domestic not-for-profit corporation acting under a plan of merger approved pursuant to s. 617.1103 shall be governed by the provisions of ss. 607.1108, 607.1109, and 607.11101.

(2) Pursuant to a plan of merger complying and approved in accordance with this section, one or more domestic corporations may merge with or into one or more other business entities formed, organized, or incorporated under the laws of this state or any other state, the United States, foreign country, or other foreign jurisdiction, if:

(a) Each domestic corporation which is a party to the merger complies with the applicable provisions of this chapter.

(b) Each domestic partnership that is a party to the merger complies with the applicable provisions of chapter 620.

(c) Each domestic limited liability company that is a party to the merger complies with the applicable provisions of chapter 608.

(d) The merger is permitted by the laws of the state, country, or jurisdiction under which each other business entity that is a party to the merger is formed, organized, or incorporated and each such other business entity complies with such laws in effecting the merger.

(3) The plan of merger shall set forth:

(a) The name of each domestic corporation and the name and jurisdiction of formation, organization, or incorporation of each other business entity planning to merge, and the name of the surviving or resulting domestic corporation or other business entity into which each other domestic corporation or other business entity plans to merge, which is hereinafter and in ss. 607.1109 and 607.11101 designated as the surviving entity.

(b) The terms and conditions of the merger.

(c) The manner and basis of converting the shares of each domestic corporation that is a party to the merger and the partnership interests, interests, shares, obligations or other securities of each other business entity that is a party to the merger into partnership interests, interests, shares, obligations or other securities of the surviving entity or any other domestic corporation or other business entity or, in whole or in part, into cash or other property, and the manner and basis of converting rights to acquire the shares of each domestic corporation that is a party to the merger and rights to acquire partnership interests, interests, shares, obligations or other securities of each other business entity that is a party to the merger into rights to acquire partnership interests, interests, shares, obligations or other securities of the surviving entity or any other domestic corporation or other business entity or, in whole or in part, into cash or other property.

(d) If a partnership is to be the surviving entity, the names and business addresses of the general partners of the surviving entity.

(e) If a limited liability company is to be the surviving entity and management thereof is vested in one or more managers, the names and business addresses of such managers.

(f) All statements required to be set forth in the plan of merger by the laws under which each other business entity that is a party to the merger is formed, organized, or incorporated.

(4) The plan of merger may set forth:

(a) If a domestic corporation is to be the surviving entity, any amendments to, or a restatement of, the articles of incorporation of the surviving entity, and such amendments or restatement shall be effective at the effective date of the merger.

(b) The effective date of the merger, which may be on or after the date of filing the certificate of merger.

(c) Any other provisions relating to the merger.

(5) The plan of merger required by subsection (3) shall be adopted and approved by each domestic corporation that is a party to the merger in the same manner as is provided in s. 607.1103. Notwithstanding the foregoing, if the surviving entity is a partnership, no shareholder of a domestic corporation that is a party to the merger shall, as a result of the merger, become a general partner of the surviving entity, unless such shareholder specifically consents in writing to becoming a general partner of

the surviving entity, and unless such written consent is obtained from each such shareholder who, as a result of the merger, would become a general partner of the surviving entity, such merger shall not become effective under s. 607.11101. Any shareholder providing such consent in writing shall be deemed to have voted in favor of the plan of merger for purposes of s. 607.1103.

(6) Sections 607.1103 and 607.1301-607.1333 shall, insofar as they are applicable, apply to mergers of one or more domestic corporations with or into one or more other business entities.

(7) Notwithstanding any provision of this section or ss. 607.1109 and 607.11101, any merger consisting solely of the merger of one or more domestic corporations with or into one or more foreign corporations shall be consummated solely in accordance with the requirements of s. 607.1107.

607.1109 Articles of merger.—

(1) After a plan of merger is approved by each domestic corporation and other business entity that is a party to the merger, the surviving entity shall deliver to the Department of State for filing articles of merger, which shall be executed by each domestic corporation as required by s. 607.0120 and by each other business entity as required by applicable law, and which shall set forth:

(a) The plan of merger.

(b) A statement that the plan of merger was approved by each domestic corporation that is a party to the merger in accordance with the applicable provisions of this chapter, and, if applicable, a statement that the written consent of each shareholder of such domestic corporation who, as a result of the merger, becomes a general partner of the surviving entity has been obtained pursuant to s. 607.1108(5).

(c) A statement that the plan of merger was approved by each domestic partnership that is a party to the merger in accordance with the applicable provisions of chapter 620.

(d) A statement that the plan of merger was approved by each domestic limited liability company that is a party to the merger in accordance with the applicable provisions of chapter 608.

(e) A statement that the plan of merger was approved by each other business entity that is a party to the merger, other than domestic corporations, limited liability companies, and partnerships formed, organized, or incorporated under the laws of this state, in accordance with the applicable laws of the state, country, or jurisdiction under which such other business entity is formed, organized, or incorporated.

(f) The effective date of the merger, which may be on or after the date of filing the articles of merger, provided, if the articles of merger do not provide for an effective date of the merger, the effective date shall be the date on which the articles of merger are filed.

(g) If the surviving entity is another business entity formed, organized, or incorporated under the laws of any state, country, or jurisdiction other than this state:

1. The address, including street and number, if any, of its principal office under the laws of the state, country, or jurisdiction in which it was formed, organized, or incorporated.

2. A statement that the surviving entity is deemed to have appointed the Secretary of State as its agent for service of process in a proceeding to enforce any obligation or the rights of dissenting shareholders of each domestic corporation that is a party to the merger.

3. A statement that the surviving entity has agreed to promptly pay to the dissenting shareholders of each domestic corporation that is a party to the merger the amount, if any, to which they are entitled under s. 607.1302.

(2) A copy of the articles of merger, certified by the Department of State, may be filed in the office of the official who is the record-ing officer of each county in this state in which real property of a party to the merger other than the surviving entity is situated.

607.11101 Effect of merger of domestic corporation and other business entity.—When a merger becomes effective:

(1) Every domestic corporation and other business entity that is a party to the merger merges into the surviving entity and the separate existence of every domestic corporation and other business entity that is a party to the merger except the surviving entity ceases.

(2) The title to all real estate and other property, or any interest therein, owned by each domestic corporation and other business entity that is a party to the merger is vested in the surviving entity without reversion or impairment. The surviving entity shall record a certified copy of the articles of merger in any county in which a merging entity holds an interest in real property.

(3) The surviving entity shall thereafter be responsible and liable for all the liabilities and obligations of each domestic corporation and other business entity that is a party to the merger, including liabilities arising out of the appraisal rights with respect to such merger under applicable law.

(4) Any claim existing or action or proceeding pending by or against any domestic corporation or other business entity that is a party to the merger may be continued as if the merger did not occur or the surviving entity may be substituted in the proceeding for the domestic corporation or other business entity which ceased existence.

(5) Neither the rights of creditors nor any liens upon the property of any domestic corporation or other business entity shall be impaired by such merger.

(6) If a domestic corporation is the surviving entity, the articles of incorporation of such corporation in effect immediately prior to the time the merger becomes effective shall be the articles of incorporation of the surviving entity, except as amended or restated to the extent provided in the plan of merger.

(7) The shares, partnership interests, interests, obligations, or other securities, and the rights to acquire shares, partnership interests, interests, obligations, or other securities, of each domestic corporation and other business entity that is a party to the merger shall be converted into shares, partnership interests, interests, obligations, or other securities, or rights to such securities, of the surviving entity or any other domestic corporation or other business entity or, in whole or in part, into cash or other property as provided in the plan of merger, and the former holders of shares, partnership interests, interests, obligations, or other securities, or rights to such securities, shall be entitled only to the rights provided in the plan of merger and to their appraisal rights, if any, under ss. 607.1301-607.1333, s. 608.4384, s. 620.205, or other applicable law.

607.1201 Sale of assets in regular course of business and mortgage of assets.—

(1) A corporation may, on the terms and conditions and for the consideration determined by the board of directors:

(a) Sell, lease, exchange, or otherwise dispose of all, or substantially all, of its property in the usual and regular course of business;

(b) Mortgage, pledge, dedicate to the repayment of indebtedness (whether with or without recourse), create a security interest in, or otherwise encumber any or all of its property whether or not in the usual and regular course of business; or

(c) Transfer any or all of its property to a corporation all the shares of which are owned by the corporation.

(2) Unless the articles of incorporation require it, approval by the shareholders of a transaction described in subsection (1) is not required.

607.1202 Sale of assets other than in regular course of business.—

(1) A corporation may sell, lease, exchange, or otherwise dispose of all, or substantially all, of its property (with or without the good will), otherwise than in the usual and regular course of business, on the terms and conditions and for the consideration determined by the corporation's board of directors, if the board of directors proposes and its shareholders of record approve the proposed transaction.

(2) For a transaction to be authorized:

(a) The board of directors must recommend the proposed transaction to the shareholders of record unless the board of directors determines that it should make no recommendation because of conflict of interest or other special circumstances and communicates the basis for its determination to the shareholders of record with the submission of the proposed transaction; and

(b) The shareholders entitled to vote must approve the transaction as provided in subsection (5).

(3) The board of directors may condition its submission of the proposed transaction on any basis.

(4) The corporation shall notify each shareholder of record, whether or not entitled to vote, of the proposed shareholders' meeting in accordance with s. 607.0705. The notice shall also state that the purpose, or one of the purposes, of the meeting is to consider the sale, lease, exchange, or other disposition of all, or substantially all, the property of the corporation, regardless of whether or not the meeting is an annual or a special meeting, and shall contain or be accompanied by a description of the transaction. Furthermore, the notice shall contain a clear and concise statement that, if the transaction is effected, shareholders dissenting therefrom are or may be entitled, if they comply with the provisions of this act regarding appraisal rights, to be paid the fair value of their shares and such notice shall be accompanied by a copy of ss. 607.1301- 607.1333.

(5) Unless this act, the articles of incorporation, or the board of directors (acting pursuant to subsection (3)) requires a greater vote or a vote by voting groups, the transaction to be authorized shall be approved by a majority of all the votes entitled to be cast on the transaction.

(6) Any plan or agreement providing for a sale, lease, exchange, or other disposition of property, or any resolution of the board of directors or shareholders approving such transaction, may authorize the board of directors of the corporation to amend the terms thereof at any time prior to the consummation of such transaction. An amendment made subsequent to the approval of the transaction by the shareholders of the corporation may not:

(a) Change the amount or kind of shares, securities, cash, property, or rights to be received in exchange for the corporation's property; or

(b) Change any other terms and conditions of the transaction if such change would materially and adversely affect the shareholders or the corporation.

(7) Unless a plan or agreement providing for a sale, lease, exchange, or other disposition of property, or any resolution of the board of directors or shareholders approving such transaction, prohibits abandonment of the transaction without shareholder approval after a transaction has been authorized, the planned transaction may be abandoned (subject to any contractual rights) at any time prior to consummation thereof, without further shareholder action, in accordance with the procedure set forth in the plan, agreement, or resolutions providing for or approving such transaction or, if none is set forth, in the manner determined by the board of directors.

(8) A transaction that constitutes a distribution is governed by s. 607.06401 and not by this section.

607.1301 Appraisal rights; definitions.—

The following definitions apply to ss. 607.1302-607.1333:

(1) "Affiliate" means a person that directly or indirectly through one or more intermediaries controls, is controlled by, or is under common control with another person or is a senior executive thereof. For purposes of s. 607.1302(2)(d), a person is deemed to be an affiliate of its senior executives.

(2) "Beneficial shareholder" means a person who is the beneficial owner of shares held in a voting trust or by a nominee on the beneficial owner's behalf.

(3) "Corporation" means the issuer of the shares held by a shareholder demanding appraisal and, for matters covered in ss. 607.1322-607.1333, includes the surviving entity in a merger.

(4) "Fair value" means the value of the corporation's shares determined:

(a) Immediately before the effectuation of the corporate action to which the shareholder objects.

(b) Using customary and current valuation concepts and techniques generally employed for similar businesses in the context of the transaction requiring appraisal, excluding any appreciation or depreciation in anticipation of the corporate action unless exclusion would be inequitable to the corporation and its remaining shareholders.

(5) "Interest" means interest from the effective date of the corporate action until the date of payment, at the rate of interest on judgments in this state on the effective date of the corporate action.

(6) "Preferred shares" means a class or series of shares the holders of which have preference over any other class or series with respect to distributions.

(7) "Record shareholder" means the person in whose name shares are registered in the records of the corporation or the beneficial owner of shares to the extent of the rights granted by a nominee certificate on file with the corporation.

(8) "Senior executive" means the chief executive officer, chief operating officer, chief financial officer, or anyone in charge of a principal business unit or function.

(9) "Shareholder" means both a record shareholder and a beneficial shareholder.

607.1302 Right of shareholders to appraisal.—

(1) A shareholder is entitled to appraisal rights, and to obtain payment of the fair value of that shareholder's shares, in the event of any of the following corporate actions:

(a) Consummation of a merger to which the corporation is a party if shareholder approval is required for the merger by s. 607.1103 and the shareholder is entitled to vote on the merger or if the corporation is a subsidiary and the merger is governed by s. 607.1104;

(b) Consummation of a share exchange to which the corporation is a party as the corporation whose shares will be acquired if the shareholder is entitled to vote on the exchange, except that appraisal rights shall not be available to any shareholder of the corporation with respect to any class or series of shares of the corporation that is not exchanged;

(c) Consummation of a disposition of assets pursuant to s. 607.1202 if the shareholder is entitled to vote on the disposition, including a sale in dissolution but not including a sale pursuant to court order or a sale for cash pursuant to a plan by which all or substantially all of the net proceeds of the sale will be distributed to the shareholders within 1 year after the date of sale;

(d) Any other amendment to the articles of incorporation, merger, share exchange, or disposition of assets to the extent provided by the articles of incorporation, bylaws, or a resolution of the board of directors, except that no bylaw or board resolution providing for appraisal rights may be amended or otherwise altered except by shareholder approval; or

(e) With regard to shares issued prior to October 1, 2003, any amendment of the articles of incorporation if the shareholder is entitled to vote on the amendment and if such amendment would adversely affect such shareholder by:

1. Altering or abolishing any preemptive rights attached to any of his or her shares;

2. Altering or abolishing the voting rights pertaining to

any of his or her shares, except as such rights may be affected by the voting rights of new shares then being authorized of any existing or new class or series of shares;

3. Effecting an exchange, cancellation, or reclassification of any of his or her shares, when such exchange, cancellation, or reclassification would alter or abolish the shareholder's voting rights or alter his or her percentage of equity in the corporation, or effecting a reduction or cancellation of accrued dividends or other arrearages in respect to such shares;

4. Reducing the stated redemption price of any of the shareholder's redeemable shares, altering or abolishing any provision relating to any sinking fund for the redemption or purchase of any of his or her shares, or making any of his or her shares subject to redemption when they are not otherwise redeemable;

5. Making noncumulative, in whole or in part, dividends of any of the shareholder's preferred shares which had theretofore been cumulative;

6. Reducing the stated dividend preference of any of the shareholder's preferred shares; or

7. Reducing any stated preferential amount payable on any of the shareholder's preferred shares upon voluntary or involuntary liquidation.

(2) Notwithstanding subsection (1), the availability of appraisal rights under paragraphs (1)(a), (b), (c), and (d) shall be limited in accordance with the following provisions:

(a) Appraisal rights shall not be available for the holders of shares of any class or series of shares which is:

1. Listed on the New York Stock Exchange or the American Stock Exchange or designated as a national market system security on an interdealer quotation system by the National Association of Securities Dealers, Inc.; or

2. Not so listed or designated, but has at least 2,000 shareholders and the outstanding shares of such class or series has a market value of at least $10 million, exclusive of the value of such shares held by its subsidiaries, senior executives, directors, and beneficial shareholders owning more than 10 percent of such shares.

(b) The applicability of paragraph (2)(a) shall be determined as of:

1. The record date fixed to determine the shareholders entitled to receive notice of, and to vote at, the meeting of shareholders to act upon the corporate action requiring appraisal rights; or

2. If there will be no meeting of shareholders, the close of business on the day on which the board of directors adopts the resolution recommending such corporate action.

(c) Paragraph (2)(a) shall not be applicable and appraisal rights shall be available pursuant to subsection (1) for the holders of any class or series of shares who are required by the terms of the corporate action requiring appraisal rights to accept for such shares anything other than cash or shares of any class or any series of shares of any corporation, or any other proprietary interest of any other entity, that satisfies the standards set forth in paragraph (2)(a) at the time the corporate action becomes effective.

(d) Paragraph (2)(a) shall not be applicable and appraisal rights shall be available pursuant to subsection (1) for the holders of any class or series of shares if:

1. Any of the shares or assets of the corporation are being acquired or converted, whether by merger, share exchange, or otherwise, pursuant to the corporate action by a person, or by an affiliate of a person, who:

a. Is, or at any time in the 1-year period immediately preceding approval by the board of directors of the corporate action requiring appraisal rights was, the beneficial owner of 20 percent or more of the voting power of the corporation, excluding any shares acquired pursuant to an offer for all shares having voting power if such offer was made within 1 year prior to the corporate action requiring appraisal rights for consideration of the same kind and of a value equal to or less than that paid in connection with the corporate action; or

b. Directly or indirectly has, or at any time in the 1-year period immediately preceding approval by the board of directors of the corporation of the corporate action requiring appraisal rights had, the power, contractually or otherwise, to cause the appointment or election of 25 percent or more of the directors to the board of directors of the corporation; or

2. Any of the shares or assets of the corporation are being acquired or converted, whether by merger, share exchange, or otherwise, pursuant to such corporate action by a person, or by an affiliate of a person, who is, or at any time in the 1-year period immediately preceding approval by the board of directors of the corporate action requiring appraisal rights was, a senior executive or director of the corporation or a senior executive of any affiliate thereof, and that senior executive or director will receive, as a result of the corporate action, a financial benefit not generally available to other shareholders as such, other than:

a. Employment, consulting, retirement, or similar benefits established separately and not as part of or in contemplation of the corporate action;

b. Employment, consulting, retirement, or similar benefits established in contemplation of, or as part of, the corporate action that are not more favorable than those existing before the corporate action or, if more favorable, that have been approved on behalf of the corporation in the same manner as is provided in s. 607.0832; or

c. In the case of a director of the corporation who will, in the corporate action, become a director of the acquiring entity in the corporate action or one of its affiliates, rights and benefits as a director that are provided on the same basis as those afforded by the acquiring entity generally to other directors of such entity or such affiliate.

(e) For the purposes of paragraph (2)(d) only, the term "beneficial owner" means any person who, directly or indirectly, through any contract, arrangement, or understanding, other than a revocable proxy, has or shares the power to vote, or to direct the voting of, shares, provided that a member of a national securities exchange shall not be deemed to be a beneficial owner of securities held directly or indirectly by it on behalf of another person solely because such member is the record holder of such securities if the member is precluded by the rules of such exchange from voting without instruction on contested matters or matters that may affect substantially the rights or privileges of the holders of the securities to be voted. When two or more persons agree to act together for the purpose of voting their shares of the corporation, each member of the group formed thereby shall be deemed to have acquired beneficial ownership, as of the date of such agreement, of all voting shares of the corporation beneficially owned by any member of the group.

(3) Notwithstanding any other provision of this section, the articles of incorporation as originally filed or any amendment thereto may limit or eliminate appraisal rights for any class or series of preferred shares, but any such limitation or elimination contained in an amendment to the articles of incorporation that limits or eliminates appraisal rights for any of such shares that are outstanding immediately prior to the effective date of such amendment or that the corporation is or may be required to issue or sell thereafter pursuant to any conversion, exchange, or other right existing immediately before the effective date of such

amendment shall not apply to any corporate action that becomes effective within 1 year of that date if such action would otherwise afford appraisal rights.

(4) A shareholder entitled to appraisal rights under this chapter may not challenge a completed corporate action for which appraisal rights are available unless such corporate action:

(a) Was not effectuated in accordance with the applicable provisions of this section or the corporation's articles of incorporation, bylaws, or board of directors' resolution

authorizing the corporate action; or

(b) Was procured as a result of fraud or material misrepresentation.

607.1303 Assertion of rights by nominees and beneficial

owners.—

(1) A record shareholder may assert appraisal rights as to fewer than all the shares registered in the record shareholder's name but owned by a beneficial shareholder only if the record shareholder objects with respect to all shares of the class or series owned by the beneficial shareholder and notifies the corporation in writing of the name and address of each beneficial shareholder on whose behalf appraisal rights are being asserted. The rights of a record shareholder who asserts appraisal rights for only part of the shares held of record in the record shareholder's name under this subsection shall be determined as if the shares as to which the record shareholder objects and the record shareholder's other shares were registered in the names of different record shareholders.

(2) A beneficial shareholder may assert appraisal rights as to shares of any class or series held on behalf of the shareholder only if such shareholder:

(a) Submits to the corporation the record shareholder's written consent to the assertion of such rights no later than the date referred to in s. 607.1322(2)(b)2.

(b) Does so with respect to all shares of the class or series that are beneficially owned by the beneficial shareholder.

607.1320 Notice of appraisal rights.—

(1) If proposed corporate action described in s. 607.1302(1) is to be submitted to a vote at a shareholders' meeting, the meeting notice must state that the corporation has concluded that shareholders are, are not, or may be entitled to assert appraisal rights under this chapter. If the corporation concludes that appraisal rights are or may be available, a copy of ss. 607.1301-607.1333 must accompany the meeting notice sent to those record shareholders entitled to exercise appraisal rights.

(2) In a merger pursuant to s. 607.1104, the parent corporation must notify in writing all record shareholders of the subsidiary who are entitled to assert appraisal rights that the corporate action became effective. Such notice must be sent within 10 days after the corporate action became effective and include the materials described in s. 607.1322.

(3) If the proposed corporate action described in s. 607.1302(1) is to be approved other than by a shareholders' meeting, the notice referred to in s. 607.1320(1) must be sent to all shareholders at the time that consents are first solicited pursuant to s. 607.0704, whether or not consents are solicited from all shareholders, and include the materials described in s. 607.1322.

607.1321 Notice of intent to demand payment.—

(1) If proposed corporate action requiring appraisal rights under s. 607.1302 is submitted to a vote at a shareholders' meeting, or is submitted to a shareholder pursuant to a consent vote under s. 607.0704, a shareholder who wishes to assert appraisal rights with respect to any class or series of shares:

(a) Must deliver to the corporation before the vote is taken, or within 20 days after receiving the notice pursuant to s. 607.1320(3) if action is to be taken without a shareholder meet-

ing, written notice of the shareholder's intent to demand payment if the proposed action is effectuated.

(b) Must not vote, or cause or permit to be voted, any shares of such class or series in favor of the proposed action.

(2) A shareholder who does not satisfy the requirements of subsection (1) is not entitled to payment under this chapter.

607.1322 Appraisal notice and form.—

(1) If proposed corporate action requiring appraisal rights under s. 607.1302(1) becomes effective, the corporation must deliver a written appraisal notice and form required by paragraph (2)(a) to all shareholders who satisfied the requirements of s. 607.1321. In the case of a merger under s. 607.1104, the parent must deliver a written appraisal notice and form to all record shareholders who may be entitled to assert appraisal rights.

(2) The appraisal notice must be sent no earlier than the date the corporate action became effective and no later than 10 days after such date and must:

(a) Supply a form that specifies the date that the corporate action became effective and that provides for the shareholder to state:

1. The shareholder's name and address.

2. The number, classes, and series of shares as to which the shareholder asserts appraisal rights.

3. That the shareholder did not vote for the transaction.

4. Whether the shareholder accepts the corporation's offer as stated in subparagraph (2)(b)4.

5. If the offer is not accepted, the shareholder's estimated fair value of the shares and a demand for payment of the shareholder's estimated value plus interest.

(b) State:

1. Where the form must be sent and where certificates for certificated shares must be deposited and the date by which those certificates must be deposited, which date may not be earlier than the date for receiving the required form under subparagraph (2)(b)2.

2. A date by which the corporation must receive the form, which date may not be fewer than 40 nor more than 60 days after the date the subsection (1) appraisal notice and form are sent, and state that the shareholder shall have waived the right to demand appraisal with respect to the shares unless the form is received by the corporation by such specified date.

3. The corporation's estimate of the fair value of the shares.

4. An offer to each shareholder who is entitled to appraisal rights to pay the corporation's estimate of fair value set forth in subparagraph (2)(b)3.

5. That, if requested in writing, the corporation will provide to the shareholder so requesting, within 10 days after the date specified in subparagraph (2)(b)2., the number of shareholders who return the forms by the specified date and the total number of shares owned by them.

6. The date by which the notice to withdraw under s. 607.1323 must be received, which date must be within 20 days after the date specified in subparagraph (2)(b)2.

(c) Be accompanied by:

1. Financial statements of the corporation that issued the shares to be appraised, consisting of a balance sheet as of the end of the fiscal year ending not more than 15 months prior to the date of the corporation's appraisal notice, an income statement for that year, a cash flow statement for that year, and the latest available interim financial statements, if any.

2. A copy of ss. 607.1301-607.1333.

607.1323 Perfection of rights; right to withdraw.—

(1) A shareholder who wishes to exercise appraisal rights must execute and return the form received pursuant to s. 607.1322(1) and,

in the case of certificated shares, deposit the shareholder's certificates in accordance with the terms of the notice by the date referred to in the notice pursuant to s. 607.1322(2)(b)2. Once a shareholder deposits that shareholder's certificates or, in the case of uncertificated shares, returns the executed forms, that shareholder loses all rights as a shareholder, unless the shareholder withdraws pursuant to subsection (2).

(2) A shareholder who has complied with subsection (1) may nevertheless decline to exercise appraisal rights and withdraw from the appraisal process by so notifying the corporation in writing by the date set forth in the appraisal notice pursuant to s. 607.1322(2)(b)6. A shareholder who fails to so withdraw from the appraisal process may not thereafter withdraw without the corporation's written consent.

(3) A shareholder who does not execute and return the form and, in the case of certificated shares, deposit that shareholder's share certificates if required, each by the date set forth in the notice described in subsection (2), shall not be entitled to payment under this chapter.

607.1324 Shareholder's acceptance of corporation's offer.—

(1) If the shareholder states on the form provided in s. 607.1322(1) that the shareholder accepts the offer of the corporation to pay the corporation's estimated fair value for the shares, the corporation shall make such payment to the shareholder within 90 days after the corporation's receipt of the form from the shareholder.

(2) Upon payment of the agreed value, the shareholder shall cease to have any interest in the shares.

607.1326 Procedure if shareholder is dissatisfied with offer.—

(1) A shareholder who is dissatisfied with the corporation's offer as set forth pursuant to s. 607.1322(2)(b)4. must notify the corporation on the form provided pursuant to s. 607.1322(1) of that shareholder's estimate of the fair value of the shares and demand payment of that estimate plus interest.

(2) A shareholder who fails to notify the corporation in writing of that shareholder's demand to be paid the shareholder's stated estimate of the fair value plus interest under subsection (1) within the timeframe set forth in s. 607.1322(2)(b)2. waives the right to demand payment under this section and shall be entitled only to the payment offered by the corporation pursuant to s. 607.1322(2)(b)4.

607.1331 Court costs and counsel fees.—

(1) The court in an appraisal proceeding commenced under s. 607.1330 shall determine all costs of the proceeding, including the reasonable compensation and expenses of appraisers appointed by the court. The court shall assess the costs against the corporation, except that the court may assess costs against all or some of the shareholders demanding appraisal, in amounts the court finds equitable, to the extent the court finds such shareholders acted arbitrarily, vexatiously, or not in good faith with respect to the rights provided by this chapter.

(2) The court in an appraisal proceeding may also assess the fees and expenses of counsel and experts for the respective parties, in amounts the court finds equitable:

(a) Against the corporation and in favor of any or all shareholders demanding appraisal if the court finds the corporation did not substantially comply with ss. 607.1320 and 607.1322; or

(b) Against either the corporation or a shareholder demanding appraisal, in favor of any other party, if the court finds that the party against whom the fees and expenses are assessed acted arbitrarily, vexatiously, or not in good faith with respect to the rights provided by this chapter.

(3) If the court in an appraisal proceeding finds that the services of counsel for any shareholder were of substantial benefit to other shareholders similarly situated, and that the fees for those services should not be assessed against the corporation, the court may award to such counsel reasonable fees to be paid out of the amounts awarded the shareholders who were benefited.

(4) To the extent the corporation fails to make a required payment pursuant to s. 607.1324, the shareholder may sue directly for the amount owed and, to the extent successful, shall be entitled to recover from the corporation all costs and expenses of the suit, including counsel fees.

607.1332 Disposition of acquired shares.—Shares acquired by a corporation pursuant to payment of the agreed value thereof or pursuant to payment of the judgment entered therefor, as provided in this chapter, may be held and disposed of by such corporation as authorized but unissued shares of the corporation, except that, in the case of a merger or share exchange, they may be held and disposed of as the plan of merger or share exchange otherwise provides. The shares of the surviving corporation into which the shares of such shareholders demanding appraisal rights would have been converted had they assented to the merger shall have the status of authorized but unissued shares of the surviving corporation.

607.1333. Limitation on corporate payment.—

(1) No payment shall be made to a shareholder seeking appraisal rights if, at the time of payment, the corporation is unable to meet the distribution standards of s. 607.06401. In such event, the shareholder shall, at the shareholder's option:

(a) Withdraw his or her notice of intent to assert appraisal rights, which shall in such event be deemed withdrawn with the consent of the corporation; or

(b) Retain his or her status as a claimant against the corporation and, if it is liquidated, be subordinated to the rights of creditors of the corporation, but have rights superior to the shareholders not asserting appraisal rights, and if it is not liquidated, retain his or her right to be paid for the shares, which right the corporation shall be obliged to satisfy when the restrictions of this section do not apply.

(2) The shareholder shall exercise the option under paragraph (1)(a) or (b) by written notice filed with the corporation within 30 days after the corporation has given written notice that the payment for shares cannot be made because of the restrictions of this section. If the shareholder fails to exercise the option, the shareholder shall be deemed to have withdrawn his or her notice of intent to assert appraisal rights.

607.1401 Dissolution by incorporators or directors.—A majority of the incorporators or directors of a corporation that has not issued shares or has not commenced business may dissolve the corporation by delivering to the Department of State for filing articles of dissolution that set forth:

(1) The name of the corporation;

(2) The date of filing of its articles of incorporation;

(3) Either:

(a) That none of the corporation's shares have been issued, or

(b) That the corporation has not commenced business;

(4) That no debt of the corporation remains unpaid;

(5) That the net assets of the corporation remaining after winding up have been distributed to the shareholders, if shares were issued; and

(6) That a majority of the incorporators or directors authorized the dissolution.

607.1402 Dissolution by board of directors and shareholders; dissolution by written consent of shareholders.—

(1) A corporation's board of directors may propose dissolution for submission to the shareholders.

(2) For a proposal to dissolve to be adopted:

(a) The board of directors must recommend dissolution to the shareholders, unless the board of directors determines that because of conflict of interest or other special circumstances it should make no recommendation and communicates the basis for its determination to the shareholders; and

(b) The shareholders entitled to vote must approve the proposal to dissolve as provided in subsection (5).

(3) The board of directors may condition its submission of the proposal for dissolution on any basis.

(4) The corporation shall notify each shareholder of record, whether or not entitled to vote, of the proposed shareholders' meeting in accordance with s. 607.0705. The notice must also state that the purpose, or one of the purposes, of the meeting is to consider dissolving the corporation.

(5) Unless the articles of incorporation or the board of directors (acting pursuant to subsection (3)) require a greater vote or a vote by voting groups, the proposal to dissolve to be adopted must be approved by a majority of all the votes entitled to be cast on that proposal.

(6) Alternatively, without action of the board of directors, action to dissolve a corporation may be taken by the written consent of the shareholders pursuant to s. 607.0704.

607.1403 Articles of dissolution.—

(1) At any time after dissolution is authorized, the corporation may dissolve by delivering to the Department of State for filing articles of dissolution which shall be executed in accordance with s. 607.0120 and which shall set forth:

(a) The name of the corporation;

(b) The date dissolution was authorized;

(c) If dissolution was approved by the shareholders, a statement that the number cast for dissolution by the shareholders was sufficient for approval.

(d) If dissolution was approved by the shareholders and if voting by voting groups was required, a statement that the number cast for dissolution by the shareholders was sufficient for approval must be separately provided for each voting group entitled to vote separately on the plan to dissolve.

(2) A corporation is dissolved upon the effective date of its articles of dissolution.

607.1404 Revocation of dissolution.—

(1) A corporation may revoke its dissolution at any time prior to the expiration of 120 days following the effective date of the articles of dissolution.

(2) Revocation of dissolution must be authorized in the same manner as the dissolution was authorized unless that authorization permitted revocation by action of the board of directors alone, in which event the board of directors may revoke the dissolution without shareholder action.

(3) After the revocation of dissolution is authorized, the corporation may revoke the dissolution by delivering to the Department of State for filing articles of revocation of dissolution, together with a copy of its articles of dissolution, that set forth:

(a) The name of the corporation;

(b) The effective date of the dissolution that was revoked;

(c) The date that the revocation of dissolution was authorized;

(d) If the corporation's board of directors or incorporators revoked the dissolution, a statement to that effect;

(e) If the corporation's board of directors revoked a dissolution authorized by the shareholders, a statement that revocation was permitted by action by the board of directors alone pursuant to that authorization; and

(f) If shareholder action was required to revoke the dissolution, the information required by s. 607.1403(1)(c) or (d).

(4) Revocation of dissolution is effective upon the effective date of the articles of revocation of dissolution.

(5) When the revocation of dissolution is effective, it relates back to and takes effect as of the effective date of the dissolution and the corporation resumes carrying on its business as if dissolution had never occurred.

607.1405 Effect of dissolution.—

(1) A dissolved corporation continues its corporate existence but may not carry on any business except that appropriate to wind up and liquidate its business and affairs, including:

(a) Collecting its assets;

(b) Disposing of its properties that will not be distributed in kind to its shareholders;

(c) Discharging or making provision for discharging its liabilities;

(d) Distributing its remaining property among its shareholders according to their interests; and

(e) Doing every other act necessary to wind up and liquidate its business and affairs.

(2) Dissolution of a corporation does not:

(a) Transfer title to the corporation's property;

(b) Prevent transfer of its shares or securities, although the authorization to dissolve may provide for closing the corporation's share transfer records;

(c) Subject its directors or officers to standards of conduct different from those prescribed in ss. 607.0801-607.0850 except as provided in s. 607.1421(4);

(d) Change quorum or voting requirements for its board of directors or shareholders; change provisions for selection, resignation, or removal of its directors or officers or both; or change provisions for amending its bylaws;

(e) Prevent commencement of a proceeding by or against the corporation in its corporate name;

(f) Abate or suspend a proceeding pending by or against the corporation on the effective date of dissolution; or

(g) Terminate the authority of the registered agent of the corporation.

(3) The directors, officers, and agents of a corporation dissolved pursuant to s. 607.1403 shall not incur any personal liability thereby by reason of their status as directors, officers, and agents of a dissolved corporation, as distinguished from a corporation which is not dissolved.

(4) The name of a dissolved corporation shall not be available for assumption or use by another corporation until 120 days after the effective date of dissolution unless the dissolved corporation provides the Department of State with an affidavit, executed pursuant to s. 607.0120, permitting the immediate assumption or use of the name by another corporation.

(5) For purposes of this section, the circuit court may appoint a trustee for any property owned or acquired by the corporation who may engage in any act permitted under subsection (1) if any director or officer of the dissolved corporation is unwilling or unable to serve or cannot be located.

607.1406 Known claims against dissolved corporation.—

(1) A dissolved corporation or successor entity, as defined in subsection (15), may dispose of the known claims against it by following the procedures described in subsections (2), (3), and (4).

(2) The dissolved corporation or successor entity shall deliver to each of its known claimants written notice of the dissolution at any time after its effective date. The written notice shall:

(a) Provide a reasonable description of the claim that the claimant may be entitled to assert;

(b) State whether the claim is admitted or not admitted, in whole or in part, and, if admitted:

1. The amount that is admitted, which may be as of a given date; and

2. Any interest obligation if fixed by an instrument of indebtedness;

(c) Provide a mailing address where a claim may be sent;

(d) State the deadline, which may not be fewer than 120 days after the effective date of the written notice, by which confirmation of the claim must be delivered to the dissolved corporation or successor entity; and

(e) State that the corporation or successor entity may make distributions thereafter to other claimants and the corporation's shareholders or persons interested as having been such without further notice.

(3) A dissolved corporation or successor entity may reject, in whole or in part, any claim made by a claimant pursuant to this subsection by mailing notice of such rejection to the claimant within 90 days after receipt of such claim and, in all events, at least 150 days before expiration of 3 years following the effective date of dissolution. A notice sent by the dissolved corporation or successor entity pursuant to this subsection shall be accompanied by a copy of this section.

(4) A dissolved corporation or successor entity electing to follow the procedures described in subsections (2) and (3) shall also give notice of the dissolution of the corporation to persons with known claims, that are contingent upon the occurrence or nonoccurrence of future events or otherwise conditional or unmatured, and request that such persons present such claims in accordance with the terms of such notice. Such notice shall be in substantially the form, and sent in the same manner, as described in subsection (2).

(5) A dissolved corporation or successor entity shall offer any claimant whose known claim is contingent, conditional, or unmatured such security as the corporation or such entity determines is sufficient to provide compensation to the claimant if the claim matures. The dissolved corporation or successor entity shall deliver such offer to the claimant within 90 days after receipt of such claim and, in all events, at least 150 days before expiration of 3 years following the effective date of dissolution. If the claimant offered such security does not deliver in writing to the dissolved corporation or successor entity a notice rejecting the offer within 120 days after receipt of such offer for security, the claimant is deemed to have accepted such security as the sole source from which to satisfy his or her claim against the corporation.

(6) A dissolved corporation or successor entity which has given notice in accordance with subsections (2) and (4) shall petition the circuit court in the county where the corporation's principal office is located or was located at the effective date of dissolution to determine the amount and form of security that will be sufficient to provide compensation to any claimant who has rejected the offer for security made pursuant to subsection (5).

(7) A dissolved corporation or successor entity which has given notice in accordance with subsection (2) shall petition the circuit court in the county where the corporation's principal office is located or was located at the effective date of dissolution to determine the amount and form of security which will be sufficient to provide compensation to claimants whose claims are known to the corporation or successor entity but whose identities are unknown. The court shall appoint a guardian ad litem to represent all claimants whose identities are unknown in any proceeding brought under this subsection. The reasonable fees and expenses of such guardian, including all reasonable expert witness fees, shall be paid by the petitioner in such proceeding.

(8) The giving of any notice or making of any offer pursuant to the provisions of this section shall not revive any claim then barred or constitute acknowledgment by the dissolved corporation or successor entity that any person to whom such notice is sent is a proper claimant and shall not operate as a waiver of any defense or counterclaim in respect of any claim asserted by any person to whom such notice is sent.

(9) A dissolved corporation or successor entity which has followed the procedures described in subsections (2)-(7):

(a) Shall pay the claims admitted or made and not rejected in accordance with subsection (3);

(b) Shall post the security offered and not rejected pursuant to subsection (5);

(c) Shall post any security ordered by the circuit court in any proceeding under subsections (6) and (7); and

(d) Shall pay or make provision for all other known obligations of the corporation or such successor entity. Such claims or obligations shall be paid in full, and any such provision for payments shall be made in full if there are sufficient funds. If there are insufficient funds, such claims and obligations shall be paid or provided for according to their priority and, among claims of equal priority, ratably to the extent of funds legally available therefor. Any remaining funds shall be distributed to the shareholders of the dissolved corporation; however, such distribution may not be made before the expiration of 150 days from the date of the last notice of rejections given pursuant to subsection (3). In the absence of actual fraud, the judgment of the directors of the dissolved corporation or the governing persons of such successor entity as to the provisions made for the payment of all obligations under paragraph (d) is conclusive.

(10) A dissolved corporation or successor entity which has not followed the procedures described in subsections (2) and (3) shall pay or make reasonable provision to pay all known claims and obligations, including all contingent, conditional, or unmatured claims known to the corporation or such successor entity and all claims which are known to the dissolved corporation or such successor entity but for which the identity of the claimant is unknown. Such claims shall be paid in full, and any such provision for payment made shall be made in full if there are sufficient funds. If there are insufficient funds, such claims and obligations shall be paid or provided for according to their priority and, among claims of equal priority, ratably to the extent of funds legally available therefor. Any remaining funds shall be distributed to the shareholders of the dissolved corporation.

(11) Directors of a dissolved corporation or governing persons of a successor entity which has complied with subsection (9) or subsection (10) are not personally liable to the claimants of the dissolved corporation.

(12) A shareholder of a dissolved corporation the assets of which were distributed pursuant to subsection (9) or subsection (10) is not liable for any claim against the corporation in an amount in excess of such shareholder's pro rata share of the claim or the amount distributed to the shareholder, whichever is less.

(13) A shareholder of a dissolved corporation, the assets of which were distributed pursuant to subsection (9) is not liable for any claim against the corporation, which claim is known to the corporation or successor entity, on which a proceeding is not begun prior to the expiration of 3 years following the effective date of dissolution.

(14) The aggregate liability of any shareholder of a dissolved corporation for claims against the dissolved corporation arising under this section, s. 607.1407, or otherwise, may not exceed the amount distributed to the shareholder in dissolution.

(15) As used in this section or s. 607.1407, the term "successor entity" includes any trust, receivership, or other legal entity governed by the laws of this state to which the remaining assets and liabilities of a dissolved corporation are transferred and which exists solely for the purposes of prosecuting and defending suits by

or against the dissolved corporation, enabling the dissolved corporation to settle and close the business of the dissolved corporation, to dispose of and convey the property of the dissolved corporation, to discharge the liabilities of the dissolved corporation, and to distribute to the dissolved corporation's shareholders any remaining assets, but not for the purpose of continuing the business for which the dissolved corporation was organized.

607.1407 Unknown claims against dissolved corporation.—

A dissolved corporation or successor entity, as defined in s. 607.1406(15), may choose to execute one of the following procedures to resolve payment of unknown claims.

(1) A dissolved corporation or successor entity may file notice of its dissolution with the Department of State on the form prescribed by the Department of State and request that persons with claims against the corporation which are not known to the corporation or successor entity present them in accordance with the notice. The notice shall:

(a) State the name of the corporation and the date of dissolution;

(b) Describe the information that must be included in a claim and provide a mailing address to which the claim may be sent; and

(c) State that a claim against the corporation under this subsection will be barred unless a proceeding to enforce the claim is commenced within 4 years after the filing of the notice.

(2) A dissolved corporation or successor entity may, within 10 days of adopting the articles of dissolution, publish a "Notice of Corporate Dissolution." The notice shall appear once a week for 2 consecutive weeks in a newspaper of general circulation in a county in the state wherein the corporation owns real or personal property. Such newspaper shall meet the requirements as are prescribed by law for such purposes. The notice shall:

(a) State the name of the corporation and the date of dissolution;

(b) Describe the information that must be included in a claim and provide a mailing address to which the claim may be sent; and

(c) State that a claim against the corporation under this subsection will be barred unless a proceeding to enforce the claim is commenced within 4 years after the filing of the notice.

(3) If the dissolved corporation or successor entity complies with subsections (1) or (2), the claim of each of the following claimants is barred unless the claimant commences a proceeding to enforce the claim against the dissolved corporation within 4 years after the filing date:

(a) A claimant who did not receive written notice under s. 607.1406(9), or whose claim was not provided for under s. 607.1456(10), whether such claim is based on an event occurring before or after the effective date of dissolution.

(b) A claimant whose claim was timely sent to the dissolved corporation but on which no action was taken.

(4) A claim may be entered under this section:

(a) Against the dissolved corporation, to the extent of its undistributed assets; or

(b) If the assets have been distributed in liquidation, against a shareholder of the dissolved corporation to the extent of such shareholder's pro rata share of the claim or the corporate assets distributed to such shareholder in liquidation, whichever is less, provided that the aggregate liability of any shareholder of a dissolved corporation arising under this section, s. 607.1406, or otherwise may not exceed the amount distributed to the shareholder in dissolution. Nothing in this section shall preclude or relieve the corporation from its notification to claimants otherwise set forth in this chapter.

607.1420 Grounds for administrative dissolution.—

(1) The Department of State may commence a proceeding under s. 607.1421 to administratively dissolve a corporation if:

(a) The corporation has failed to file its annual report or pay the annual report filing fee within the time required by this act;

(b) The corporation is without a registered agent or registered office in this state for 30 days or more;

(c) The corporation does not notify the Department of State within 30 days that its registered agent or registered office has been changed, that its registered agent has resigned, or that its registered office has been discontinued;

(d) The corporation has failed to answer truthfully and fully, within the time prescribed by this act, interrogatories propounded by the Department of State; or

(e) The corporation's period of duration stated in its articles of incorporation has expired.

(2) The foregoing enumeration in subsection (1) of grounds for administrative dissolution shall not exclude actions or special proceedings by the Department of Legal Affairs or any state officials for the annulment or dissolution of a corporation for other causes as provided in any other statute of this state.

607.1421 Procedure for and effect of administrative dissolution.—

(1) If the Department of State determines that one or more grounds exist under s. 607.1420 for dissolving a corporation, it shall serve the corporation with written notice of its determination under s. 607.0504(2), stating the grounds therefor.

(2) If the corporation does not correct each ground for dissolution or demonstrate to the reasonable satisfaction of the Department of State that each ground determined by the department does not exist within 60 days of issuance of the notice, the department shall administratively dissolve the corporation by issuing a certificate of dissolution that recites the ground or grounds for dissolution and its effective date.

(3) A corporation administratively dissolved continues its corporate existence but may not carry on any business except that necessary to wind up and liquidate its business and affairs under s. 607.1405 and notify claimants under s. 607.1406.

(4) A director, officer, or agent of a corporation dissolved pursuant to this section, purporting to act on behalf of the corporation, is personally liable for the debts, obligations, and liabilities of the corporation arising from such action and incurred subsequent to the corporation's administrative dissolution only if he or she has actual notice of the administrative dissolution at the time such action is taken; but such liability shall be terminated upon the ratification of such action by the corporation's board of directors or shareholders subsequent to the reinstatement of the corporation under ss. 607.1401-607.14401.

(5) The administrative dissolution of a corporation does not terminate the authority of its registered agent.

607.1422 Reinstatement following administrative dissolution.—

(1) A corporation administratively dissolved under s. 607.1421 may apply to the Department of State for reinstatement at any time after the effective date of dissolution. The corporation must submit a reinstatement form prescribed and furnished by the Department of State or a current uniform business report signed by the registered agent and an officer or director and all fees then owed by the corporation, computed at the rate provided by law at the time the corporation applies for reinstatement.

(2) If the Department of State determines that the application contains the information required by subsection (1) and that the information is correct, it shall reinstate the corporation.

(3) When the reinstatement is effective, it relates back to and takes effect as of the effective date of the administrative dissolution and the corporation resumes carrying on its business as if the administrative dissolution had never occurred.

(4) The name of the dissolved corporation shall not be available for assumption or use by another corporation until 1 year after the

effective date of dissolution unless the dissolved corporation provides the Department of State with an affidavit executed as required by s. 607.0120 permitting the immediate assumption or use of the name by another corporation.

(5) If the name of the dissolved corporation has been lawfully assumed in this state by another corporation, the Department of State shall require the dissolved corporation to amend its articles of incorporation to change its name before accepting its application for reinstatement.

607.1423 Appeal from denial of reinstatement.—

(1) If the Department of State denies a corporation's application for reinstatement following administrative dissolution, it shall serve the corporation under s. 607.0504(2) with a written notice that explains the reason or reasons for denial.

(2) After exhaustion of administrative remedies, the corporation may appeal the denial of reinstatement to the appropriate court as provided in s. 120.68 within 30 days after service of the notice of denial is perfected. The corporation appeals by petitioning the court to set aside the dissolution and attaching to the petition copies of the Department of State's certificate of dissolution, the corporation's application for reinstatement, and the department's notice of denial.

(3) The court may summarily order the Department of State to reinstate the dissolved corporation or may take other action the court considers appropriate.

(4) The court's final decision may be appealed as in other civil proceedings.

607.1430 Grounds for judicial dissolution.—A circuit court may dissolve a corporation or order such other remedy as provided in s. 607.1434:

(1)(a) In a proceeding by the Department of Legal Affairs if it is established that:

1. The corporation obtained its articles of incorporation through fraud; or

2. The corporation has continued to exceed or abuse the authority conferred upon it by law.

(b) The enumeration in paragraph (a) of grounds for involuntary dissolution does not exclude actions or special proceedings by the Department of Legal Affairs or any state official for the annulment or dissolution of a corporation for other causes as provided in any other statute of this state;

(2) In a proceeding by a shareholder if it is established that:

(a) The directors are deadlocked in the management of the corporate affairs, the shareholders are unable to break the deadlock, and irreparable injury to the corporation is threatened or being suffered; or

(b) The shareholders are deadlocked in voting power and have failed to elect successors to directors whose terms have expired or would have expired upon qualification of their successors;

(3) In a proceeding by a shareholder or group of shareholders in a corporation having 35 or fewer shareholders if it is established that:

(a) The corporate assets are being misapplied or wasted, causing material injury to the corporation; or

(b) The directors or those in control of the corporation have acted, are acting, or are reasonably expected to act in a manner that is illegal or fraudulent;

(4) In a proceeding by a creditor if it is established that:

(a) The creditor's claim has been reduced to judgment, the execution on the judgment returned unsatisfied, and the corporation is insolvent; or

(b) The corporation has admitted in writing that the creditor's claim is due and owing and the corporation is insolvent; or

(5) In a proceeding by the corporation to have its voluntary dissolution continued under court supervision.

607.1431 Procedure for judicial dissolution.—

(1) Venue for a proceeding brought under s. 607.1430 lies in the circuit court of the county where the corporation's principal office is or was last located, as shown by the records of the Department of State, or, if none in this state, where its registered office is or was last located.

(2) It is not necessary to make shareholders parties to a proceeding to dissolve a corporation unless relief is sought against them individually.

(3) A court in a proceeding brought to dissolve a corporation may issue injunctions, appoint a receiver or custodian pendente lite with all powers and duties the court directs, take other action required to preserve the corporate assets wherever located, and carry on the business of the corporation until a full hearing can be held.

(4) If the court determines that any party has commenced, continued, or participated in an action under s. 607.1430 and has acted arbitrarily, frivolously, vexatiously, or not in good faith, the court may, in its discretion, award attorney's fees and other reasonable expenses to the other parties to the action who have been affected adversely by such actions.

607.1432 Receivership or custodianship.—

(1) A court in a judicial proceeding brought to dissolve a corporation may appoint one or more receivers to wind up and liquidate, or one or more custodians to manage, the business and affairs of the corporation. The court shall hold a hearing, after notifying all parties to the proceeding and any interested persons designated by the court, before appointing a receiver or custodian. The court appointing a receiver or custodian has exclusive jurisdiction over the corporation and all of its property wherever located.

(2) The court may appoint a natural person or a corporation authorized to act as a receiver or custodian. The corporation may be a domestic corporation or a foreign corporation authorized to transact business in this state. The court may require the receiver or custodian to post bond, with or without sureties, in an amount the court directs.

(3) The court shall describe the powers and duties of the receiver or custodian in its appointing order, which may be amended from time to time. Among other powers:

(a) The receiver:

1. May dispose of all or any part of the assets of the corporation wherever located, at a public or private sale, if authorized by the court; and

2. May sue and defend in his or her own name as receiver of the corporation in all courts of this state.

(b) The custodian may exercise all of the powers of the corporation, through or in place of its board of directors or officers, to the extent necessary to manage the affairs of the corporation in the best interests of its shareholders and creditors.

(4) The court during a receivership may redesignate the receiver a custodian, and during a custodianship may redesignate the custodian a receiver, if doing so is in the best interests of the corporation and its shareholders and creditors.

(5) The court from time to time during the receivership or custodianship may order compensation paid and expense disbursements or reimbursements made to the receiver or custodian and his or her counsel from the assets of the corporation or proceeds from the sale of the assets.

(6) The court has jurisdiction to appoint an ancillary receiver for the assets and business of a corporation. The ancillary receiver shall serve ancillary to a receiver located in any other state, whenever the court deems that circumstances exist requiring the

appointment of such a receiver. The court may appoint such an ancillary receiver for a foreign corporation even though no receiver has been appointed elsewhere. Such receivership shall be converted into an ancillary receivership when an order entered by a court of competent jurisdiction in the other state provides for a receivership of the corporation.

607.1433 Judgment of dissolution.—

(1) If after a hearing the court determines that one or more grounds for judicial dissolution described in s. 607.1430 exist, it may enter a judgment dissolving the corporation and specifying the effective date of the dissolution, and the clerk of the court shall deliver a certified copy of the judgment to the Department of State, which shall file it.

(2) After entering the judgment of dissolution, the court shall direct the winding up and liquidation of the corporation's business and affairs in accordance with s. 607.1405 and the notification of claimants in accordance with s. 607.1406, subject to the provisions of subsection (3).

(3) In a proceeding for judicial dissolution, the court may require all creditors of the corporation to file with the clerk of the court or with the receiver, in such form as the court may prescribe, proofs under oath of their respective claims. If the court requires the filing of claims, it shall fix a date, which shall be not less than 4 months from the date of the order, as the last day for filing of claims. The court shall prescribe the method by which such notice of the deadline for filing claims shall be given to creditors and claimants. Prior to the date so fixed, the court may extend the time for the filing of claims by court order. Creditors and claimants failing to file proofs of claim on or before the date so fixed may be barred, by order of court, from participating in the distribution of the assets of the corporation. Nothing in this section affects the enforceability of any recorded mortgage or lien or the perfected security interest or rights of a person in possession of real or personal property.

607.1434 Alternative remedies to judicial dissolution.—In an action for dissolution pursuant to s. 607.1430, the court may, upon a showing of sufficient merit to warrant such remedy:

(1) Appoint a receiver or custodian pendente lite as provided in s. 607.1432;

(2) Appoint a provisional director as provided in s. 607.1435;

(3) Order a purchase of the complaining shareholder's shares pursuant to s. 607.1436; or

(4) Upon proof of good cause, make any order or grant any equitable relief other than dissolution or liquidation as in its discretion it may deem appropriate.

607.1435 Provisional director.—

(1) A provisional director may be appointed in the discretion of the court if it appears that such action by the court will remedy the grounds alleged by the complaining shareholder to support the jurisdiction of the court under s. 607.1430. A provisional director may be appointed notwithstanding the absence of a vacancy on the board of directors, and such director shall have all the rights and powers of a duly elected director, including the right to notice of and to vote at meetings of directors, until such time as the provisional director is removed by order of the court or, unless otherwise ordered by a court, removed by a vote of the shareholders sufficient either to elect a majority of the board of directors or, if greater than majority voting is required by the articles of incorporation or the bylaws, to elect the requisite number of directors needed to take action. A provisional director shall be an impartial person who is neither a shareholder nor a creditor of the corporation or of any subsidiary or affiliate of the corporation, and whose further qualifications, if any, may be determined by the court.

(2) A provisional director shall report from time to time to the court concerning the matter complained of, or the status of the deadlock, if any, and of the status of the corporation's business, as the court shall direct. No provisional director shall be liable for any action taken or decision made, except as directors may be liable under s. 607.0831. In addition, the provisional director shall submit to the court, if so directed, recommendations as to the appropriate disposition of the action. Whenever a provisional director is appointed, any officer or director of the corporation may, from time to time, petition the court for instructions clarifying the duties and responsibilities of such officer or director.

(3) In any proceeding under this section, the court shall allow reasonable compensation to the provisional director for services rendered and reimbursement or direct payment of reasonable costs and expenses, which amounts shall be paid by the corporation.

607.1436 Election to purchase instead of dissolution.—

(1) In a proceeding under s. 607.1430(2) or (3) to dissolve a corporation, the corporation may elect or, if it fails to elect, one or more shareholders may elect to purchase all shares owned by the petitioning shareholder at the fair value of the shares. An election pursuant to this section shall be irrevocable unless the court determines that it is equitable to set aside or modify the election.

(2) An election to purchase pursuant to this section may be filed with the court at any time within 90 days after the filing of the petition under s. 607.1430(2) or (3) or at such later time as the court in its discretion may allow. If the election to purchase is filed by one or more shareholders, the corporation shall, within 10 days thereafter, give written notice to all shareholders, other than the petitioner. The notice must state the name and number of shares owned by the petitioner and the name and number of shares owned by each electing shareholder and must advise the recipients of their right to join in the election to purchase shares in accordance with this section. Shareholders who wish to participate must file notice of their intention to join in the purchase no later than 30 days after the effective date of the notice to them. All shareholders who have filed an election or notice of their intention to participate in the election to purchase thereby become parties to the proceeding and shall participate in the purchase in proportion to their ownership of shares as of the date the first election was filed, unless they otherwise agree or the court otherwise directs. After an election has been filed by the corporation or one or more shareholders, the proceeding under s. 607.1430(2) or (3) may not be discontinued or settled, nor may the petitioning shareholder sell or otherwise dispose of his or her shares, unless the court determines that it would be equitable to the corporation and the shareholders, other than the petitioner, to permit such discontinuance, settlement, sale, or other disposition.

(3) If, within 60 days after the filing of the first election, the parties reach agreement as to the fair value and terms of the purchase of the petitioner's shares, the court shall enter an order directing the purchase of petitioner's shares upon the terms and conditions agreed to by the parties.

(4) If the parties are unable to reach an agreement as provided for in subsection (3), the court, upon application of any party, shall stay the s. 607.1430 proceedings and determine the fair value of the petitioner's shares as of the day before the date on which the petition under s. 607.1430 was filed or as of such other date as the court deems appropriate under the circumstances.

(5) Upon determining the fair value of the shares, the court shall enter an order directing the purchase upon such terms and conditions as the court deems appropriate, which may include payment of the purchase price in installments, when necessary in the interests of equity, provision for security to assure payment of the purchase price and any additional costs, fees, and expenses as may have been awarded, and, if the shares are to be purchased by shareholders, the allocation of shares among such shareholders. In allocating petitioner's shares among holders of different classes of shares, the court shall attempt to preserve the existing distribution

of voting rights among holders of different classes insofar as practicable and may direct that holders of a specific class or classes shall not participate in the purchase. Interest may be allowed at the rate and from the date determined by the court to be equitable; however, if the court finds that the refusal of the petitioning shareholder to accept an offer of payment was arbitrary or otherwise not in good faith, no interest shall be allowed. If the court finds that the petitioning shareholder had probable grounds for relief under s. 607.1430(3), it may award to the petitioning shareholder reasonable fees and expenses of counsel and of any experts employed by petitioner.

(6) Upon entry of an order under subsection (3) or subsection (5), the court shall dismiss the petition to dissolve the corporation under s. 607.1430 and the petitioning shareholder shall no longer have any rights or status as a shareholder of the corporation, except the right to receive the amounts awarded by the order of the court, which shall be enforceable in the same manner as any other judgment.

(7) The purchase ordered pursuant to subsection (5) shall be made within 10 days after the date the order becomes final unless, before that time, the corporation files with the court a notice of its intention to adopt articles of dissolution pursuant to ss. 607.1402 and 607.1403, which articles shall then be adopted and filed within 50 days thereafter. Upon filing of such articles of dissolution, the corporation shall be dissolved in accordance with the provisions of ss. 607.1405 and 607.1406, and the order entered pursuant to subsection (5) shall no longer be of any force or effect, except that the court may award the petitioning shareholder reasonable fees and expenses of counsel and any experts in accordance with the provisions of subsection (5) and the petitioner may continue to pursue any claims previously asserted on behalf of the corporation.

(8) Any payment by the corporation pursuant to an order under subsection (3) or subsection (5), other than an award of fees and expenses pursuant to subsection (5), is subject to the provisions of s. 607.06401.

607.14401 Deposit with Department of Banking and Finance.— Assets of a dissolved corporation that should be transferred to a creditor, claimant, or shareholder of the corporation who cannot be found or who is not competent to receive them shall be deposited, within 6 months from the date fixed for the payment of the final liquidating distribution, with the Department of Banking and Finance, where such assets shall be held as abandoned property. When the creditor, claimant, or shareholder furnishes satisfactory proof of entitlement to the amount or assets deposited, the Department of Banking and Finance shall pay the creditor, claimant, or shareholder or his or her representative that amount or those assets.

607.1440.

607.1501 Authority of foreign corporation to transact business required.—

(1) A foreign corporation may not transact business in this state until it obtains a certificate of authority from the Department of State.

(2) The following activities, among others, do not constitute transacting business within the meaning of subsection (1):

(a) Maintaining, defending, or settling any proceeding.

(b) Holding meetings of the board of directors or shareholders or carrying on other activities concerning internal corporate affairs.

(c) Maintaining bank accounts.

(d) Maintaining officers or agencies for the transfer, exchange, and registration of the corporation's own securities or maintaining trustees or depositaries with respect to those securities.

(e) Selling through independent contractors.

(f) Soliciting or obtaining orders, whether by mail or through employees, agents, or otherwise, if the orders require acceptance outside this state before they become contracts.

(g) Creating or acquiring indebtedness, mortgages, and security interests in real or personal property.

(h) Securing or collecting debts or enforcing mortgages and security interests in property securing the debts.

(i) Transacting business in interstate commerce.

(j) Conducting an isolated transaction that is completed within 30 days and that is not one in the course of repeated transactions of a like nature.

(k) Owning and controlling a subsidiary corporation incorporated in or transacting business within this state or voting the stock of any corporation which it has lawfully acquired.

(l) Owning a limited partnership interest in a limited partnership that is doing business within this state, unless such limited partner manages or controls the partnership or exercises the powers and duties of a general partner.

(m) Owning, without more, real or personal property.

(3) The list of activities in subsection (2) is not exhaustive.

(4) This section has no application to the question of whether any foreign corporation is subject to service of process and suit in this state under any law of this state.

607.1502 Consequences of transacting business without authority.—

(1) A foreign corporation transacting business in this state without a certificate of authority may not maintain a proceeding in any court in this state until it obtains a certificate of authority.

(2) The successor to a foreign corporation that transacted business in this state without a certificate of authority and the assignee of a cause of action arising out of that business may not maintain a proceeding based on that cause of action in any court in this state until the foreign corporation or its successor obtains a certificate of authority.

(3) A court may stay a proceeding commenced by a foreign corporation or its successor or assignee until it determines whether the foreign corporation or its successor requires a certificate of authority. If it so determines, the court may further stay the proceeding until the foreign corporation or its successor obtains the certificate.

(4) A foreign corporation which transacts business in this state without authority to do so shall be liable to this state for the years or parts thereof during which it transacted business in this state without authority in an amount equal to all fees and taxes which would have been imposed by this act upon such corporation had it duly applied for and received authority to transact business in this state as required by this act. In addition to the payments thus prescribed, such corporation shall be liable for a civil penalty of not less than $500 or more than $1,000 for each year or part thereof during which it transacts business in this state without a certificate of authority. The Department of State may collect all penalties due under this subsection and may bring an action in circuit court to recover all penalties and fees due and owing the state.

(5) Notwithstanding subsections (1) and (2), the failure of a foreign corporation to obtain a certificate of authority does not impair the validity of any of its contracts, deeds, mortgages, security interests, or corporate acts or prevent it from defending any proceeding in this state.

607.1503 Application for certificate of authority.—

(1) A foreign corporation may apply for a certificate of authority to transact business in this state by delivering an application to the Department of State for filing. Such application shall be made on forms prescribed and furnished by the Department of State and shall set forth:

(a) The name of the foreign corporation as long as its name satisfies the requirements of s. 607.0401, but if its name does not satisfy such requirements, a corporate name that satisfies the requirements of s. 607.1506;

(b) The jurisdiction under the law of which it is incorporated;

(c) Its date of incorporation and period of duration;

(d) The street address of its principal office;

(e) The address of its registered office in this state and the name of its registered agent at that office;

(f) The names and usual business addresses of its current directors and officers;

(g) Such additional information as may be necessary or appropriate in order to enable the Department of State to determine whether such corporation is entitled to file an application for authority to transact business in this state and to determine and assess the fees and taxes payable as prescribed in this act.

(2) The foreign corporation shall deliver with the completed application a certificate of existence (or a document of similar import) duly authenticated, not more than 90 days prior to delivery of the application to the Department of State, by the secretary of state or other official having custody of corporate records in the jurisdiction under the law of which it is incorporated. A translation of the certificate, under oath of the translator, must be attached to a certificate which is in a language other than the English language.

(3) A foreign corporation shall not be denied authority to transact business in this state by reason of the fact that the laws of the jurisdiction under which such corporation is organized governing its organization and internal affairs differ from the laws of this state.

607.1504 Amended certificate of authority.—

(1) A foreign corporation authorized to transact business in this state shall make application to the Department of State to obtain an amended certificate of authority if it changes:

(a) Its corporate name;

(b) The period of its duration; or

(c) The jurisdiction of its incorporation.

(2) Such application shall be made within 90 days after the occurrence of any change mentioned in subsection (1), shall be made on forms prescribed by the Department of State and shall be executed in accordance with s. 607.0120. The foreign corporation shall deliver with the completed application, a certificate, or a document of similar import, authenticated as of a date not more than 90 days prior to delivery of the application to the Department of State by the Secretary of State or other official having custody of corporate records in the jurisdiction under the laws of which it is incorporated, evidencing the amendment. A translation of the certificate, under oath or affirmation of the translator, must be attached to a certificate that is in a language other than English. The application shall set forth:

(a) The name of the foreign corporation as it appears on the records of the Department of State.

(b) The jurisdiction of its incorporation.

(c) The date it was authorized to do business in this state.

(d) If the name of the foreign corporation has been changed, the name relinquished, the new name, a statement that the change of name has been effected under the laws of the jurisdiction of its incorporation, and the date the change was effected.

(e) If the amendment changes its period of duration, a statement of such change.

(f) If the amendment changes the jurisdiction of incorporation, a statement of such change.

(3) The requirements of s. 607.1503 for obtaining an original certificate of authority apply to obtaining an amended certificate under this section.

607.1505 Effect of certificate of authority.—

(1) A certificate of authority authorizes the foreign corporation to which it is issued to transact business in this state subject, however, to the right of the Department of State to suspend or revoke the certificate as provided in this act.

(2) A foreign corporation with a valid certificate of authority has the same but no greater rights and has the same but no greater privileges as, and except as otherwise provided by this act is subject to the same duties, restrictions, penalties, and liabilities now or later imposed on, a domestic corporation of like character.

(3) This act does not authorize this state to regulate the organization or internal affairs of a foreign corporation authorized to transact business in this state.

607.1506 Corporate name of foreign corporation.—

(1) A foreign corporation is not entitled to file an application for a certificate of authority unless the corporate name of such corporation satisfies the requirements of s. 607.0401. If the corporate name of a foreign corporation does not satisfy the requirements of s. 607.0401, the foreign corporation, to obtain or maintain a certificate of authority to transact business in this state:

(a) May add the word "corporation," "company," or "incorporated" or the abbreviation "corp.," "Inc.," "Co.," or

the designation "Corp," "Inc," or "Co," as will clearly indicate that it is a corporation instead of a natural person, partnership, or other business entity; or

(b) May use an alternate name to transact business in this state if its real name is unavailable. Any such alternate corporate name, adopted for use in this state, shall be cross-referenced to the real corporate name in the records of the Division of Corporations. If the corporation's real corporate name becomes available in this state or the corporation chooses to change its alternate name, a copy of the resolution of its board of directors changing or withdrawing the alternate name, executed as required by s. 607.0120, shall be delivered for filing.

(2) The corporate name (including the alternate name) of a foreign corporation must be distinguishable upon the records of the Division of Corporations from:

(a) Any corporate name of a corporation incorporated or authorized to transact business in this state;

(b) The alternate name of another foreign corporation authorized to transact business in this state;

(c) The corporate name of a not-for-profit corporation incorporated or authorized to transact business in this state; and

(d) The names of all other entities or filings, except fictitious name registrations pursuant to s. 865.09, organized or registered under the laws of this state that are on file with the Division of Corporations.

(3) If a foreign corporation authorized to transact business in this state changes its corporate name to one that does not satisfy the requirements of s. 607.0401, it may not transact business in this state under the changed name until it adopts a name satisfying the requirements of s. 607.0401 and obtains an amended certificate of authority under s. 607.1504.

607.1507 Registered office and registered agent of foreign corporation.—

(1) Each foreign corporation authorized to transact business in this state must continuously maintain in this state:

(a) A registered office that may be the same as any of its places of business; and

(b) A registered agent, who may be:

1. An individual who resides in this state and whose business office is identical with the registered office;

2. A corporation or not-for-profit corporation as defined in chapter 617, the business office of which is identical with the registered office; or

3. Another foreign corporation or foreign not-for-profit corporation authorized pursuant to this chapter or chapter 617, to transact business or conduct its affairs in this state the business office of which is identical with the registered office.

(2) A registered agent appointed pursuant to this section or a successor registered agent appointed pursuant to s. 607.1508 on whom process may be served shall each file a statement in writing with the Department of State, in such form and manner as shall be prescribed by the department, accepting the appointment as a registered agent simultaneously with his or her being designated. Such statement of acceptance shall state that the registered agent is familiar with, and accepts, the obligations of that position.

607.1508 Change of registered office and registered agent of foreign corporation.—

(1) A foreign corporation authorized to transact business in this state may change its registered office or registered agent by delivering to the Department of State for filing a statement of change that sets forth:

(a) Its name;

(b) The street address of its current registered office;

(c) If the current registered office is to be changed, the street address of its new registered office;

(d) The name of its current registered agent;

(e) If the current registered agent is to be changed, the name of its new registered agent and the new agent's written consent (either on the statement or attached to it) to the appointment;

(f) That, after the change or changes are made, the street address of its registered office and the business office of its registered agent will be identical; and

(g) That such change was authorized by resolution duly adopted by its board of directors or by an officer of the corporation so authorized by the board of directors.

(2) If a registered agent changes the street address of her or his business office, she or he may change the street address of the registered office of any foreign corporation for which she or he is the registered agent by notifying the corporation in writing of the change and signing (either manually or in facsimile) and delivering to the Department of State for filing a statement of change that complies with the requirements of paragraphs (1)(a)-(f) and recites that the corporation has been notified of the change.

607.1509 Resignation of registered agent of foreign corporation.—

(1) The registered agent of a foreign corporation may resign his or her agency appointment by signing and delivering to the Department of State for filing a statement of resignation and mailing a copy of such statement to the corporation at the corporation's principal office address shown in its most recent annual report or, if none, shown in its application for a certificate of authority or other most recently filed document. The statement of resignation must state that a copy of such statement has been mailed to the corporation at the address so stated. The statement of resignation may include a statement that the registered office is also discontinued.

(2) The agency appointment is terminated as of the 31st day after the date on which the statement was filed and, unless otherwise provided in the statement, termination of the agency acts as a termination of the registered office.

607.15101 Service of process, notice, or demand on a foreign corporation.—

(1) The registered agent of a foreign corporation authorized to transact business in this state is the corporation's agent for service of process, notice, or demand required or permitted by law to be served on the foreign corporation.

(2) A foreign corporation may be served by registered or certified mail, return receipt requested, addressed to the secretary of the foreign corporation at its principal office shown in its application for a certificate of authority or in its most recent annual report if the foreign corporation:

(a) Has no registered agent or its registered agent cannot with reasonable diligence be served;

(b) Has withdrawn from transacting business in this state under s. 607.1520; or

(c) Has had its certificate of authority revoked under s. 607.1531.

(3) Service is perfected under subsection (2) at the earliest of:

(a) The date the foreign corporation receives the mail;

(b) The date shown on the return receipt, if signed on behalf of the foreign corporation; or

(c) Five days after its deposit in the United States mail, as evidenced by the postmark, if mailed postpaid and correctly addressed.

(4) This section does not prescribe the only means, or necessarily the required means, of serving a foreign corporation. Process against any foreign corporation may also be served in accordance with chapter 48 or chapter 49.

(5) Any notice to or demand on a foreign corporation made pursuant to this act may be made in accordance with the procedures for notice to or demand on domestic corporations under s. 607.0504.

607.1510.

607.1520 Withdrawal of foreign corporation.—

(1) A foreign corporation authorized to transact business in this state may not withdraw from this state until it obtains a certificate of withdrawal from the Department of State.

(2) A foreign corporation authorized to transact business in this state may apply for a certificate of withdrawal by delivering an application to the Department of State for filing. The application shall be made on forms prescribed and furnished by the Department of State and shall set forth:

(a) The name of the foreign corporation and the jurisdiction under the law of which it is incorporated;

(b) That it is not transacting business in this state and that it surrenders its authority to transact business in this state;

(c) That it revokes the authority of its registered agent to accept service on its behalf and appoints the Department of State as its agent for service of process based on a cause of action arising during the time it was authorized to transact business in this state;

(d) A mailing address to which the Department of State may mail a copy of any process served on it under paragraph (c); and

(e) A commitment to notify the Department of State in the future of any change in its mailing address.

(3) After the withdrawal of the corporation is effective, service of process on the Department of State under this section is service on the foreign corporation. Upon receipt of the process, the Department of State shall mail a copy of the process to the foreign corporation at the mailing address set forth under subsection (2).

607.1530 Grounds for revocation of authority to transact business.—The Department of State may commence a proceeding under s. 607.1531 to revoke the certificate of authority of a foreign corporation authorized to transact business in this state if:

(1) The foreign corporation has failed to file its annual report with the Department of State within the time required by this act.

(2) The foreign corporation does not pay, within the time required by this act, any fees, taxes, or penalties imposed by this act or other law.

(3) The foreign corporation is without a registered agent or registered office in this state for 30 days or more.

(4) The foreign corporation does not notify the Department of State under s. 607.1508 or s. 607.1509 that its registered agent has resigned or that its registered office has been discontinued within 30 days of the resignation or discontinuance.

(5) An incorporator, director, officer, or agent of the foreign corporation signed a document she or he knew was false in any material respect with intent that the document be delivered to the Department of State for filing.

(6) The Department of State receives a duly authenticated certificate from the secretary of state or other official having custody of corporate records in the jurisdiction under the law of which the foreign corporation is incorporated stating that it has been dissolved or disappeared as the result of a merger.

(7) The foreign corporation has failed to answer truthfully and fully, within the time prescribed by this act, interrogatories propounded by the Department of State.

607.1531 Procedure for and effect of revocation.—

(1) If the Department of State determines that one or more grounds exist under s. 607.1530 for revocation of a certificate of authority, the Department of State shall serve the foreign corporation with written notice of such determination under s. 607.15101.

(2) If the foreign corporation does not correct each ground for revocation or demonstrate to the reasonable satisfaction of the Department of State that each ground determined by the Department of State does not exist within 60 days after issuance of notice is perfected under s. 607.15101, the Department of State shall revoke the foreign corporation's certificate of authority by signing a certificate of revocation that recites the ground or grounds for revocation and its effective date.

(3) The authority of a foreign corporation to transact business in this state ceases on the date shown on the certificate revoking its certificate of authority.

(4) Revocation of a foreign corporation's certificate of authority does not terminate the authority of the registered agent of the corporation.

607.15315 Revocation; application for reinstatement.—

(1)(a) A foreign corporation the certificate of authority of which has been revoked pursuant to s. 607.1531 may apply to the Department of State for reinstatement at any time after the effective date of revocation of authority. The application must:

1. Recite the name of the foreign corporation and the effective date of its revocation of authority;

2. State that the ground or grounds for revocation of authority either did not exist or have been eliminated and that no further grounds currently exist for revocation of authority;

3. State that the foreign corporation's name satisfies the requirements of s. 607.1506; and

4. State that all fees owed by the corporation and computed at the rate provided by law at the time the foreign corporation applies for reinstatement have been paid; or

(b) As an alternative, the foreign corporation may submit a current annual report, signed by the registered agent and an officer or director, which substantially complies with the requirements of paragraph (a).

(2) If the Department of State determines that the application contains the information required by subsection (1) and that the information is correct, it shall cancel the certificate of revocation of authority and prepare a certificate of reinstatement that recites its determination and prepare a certificate of reinstatement, file

the original of the certificate, and serve a copy on the corporation under s. 607.0504(2).

(3) When the reinstatement is effective, it relates back to and takes effect as of the effective date of the revocation of authority and the foreign corporation resumes carrying on its business as if the revocation of authority had never occurred.

(4) The name of the foreign corporation the certificate of authority of which has been revoked is not available for assumption or use by another corporation until 1 year after the effective date of revocation of authority unless the corporation provides the Department of State with an affidavit executed as required by s. 607.0120 permitting the immediate assumption or use of the name by another corporation.

(5) If the name of the foreign corporation has been lawfully assumed in this state by another corporation, the Department of State shall require the foreign corporation to comply with s. 607.1506 before accepting its application for reinstatement.

607.1532 Appeal from revocation.—

(1) If the Department of State revokes the authority of any foreign corporation to transact business in this state pursuant to the provisions of this act, such foreign corporation may likewise appeal to the circuit court of the county where the registered office of such corporation in this state is situated by filing with the clerk of such court a petition setting forth a copy of its application for authority to transact business in this state and a copy of the certificate of revocation given by the Department of State, whereupon the matter shall be tried de novo by the court, and the court shall either sustain the action of the Department of State or direct the department to take such action as the court deems proper.

(2) Appeals from all final orders and judgments entered by the circuit court under this section in review of any ruling or decision of the Department of State may be taken as in other civil actions.

607.1601 Corporate records.—

(1) A corporation shall keep as permanent records minutes of all meetings of its shareholders and board of directors, a record of all actions taken by the shareholders or board of directors without a meeting, and a record of all actions taken by a committee of the board of directors in place of the board of directors on behalf of the corporation.

(2) A corporation shall maintain accurate accounting records.

(3) A corporation or its agent shall maintain a record of its shareholders in a form that permits preparation of a list of the names and addresses of all shareholders in alphabetical order by class of shares showing the number and series of shares held by each.

(4) A corporation shall maintain its records in written form or in another form capable of conversion into written form within a reasonable time.

(5) A corporation shall keep a copy of the following records:

(a) Its articles or restated articles of incorporation and all amendments to them currently in effect;

(b) Its bylaws or restated bylaws and all amendments to them currently in effect;

(c) Resolutions adopted by its board of directors creating one or more classes or series of shares and fixing their relative rights, preferences, and limitations, if shares issued pursuant to those resolutions are outstanding;

(d) The minutes of all shareholders' meetings and records of all action taken by shareholders without a meeting for the past 3 years;

(e) Written communications to all shareholders generally or all shareholders of a class or series within the past 3 years, including the financial statements furnished for the past 3 years under s. 607.1620;

(f) A list of the names and business street addresses of its current directors and officers; and

(g) Its most recent annual report delivered to the Department of State under s. 607.1622.

607.1602 Inspection of records by shareholders.—

(1) A shareholder of a corporation is entitled to inspect and copy, during regular business hours at the corporation's principal office, any of the records of the corporation described in s. 607.1601(5) if the shareholder gives the corporation written notice of his or her demand at least 5 business days before the date on which he or she wishes to inspect and copy.

(2) A shareholder of a corporation is entitled to inspect and copy, during regular business hours at a reasonable location specified by the corporation, any of the following records of the corporation if the shareholder meets the requirements of subsection (3) and gives the corporation written notice of his or her demand at least 5 business days before the date on which he or she wishes to inspect and copy:

(a) Excerpts from minutes of any meeting of the board of directors, records of any action of a committee of the board of directors while acting in place of the board of directors on behalf of the corporation, minutes of any meeting of the shareholders, and records of action taken by the shareholders or board of directors without a meeting, to the extent not subject to inspection under subsection (1);

(b) Accounting records of the corporation;

(c) The record of shareholders; and

(d) Any other books and records.

(3) A shareholder may inspect and copy the records described in subsection (2) only if:

(a) The shareholder's demand is made in good faith and for a proper purpose;

(b) The shareholder describes with reasonable particularity his or her purpose and the records he or she desires to inspect; and

(c) The records are directly connected with the shareholder's purpose.

(4) A shareholder of a Florida corporation, or a shareholder of a foreign corporation authorized to transact business in this state who resides in this state, is entitled to inspect and copy, during regular business hours at a reasonable location in this state specified by the corporation, a copy of the records of the corporation described in s. 607.1601(5)(b) and (f), if the shareholder gives the corporation written notice of his or her demand at least 15 business days before the date on which he or she wishes to inspect and copy.

(5) This section does not affect:

(a) The right of a shareholder to inspect and copy records under s. 607.0720 or, if the shareholder is in litigation with the corporation, to the same extent as any other litigant;

(b) The power of a court, independently of this act, to compel the production of corporate records for examination.

(6) A corporation may deny any demand for inspection made pursuant to subsection (2) if the demand was made for an improper purpose, or if the demanding shareholder has within 2 years preceding his or her demand sold or offered for sale any list of shareholders of the corporation or any other corporation, has aided or abetted any person in procuring any list of shareholders for any such purpose, or has improperly used any information secured through any prior examination of the records of the corporation or any other corporation.

(7) A shareholder may not sell or otherwise distribute any information or records inspected under this section, except to the extent that such use is for a proper purpose as defined in subsection (3). Any person who violates this provision shall be subject to a civil penalty of $5,000.

(8) For purposes of this section, the term "shareholder" includes a beneficial owner whose shares are held in a voting trust or by a nominee on his or her behalf.

(9) For purposes of this section, a "proper purpose" means a purpose reasonably related to such person's interest as a shareholder.

607.1603 Scope of inspection right.—

(1) A shareholder's agent or attorney has the same inspection and copying rights as the shareholder he or she represents.

(2) The right to copy records under s. 607.1602 includes, if reasonable, the right to receive copies made by photographic, xerographic, or other means.

(3) The corporation may impose a reasonable charge, covering the costs of labor and material, for copies of any documents provided to the shareholder. The charge may not exceed the estimated cost of production or reproduction of the records. If the records are kept in other than written form, the corporation shall convert such records into written form upon the request of any person entitled to inspect the same. The corporation shall bear the costs of converting any records described in s. 607.1601(5). The requesting shareholder shall bear the costs, including the cost of compiling the information requested, incurred to convert any records described in s. 607.1602(2).

(4) If requested by a shareholder, the corporation shall comply with a shareholder's demand to inspect the records of shareholders under s. 607.1602(2)(c) by providing him or her with a list of its shareholders of the nature described in s. 607.1601(3). Such a list must be compiled as of the last record date for which it has been compiled or as of a subsequent date if specified by the shareholder.

607.1604 Court-ordered inspection.—

(1) If a corporation does not allow a shareholder who complies with s. 607.1602(1) or (4) to inspect and copy any records required by that subsection to be available for inspection, the circuit court in the county where the corporation's principal office (or, if none in this state, its registered office) is located may summarily order inspection and copying of the records demanded at the corporation's expense upon application of the shareholder.

(2) If a corporation does not within a reasonable time allow a shareholder to inspect and copy any other record, the shareholder who complies with s. 607.1602(2) and (3), may apply to the circuit court in the county where the corporation's principal office (or, if none in this state, its registered office) is located for an order to permit inspection and copying of the records demanded. The court shall dispose of an application under this subsection on an expedited basis.

(3) If the court orders inspection or copying of the records demanded, it shall also order the corporation to pay the shareholder's costs, including reasonable attorney's fees, reasonably incurred to obtain the order and enforce its rights under this section unless the corporation, or the officer, director, or agent, as the case may be, proves that it or she or he refused inspection in good faith because it or she or he had a reasonable basis for doubt about the right of the shareholder to inspect or copy the records demanded.

(4) If the court orders inspection or copying of the records demanded, it may impose reasonable restrictions on the use or distribution of the records by the demanding shareholder.

607.1605 Inspection of records by directors.—

(1) A director of a corporation is entitled to inspect and copy the books, records, and documents of the corporation at any reasonable time to the extent reasonably related to the performance of the director's duties as a director, including duties as a member of a committee, but not for any other purpose or in any manner that would violate any duty to the corporation.

(2) (2) The circuit court of the county in which the corporation's principal office or, if none in this state, its registered office is located may order inspection and copying of the books, records, and documents at the corporation's expense, upon application of a director who has been refused such inspection rights, unless the corporation establishes that the director is not entitled to such inspection rights. The court shall dispose of an application under this subsection on an expedited basis.

(3) If an order is issued, the court may include provisions protecting the corporation from undue burden or expense and prohibiting the director from using information obtained upon exercise of the inspection rights in a manner that would violate a duty to the corporation, and may also order the corporation to reimburse the director for the director's costs, including reasonable counsel fees, incurred in connection with the application.

607.1620 Financial statements for shareholders.—

(1) Unless modified by resolution of the shareholders within 120 days of the close of each fiscal year, a corporation shall furnish its shareholders annual financial statements which may be consolidated or combined statements of the corporation and one or more of its subsidiaries, as appropriate, that include a balance sheet as of the end of the fiscal year, an income statement for that year, and a statement of cash flows for that year. If financial statements are prepared for the corporation on the basis of generally accepted accounting principles, the annual financial statements must also be prepared on that basis.

(2) If the annual financial statements are reported upon by a public accountant, his or her report must accompany them. If not, the statements must be accompanied by a statement of the president or the person responsible for the corporation's accounting records:

(a) Stating his or her reasonable belief whether the statements were prepared on the basis of generally accepted accounting principles and, if not, describing the basis of preparation; and

(b) Describing any respects in which the statements were not prepared on a basis of accounting consistent with the statements prepared for the preceding year.

(3) A corporation shall mail the annual financial statements to each shareholder within 120 days after the close of each fiscal year or within such additional time thereafter as is reasonably necessary to enable the corporation to prepare its financial statements if, for reasons beyond the corporation's control, it is unable to prepare its financial statements within the prescribed period. Thereafter, on written request from a shareholder who was not mailed the statements, the corporation shall mail him or her the latest annual financial statements.

(4) If a corporation does not comply with the shareholder's request for annual financial statements pursuant to this section within 30 days of delivery of such request to the corporation, the circuit court in the county where the corporation's principal office (or, if none in this state, its registered office) is located may, upon application of the shareholder, summarily order the corporation to furnish such financial statements. If the court orders the corporation to furnish the shareholder with the financial statements demanded, it shall also order the corporation to pay the shareholder's costs, including reasonable attorney's fees, reasonably incurred to obtain the order and otherwise enforce its rights under this section.

607.1621 Other reports to shareholders.—

(1) If a corporation indemnifies or advances expenses to any director, officer, employee, or agent under s. 607.0850 otherwise than by court order or action by the shareholders or by an insurance carrier pursuant to insurance maintained by the corporation, the corporation shall report the indemnification or advance in writing to the shareholders with or before the notice of the next shareholders' meeting, or prior to such meeting if the indemnifi-

cation or advance occurs after the giving of such notice but prior to the time such meeting is held, which report shall include a statement specifying the persons paid, the amounts paid, and the nature and status at the time of such payment of the litigation or threatened litigation.

(2) If a corporation issues or authorizes the issuance of shares for promises to render services in the future, the corporation shall report in writing to the shareholders the number of shares authorized or issued, and the consideration received by the corporation, with or before the notice of the next shareholders' meeting.

607.1622 Annual report for Department of State.—

(1) Each domestic corporation and each foreign corporation authorized to transact business in this state shall deliver to the Department of State for filing a sworn annual report on such forms as the Department of State prescribes that sets forth:

(a) The name of the corporation and the state or country under the law of which it is incorporated;

(b) The date of incorporation or, if a foreign corporation, the date on which it was admitted to do business in this state;

(c) The address of its principal office and the mailing address of the corporation;

(d) The corporation's federal employer identification number, if any, or, if none, whether one has been applied for;

(e) The names and business street addresses of its directors and principal officers;

(f) The street address of its registered office and the name of its registered agent at that office in this state;

(g) Language permitting a voluntary contribution of $5 per taxpayer, which contribution shall be transferred into the Election Campaign Financing Trust Fund. A statement providing an explanation of the purpose of the trust fund shall also be included; and

(h) Such additional information as may be necessary or appropriate to enable the Department of State to carry out the provisions of this act.

(2) Proof to the satisfaction of the Department of State that on or before May 1 such report was deposited in the United States mail in a sealed envelope, properly addressed with postage prepaid, shall be deemed compliance with this requirement.

(3) If an annual report does not contain the information required by this section, the Department of State shall promptly notify the reporting domestic or foreign corporation in writing and return the report to it for correction. If the report is corrected to contain the information required by this section and delivered to the Department of State within 30 days after the effective date of notice, it is deemed to be timely filed.

(4) Each report shall be executed by the corporation by an officer or director or, if the corporation is in the hands of a receiver or trustee, shall be executed on behalf of the corporation by such receiver or trustee, and the signing thereof shall have the same legal effect as if made under oath, without the necessity of appending such oath thereto.

(5) The first annual report must be delivered to the Department of State between January 1 and May 1 of the year following the calendar year in which a domestic corporation was incorporated or a foreign corporation was authorized to transact business. Subsequent annual reports must be delivered to the Department of State between January 1 and May 1 of the subsequent calendar years.

(6) Information in the annual report must be current as of the date the annual report is executed on behalf of the corporation.

(7) If an additional updated report is received, the department shall file the document and make the information contained therein part of the official record.

(8) Any corporation failing to file an annual report which complies with the requirements of this section shall not be permitted

to maintain or defend any action in any court of this state until such report is filed and all fees and taxes due under this act are paid and shall be subject to dissolution or cancellation of its certificate of authority to do business as provided in this act.

(9) The department shall prescribe the forms on which to make the annual report called for in this section and may substitute the uniform business report, pursuant to s. 606.06, as a means of satisfying the requirement of this part.

607.1701 Application to existing domestic corporation.—This act applies to all domestic corporations in existence on July 1, 1990, that were incorporated under any general statute of this state providing for incorporation of corporations for profit if power to amend or repeal the statute under which the corporation was incorporated was reserved.

607.1702 Application to qualified foreign corporations.—A foreign corporation authorized to transact business in this state on July 1, 1990, is subject to this act but is not required to obtain a new certificate of authority to transact business under this act.

607.1711 Application to foreign and interstate commerce.—The provisions of this act apply to commerce with foreign nations and among the several states only insofar as the same may be permitted under the Constitution and laws of the United States.

607.1801 Domestication of foreign corporations.—

(1) As used in this section, the term "corporation" includes any incorporated organization, private law corporation (whether or not organized for business purposes), public law corporation, partnership, proprietorship, joint venture, foundation, trust, association, or similar entity.

(2) Any foreign corporation may become domesticated in this state by filing with the Department of State:

(a) A certificate of domestication which shall be executed in accordance with subsection (7) and filed and recorded in accordance with s. 607.0120; and

(b) Articles of incorporation, which shall be executed, filed, and recorded in accordance with ss. 607.0120 and 607.0202.

(3) The certificate of domestication shall certify:

(a) The date on which and jurisdiction where the corporation was first formed, incorporated, or otherwise came into being;

(b) The name of the corporation immediately prior to the filing of the certificate of domestication;

(c) The name of the corporation as set forth in its articles of incorporation filed in accordance with paragraph (2)(b); and

(d) The jurisdiction that constituted the seat, siege social, or principal place of business or central administration of the corporation, or any other equivalent thereto under applicable law, immediately prior to the filing of the certificate of domestication.

(4) Upon filing with the Department of State of the certificate of domestication and articles of incorporation, the corporation shall be domesticated in this state, and the corporation shall thereafter be subject to this act, except that notwithstanding the provision of s. 607.0203 the existence of the corporation shall be deemed to have commenced on the date the corporation commenced its existence in the jurisdiction in which the corporation was first formed, incorporated, or otherwise came into being.

(5) The domestication of any corporation in this state shall not be deemed to affect any obligations or liabilities of the corporation incurred prior to its domestication.

(6) The filing of a certificate of domestication shall not affect the choice of law applicable to the corporation, except that, from the date the certificate of domestication is filed, the law of this state, including this act, shall apply to the corporation to the same extent as if the corporation has been incorporated as a corporation of this state on that date.

(7) The certificate of domestication shall be signed by any corporation officer, director, trustee, manager, partner, or other person performing functions equivalent to those of an officer or director, however named or described, and who is authorized to sign the certificate of domestication on behalf of the corporation.

607.1805 Procedures for conversion to professional service corporation.—A corporation that is organized for profit under the laws of this state and that is engaged solely in carrying out the professional services provided by a corporation organized under chapter 621 may change its corporate nature to that of a professional service corporation if it complies with chapter 621.

607.1901 Corporations Trust Fund creation; transfer of funds.—

(1) There is created a Corporations Trust Fund within the Division of Corporations of the Department of State. All funds required to be paid to the division shall be collected and deposited into this trust fund and shall be used for the purposes prescribed in subsection (2).

(2)(a) The Legislature shall appropriate from the fund such amounts as it deems necessary for the operation of the division.

(b) An amount equal to 2.9 percent of all moneys deposited each month in the fund is transferred to the Corporation Tax Administration Trust Fund created pursuant to s. 213.31.

(c) In the last six months of any fiscal year, an amount equal to 43 percent of all moneys deposited each month into the fund is transferred to the General Revenue Fund.

(d) The division shall transfer from the trust fund to the Cultural Institutions Trust Fund, quarterly, the amount of $10 from each corporate annual report fee collected by the division and prorations transferring $8 million each fiscal year, to be used as provided in s. 265.2861. Effective October 1, 2001, an additional $2 million each fiscal year shall be transferred from the Corporations Trust Fund to the Cultural Institutions Trust Fund to be used as provided in s. 265.2861. The additional $2 million is contingent upon the receipt of corresponding revenues collected under s. 55.209, as created by this act.

(e) The division shall transfer from the trust fund to the Cultural Institutions Trust Fund, quarterly, prorations transferring $250,000 each fiscal year, to be used as provided in s. 265.609.

(f) The division shall transfer from the trust fund to the Cultural Institutions Trust Fund, quarterly, prorations transferring $550,000 each fiscal year, to be used as provided in s. 265.608.

(g) The division shall transfer from the trust fund to the Historical Resources Operating Trust Fund, quarterly, prorations transferring $2 million each fiscal year, to be used as provided in s. 267.0617.

(h) The division shall transfer from the trust fund to the Historical Resources Operating Trust Fund, quarterly, prorations transferring $1.5 million each fiscal year, to be used as provided in s. 267.0619.

(i) Effective October 1, 2001, the division shall transfer from the trust fund to the department's Grants and Donations Trust Fund quarterly prorations equaling not more than $1.6 million each fiscal year, to be used in the provision of services under s. 288.816. The transfer of $1.6 million is contingent upon the receipt of corresponding revenues collected under s. 55.209, as created by this act.

(3) The unencumbered balance in the trust fund at the close of each quarter within the fiscal year may not exceed $300,000. Any funds in excess of this amount shall be transferred unallocated to the General Revenue Fund.

607.19011 Corporations Trust Fund; deposit and use of revenues collected in accordance with ch. 95-242.—All revenues collected in accordance with this act shall be deposited into the Corporations Trust Fund of the Department of State and shall be used in furtherance of the Department of State's cultural and historic preservation programs and other activities as the Legislature may direct.

607.1904 Estoppel.—No body of persons acting as a corporation shall be permitted to set up the lack of legal organization as a defense to an action against them as a corporation, nor shall any person sued on a contract made with the corporation or sued for an injury to its property or a wrong done to its interests be permitted to set up the lack of such legal organization in his or her defense.

607.1907 Effect of repeal of prior acts.—

(1) Except as provided in subsection (2), the repeal of a statute by this act does not affect:

(a) The operation of the statute or any action taken under it before its repeal, including, without limiting the generality of the foregoing, the continuing validity of any provision of the articles of incorporation or bylaws of a corporation authorized by the statute at the time of its adoption;

(b) Any ratification, right remedy, privilege, obligation, or liability acquired, accrued, or incurred under the statute before its repeal;

(c) Any violation of the statute, or any penalty, forfeiture, or punishment incurred because of the violation, before its repeal;

(d) Any proceeding, merger, consolidation, sale of assets, reorganization, or dissolution commenced under the statute before its repeal, and the proceeding, merger, consolidation, sale of assets, reorganization, or dissolution may be completed in accordance with the statute as if it had not been repealed.

(2) If a penalty or punishment imposed for violation of a statute repealed by this act is reduced by this act, the penalty or punishment if not already imposed shall be imposed in accordance with this act.

607.193 Supplemental corporate fee.—

(1) In addition to any other taxes imposed by law, an annual supplemental corporate fee of $88.75 is imposed on each business entity that is authorized to transact business in this state and is required to file an annual report with the Department of State under s. 607.1622, s. 608.452, or s. 620.177.

(2)(a) The business entity shall remit the supplemental corporate fee to the Department of State at the time it files the annual report required by s. 607.1622, s. 608.452, or s. 620.177.

(b) In addition to the fees levied under ss. 607.0122, 608.452, and 620.182 and the supplemental corporate fee, a late charge of $400 shall be imposed if the supplemental corporate fee is remitted after May 1 except in circumstances in which a business entity did not receive the uniform business report prescribed by the department.

(3) The Department of State shall adopt rules and prescribe forms necessary to carry out the purposes of this section. Notwithstanding s. 607.1901, proceeds from the supplemental corporate fee, including any late charges, shall be deposited into the General Revenue Fund.

607 and 608.

621.14 Construction of law.

621.01 Legislative intent.—It is the legislative intent to provide for the incorporation or organization as a limited liability company of an individual or group of individuals, professional corporations, or professional limited liability companies to render the same professional service to the public for which such individuals, individual shareholders of professional corporations, or members of limited liability companies are required by law to be licensed or to obtain other legal authorization.

607 for the sole and specific purpose of rendering the same and specific professional service.

608 for the sole and specific purpose of rendering the same and specific professional service.

607 or a member-employee of a limited liability company organized under chapter 608. The corporation or limited liability company shall be liable up to the full value of its property for any negligent or wrongful acts or misconduct committed by any of its officers, agents, members, managers, or employees while they are engaged on behalf of the corporation or limited liability company in the rendering of professional services.

608.406.

(3) In the case of a corporation, the use of the word "company," "corporation," or "incorporated" or any other word, abbreviation, affix, or prefix indicating that it is a corporation in the corporate name of a corporation organized under this act, other than the word "chartered" or the words "professional association" or the abbreviation "P.A.," is specifically prohibited.

(4) It shall be permissible, however, for the corporation or limited liability company to render professional services and to exercise its authorized powers under a name which is identical to its name except that the word "chartered," the words "professional association" or "professional limited company," or the abbreviations "P.A." or "P.L." may be omitted, provided that the corporation or limited liability company has first registered the name to be so used in the manner required for the registration of fictitious names.

607 and 608.—

(1) Chapter 607 is applicable to a corporation organized pursuant to this act except to the extent that any of the provisions of this act are interpreted to be in conflict with the provisions of chapter 607. In such event, the provisions and sections of this act shall take precedence with respect to a corporation organized pursuant to the provisions of this act.

(2) Chapter 608 is applicable to a limited liability company organized pursuant to this act except to the extent that any of the provisions of this act are interpreted to be in conflict with the provisions of chapter 608. In such event, the provisions and sections of this act shall take precedence with respect to a limited liability company organized pursuant to the provisions of this act.

(3) A professional corporation or limited liability company organized under this act shall exchange shares or merge only with other domestic professional corporations or limited liability companies organized under this act to render the same specific professional service, and a merger or consolidation with any foreign corporation or limited liability company is prohibited.

(4) A professional corporation or limited liability company heretofore or hereafter organized under this act may change its business purpose from the rendering of professional service to provide for any other lawful purpose by amending its certificate of incorporation in the manner required for an original incorporation under chapter 607 or by amending its certificate of organization in the manner required for an original organization under chapter 608. However, such an amendment, when filed with and accepted by the Department of State, shall remove such corporation or limited liability company from the provisions of this chapter including, but not limited to, the right to practice a profession. A change of business purpose shall not have any effect on the continued existence of the corporation or limited liability company.

History.—s. 13, ch. 61-64; ss. 10, 35, ch. 69-106; s. 2, ch. 69-288; s. 210, ch. 77-104; s. 179, ch. 90-179; s. 14, ch. 93-110; s. 87, ch. 93-284.

621.14 Construction of law.—The provisions of this act shall not be construed as repealing, modifying, or restricting the applicable provisions of law relating to incorporations, organization of limited liability companies, sales of securities, or regulating the several professions enumerated in this act except insofar as such laws conflict with the provisions of this act.

History.—s. 15, ch. 61-64; s. 15, ch. 93-110; s. 88, ch. 93-284.

APPENDIX C
BLANK FORMS

INSTRUCTIONS FOR A PROFIT CORPORATION

The following are instructions, a transmittal letter and sample articles of incorporation pursuant to Chapter 607 and 621 Florida Statutes (F.S.).

NOTE: THIS IS A BASIC FORM MEETING MINIMAL REQUIREMENTS FOR FILING ARTICLES OF INCORPORATION.

The Division of Corporations strongly recommends that corporate documents be reviewed by your legal counsel. The Division is a filing agency and as such does not render any legal, accounting, or tax advice.

This office does not provide you with corporate seals, minute books, or stock certificates. It is the responsibility of the corporation to secure these items once the corporation has been filed with this office.

Questions concerning S Corporations should be directed to the Internal Revenue Service by telephoning 1-800-829-1040. This is an IRS designation, which is not determined by this office.

A preliminary search for name availability can be made on the Internet through the Division's records at www.sunbiz.org. Preliminary name searches and name reservations are no longer available from the Division of Corporations. You are responsible for any name infringement that may result from your corporate name selection.

Pursuant to Chapter 607 or 621 F.S., the articles of incorporation **must** set forth the following:

Article I: The name of the corporation **must** include a corporate suffix such as Corporation, Corp., Incorporated, Inc., Company, or Co.

A Professional Association **must** contain the word "chartered" or "professional association" or "P.A.".

Article II: The principal place of business and mailing address of the corporation.

Article III: **Specific Purpose for a "Professional Corporation"**

Article IV: The number of shares of stock that this corporation is authorized to have **must** be stated.

CR2E010(6/01)

Article V: The names, address and titles of the Directors/Officers **(optional).** The names of officers/directors may be required to apply for a license, open a bank account, etc.

Article VI: The name and **Florida street address** of the initial Registered Agent. The Registered Agent **must** sign in the space provided and type or print his/her name accepting the designation as registered agent.

Article VII: The name and address of the Incorporator. The Incorporator **must** sign in the space provided and type or print his/her name below signature.

An Effective Date: **Add a separate article if applicable or necessary**: An effective date **may** be added to the Articles of Incorporation, otherwise the date of receipt will be the file date. (An effective date can not be more than five (5) business days prior to the date of receipt or ninety (90) days after the date of filing).
****

The fee for filing a profit corporation is:
Filing Fee $35.00
Designation of Registered Agent $35.00
Certified Copy (optional) $ 8.75 (plus $1 per page for each page over 8, not to exceed a maximum of $52.50).
Certificate of Status (optional) $ 8.75
(Make checks payable to Florida Department of State)

Mailing Address:	Street Address:
Department of State	Department of State
Division of Corporations	Division of Corporations
P.O. Box 6327	409 E. Gaines St.
Tallahassee, FL 32314	Tallahassee, FL 32399
(850) 245-6052	(850) 245-6052

TRANSMITTAL LETTER

Department of State
Division of Corporations
P. O. Box 6327
Tallahassee, FL 32314

SUBJECT: _____
(PROPOSED CORPORATE NAME – <u>MUST INCLUDE SUFFIX</u>)

Enclosed are an original and one (1) copy of the articles of incorporation and a check for:

❑ $70.00
Filing Fee

❑ $78.75
Filing Fee
& Certificate of Status

❑ $78.75
Filing Fee
& Certified Copy

❑ $87.50
Filing Fee,
Certified Copy
& Certificate of
Status

ADDITIONAL COPY REQUIRED

FROM: _____
Name (Printed or typed)

_____
Address

_____
City, State & Zip

_____
Daytime Telephone number

NOTE: Please provide the original and one copy of the articles.

ARTICLES OF INCORPORATION
In compliance with Chapter 607 and/or Chapter 621, F.S. (Profit)

ARTICLE I   NAME
The name of the corporation shall be:

ARTICLE II   PRINCIPAL OFFICE
The principal place of business/mailing address is:

ARTICLE III   PURPOSE
The purpose for which the corporation is organized is:

ARTICLE IV   SHARES
The number of shares of stock is:

ARTICLE   V   INITIAL OFFICERS/DIRECTORS (optional)
The name(s), address(es) and title(s):

ARTICLE VI   REGISTERED AGENT
The **name and Florida street address** of the registered agent is:

ARTICLE VII   INCORPORATOR
The **name and address** of the Incorporator is:

****

Having been named as registered agent to accept service of process for the above stated corporation at the place designated in this certificate, I am familiar with and accept the appointment as registered agent and agree to act in this capacity

| Signature/Registered Agent | Date |

| Signature/Incorporator | Date |

ARTICLES OF INCORPORATION

Professional Service Corporation

1.   The name of the corporation shall be: _____

_____

2.   The purpose for which this corporation is organized is _____

_____

3.   The principal place of business and mailing address of the corporation is:

_____

_____

4.   The corporation shall have the authority to issue _____ shares of common stock, in one class only, each with a par value of $_____.

5.   The registered agent of the corporation is _____ and the registered street address is _____, Florida _____.

6.   The initial Board of Directors shall have ___ member(s) whose name(s) and address(es) is/are as   follows: _____

_____

_____

_____

The number of directors may be raised or lowered by amendment of the bylaws of the corporation but shall in no case be less than one.

7.   The incorporator of this corporation is _____ whose street address is _____

Dated _____

_____
Incorporator

Having been named as registered agent and to accept service of process for the above stated corporation at the place designated in this certificate, I hereby accept the appointment as registered agent and agree to act in this capacity. I further agree to comply with the provisions of all statutes relating to the proper and complete performance of my duties, and am familiar with and accept the obligations of my position as registered agent.

Dated _____

_____
Registered Agent

A domestic or foreign corporation may correct a document filed by the Department of State within 10 business days of filing if the document contains an incorrect statement, or was defectively executed, attested, sealed, verified or acknowledged.

Pursuant to Section 607.0124 or 617.0124, Florida Statutes, a document is corrected by preparing **Articles of Correction** that:

Describe the document (including its file date), or attach a copy of it to the Articles of Correction

Specify the incorrect statement and reason it is incorrect or the manner in which the execution was defective; and

Correct the incorrect statement or defective execution.

A form for **Articles of Correction** is attached. Additional sheets can be included if necessary. Pursuant to Section 607.0120 or 617.01201, Florida Statutes, the document must be typewritten or printed and must be legible.

Filing Fee	**$35.00**
Certified Copy (Optional)	**$8.75 (plus $1 per page for each page over 8, not to exceed a maximum of $52.50**
Certificate of Status (Optional)	**$8.75**

Send one check in the total amount made payable to the Florida Department of State.

Please include a cover letter containing your telephone number, return address and certification requirements, or complete the attached transmittal letter.

Mailing Address:
Amendment Section
Division of Corporations
P.O. Box 6327
Tallahassee, Florida 32314

Street Address:
Amendment Section
Division of Corporations
409 E. Gaines Street
Tallahassee, Florida 32399

For further information, you may contact the Amendment Section at (850) 245-6050.

TRANSMITTAL LETTER

TO: Amendment Section
        Division of Corporations

SUBJECT:_____
(Name of Corporation)

DOCUMENT NUMBER:_____

The enclosed Articles of Correction and fee are submitted for filing.

Please return all correspondence concerning this matter to the following:

_____
(Name of Person)

_____
(Name of Firm/Company)

_____
(Address)

_____
(City/State and Zip Code)

For further information concerning this matter, please call:

_____ at (_____)_____
(Name of Person)   (Area Code & Daytime Telephone Number)

Enclosed is a check for the following amount:

❐ $35.00 Filing Fee   ❐ $43.75 Filing Fee & Certificate of Status

❐ $43.75 Filing Fee & Certified Copy   ❐ $52.50 Filing Fee, Certificate of Status &
                                            Certified Copy

Mailing Address: **Street Address:**
Amendment Section   Amendment Section
Division of Corporations   Division of Corporations
P.O. Box 6327   409 E. Gaines Street
Tallahassee, Florida 32314   Tallahassee, Florida 32399

ARTICLES OF CORRECTION

for

_____
Name of Corporation as currently filed with the Florida Dept. of State

_____
Document Number (if known)

Pursuant to the provisions of Section 607.0124 or 617.0124, Florida Statutes, this corporation files these Articles of Correction.

These articles of correction correct _____,
(Document Type)

filed with the Department of State on _____.
(File Date of Document)

Specify the incorrect statement and reason it is incorrect or the manner in which the execution was defective:

_____

_____

_____

_____

_____

_____

Correct the incorrect statement or defective execution:

_____

_____

_____

_____

_____

_____

_____
Signature of the Chairman or Vice Chairman of the Board of Directors, any officer, or an incorporator, if applicable.

_____   _____
Typed or printed name of signee   Title

Filing Fee: $35.00

ARTICLES OF AMENDMENT
TO
ARTICLES OF INCORPORATION
OF

_____

(present name)

_____
(Document Number of Corporation (If known)

Pursuant to the provisions of section 607.1006, Florida Statutes, this Florida profit corporation adopts the following articles of amendment to its articles of incorporation:

FIRST: Amendment(s) adopted: *(indicate article number(s) being amended, added or deleted)*

SECOND: If an amendment provides for an exchange, reclassification or cancellation of issued shares, provisions for implementing the amendment if not contained in the amendment itself, are as follows:

THIRD: The date of each amendment's adoption:_____ .

FOURTH: Adoption of Amendment(s) **(CHECK ONE)**

❑   The amendment(s) was/were approved by the shareholders. The number of votes cast for the amendment(s) was/were sufficient for approval.

❑   The amendment(s) was/were approved by the shareholders through voting groups. *The following statement must be separately provided for each voting group entitled to vote separately on the amendment(s):*

"The number of votes cast for the amendment(s) was/were sufficient
for approval by _____."
(voting group)

❑   The amendment(s) was/were adopted by the board of directors without shareholder action and shareholder action was not required.

❑   The amendment(s) was/were adopted by the incorporators without shareholder action and shareholder action was not required.

Signed this _____ day of_____, _____.

Signature_____
(By the Chairman or Vice Chairman of the Board of Directors, President or other officer if adopted by the shareholders)

OR

(By a director if adopted by the directors)

OR

(By an incorporator if adopted by the incorporators)

_____
(Typed or printed name)

_____
(Title)

Form **SS-4**

(Rev. December 2001)

Department of the Treasury
Internal Revenue Service

Application for Employer Identification Number

(For use by employers, corporations, partnerships, trusts, estates, churches, government agencies, Indian tribal entities, certain individuals, and others.)

▶ See separate instructions for each line.   ▶ Keep a copy for your records.

EIN

OMB No. 1545-0003

Type or print clearly.

1 Legal name of entity (or individual) for whom the EIN is being requested

2 Trade name of business (if different from name on line 1)

3 Executor, trustee, "care of" name

4a Mailing address (room, apt., suite no. and street, or P.O. box)

5a Street address (if different) (Do not enter a P.O. box.)

4b City, state, and ZIP code

5b City, state, and ZIP code

6 County and state where principal business is located

7a Name of principal officer, general partner, grantor, owner, or trustor

7b SSN, ITIN, or EIN

8a **Type of entity** (check only one box)

- ☐ Sole proprietor (SSN) _____
- ☐ Partnership
- ☐ Corporation (enter form number to be filed) ▶ _____
- ☐ Personal service corp.
- ☐ Church or church-controlled organization
- ☐ Other nonprofit organization (specify) ▶ _____
- ☐ Other (specify) ▶

- ☐ Estate (SSN of decedent) _____
- ☐ Plan administrator (SSN) _____
- ☐ Trust (SSN of grantor) _____
- ☐ National Guard   ☐ State/local government
- ☐ Farmers' cooperative   ☐ Federal government/military
- ☐ REMIC   ☐ Indian tribal governments/enterprises

Group Exemption Number (GEN) ▶ _____

8b If a corporation, name the state or foreign country (if applicable) where incorporated

State

Foreign country

9 **Reason for applying** (check only one box)

- ☐ Started new business (specify type) ▶_____
  _____
- ☐ Hired employees (Check the box and see line 12.)
- ☐ Compliance with IRS withholding regulations
- ☐ Other (specify) ▶

- ☐ Banking purpose (specify purpose) ▶ _____
- ☐ Changed type of organization (specify new type) ▶ _____
- ☐ Purchased going business
- ☐ Created a trust (specify type) ▶ _____
- ☐ Created a pension plan (specify type) ▶ _____

10 Date business started or acquired (month, day, year)

11 Closing month of accounting year

12 First date wages or annuities were paid or will be paid (month, day, year). **Note:** *If applicant is a withholding agent, enter date income will first be paid to nonresident alien. (month, day, year)* . . . . ▶

13 Highest number of employees expected in the next 12 months. **Note:** *If the applicant does not expect to have any employees during the period, enter "-0-."* . . . . ▶

Agricultural	Household	Other

14 Check **one** box that best describes the principal activity of your business.

- ☐ Construction
- ☐ Real estate
- ☐ Rental & leasing
- ☐ Manufacturing
- ☐ Transportation & warehousing
- ☐ Finance & insurance
- ☐ Health care & social assistance
- ☐ Accommodation & food service
- ☐ Other (specify)
- ☐ Wholesale–agent/broker
- ☐ Wholesale–other
- ☐ Retail

15 Indicate principal line of merchandise sold; specific construction work done; products produced; or services provided.

16a Has the applicant ever applied for an employer identification number for this or any other business? . . . . . ☐ **Yes**   ☐ **No**

Note: *If "Yes," please complete lines 16b and 16c.*

16b If you checked "Yes" on line 16a, give applicant's legal name and trade name shown on prior application if different from line 1 or 2 above.

Legal name ▶   Trade name ▶

16c Approximate date when, and city and state where, the application was filed. Enter previous employer identification number if known.

Approximate date when filed (mo., day, year) | City and state where filed | Previous EIN

Third Party Designee

Complete this section **only** if you want to authorize the named individual to receive the entity's EIN and answer questions about the completion of this form.

Designee's name

Designee's telephone number (include area code)
(   )

Address and ZIP code

Designee's fax number (include area code)
(   )

Under penalties of perjury, I declare that I have examined this application, and to the best of my knowledge and belief, it is true, correct, and complete.

Applicant's telephone number (include area code)
(   )

Name and title (type or print clearly) ▶

Applicant's fax number (include area code)
(   )

Signature ▶   Date ▶

For Privacy Act and Paperwork Reduction Act Notice, see separate instructions.   Cat. No. 16055N   Form **SS-4** (Rev. 12-2001)

Do I Need an EIN?

File Form SS-4 if the applicant entity does not already have an EIN but is required to show an EIN on any return, statement, or other document.[1] **See also the separate instructions for each line on Form SS-4.**

IF the applicant...	AND...	THEN...
Started a new business	Does not currently have (nor expect to have) employees	Complete lines 1, 2, 4a- 6, 8a, and 9- 16c.
Hired (or will hire) employees, including household employees	Does not already have an EIN	Complete lines 1, 2, 4a- 6, 7a- b (if applicable), 8a, 8b (if applicable), and 9- 16c.
Opened a bank account	Needs an EIN for banking purposes only	Complete lines 1- 5b, 7a- b (if applicable), 8a, 9, and 16a- c.
Changed type of organization	Either the legal character of the organization or its ownership changed (e.g., you incorporate a sole proprietorship or form a partnership)[2]	Complete lines 1- 16c (as applicable).
Purchased a going business[3]	Does not already have an EIN	Complete lines 1- 16c (as applicable).
Created a trust	The trust is other than a grantor trust or an IRA trust[4]	Complete lines 1- 16c (as applicable).
Created a pension plan as a plan administrator[5]	Needs an EIN for reporting purposes	Complete lines 1, 2, 4a- 6, 8a, 9, and 16a- c.
Is a foreign person needing an EIN to comply with IRS withholding regulations	Needs an EIN to complete a Form W-8 (other than Form W-8ECI), avoid withholding on portfolio assets, or claim tax treaty benefits[6]	Complete lines 1- 5b, 7a- b (SSN or ITIN optional), 8a- 9, and 16a- c.
Is administering an estate	Needs an EIN to report estate income on Form 1041	Complete lines 1, 3, 4a- b, 8a, 9, and 16a- c.
Is a withholding agent for taxes on non-wage income paid to an alien (i.e., individual, corporation, or partnership, etc.)	Is an agent, broker, fiduciary, manager, tenant, or spouse who is required to file **Form 1042,** Annual Withholding Tax Return for U.S. Source Income of Foreign Persons	Complete lines 1, 2, 3 (if applicable), 4a- 5b, 7a- b (if applicable), 8a, 9, and 16a- c.
Is a state or local agency	Serves as a tax reporting agent for public assistance recipients under Rev. Proc. 80-4, 1980-1 C.B. 581[7]	Complete lines 1, 2, 4a- 5b, 8a, 9, and 16a- c.
Is a single-member LLC	Needs an EIN to file **Form 8832,** Classification Election, for filing employment tax returns, **or** for state reporting purposes[8]	Complete lines 1- 16c (as applicable).
Is an S corporation	Needs an EIN to file **Form 2553,** Election by a Small Business Corporation[9]	Complete lines 1- 16c (as applicable).

[1] For example, a sole proprietorship or self-employed farmer who establishes a qualified retirement plan, or is required to file excise, employment, alcohol, tobacco, or firearms returns, must have an EIN. **A partnership, corporation, REMIC (real estate mortgage investment conduit), nonprofit organization (church, club, etc.), or farmers' cooperative must use an EIN for any tax-related purpose even if the entity does not have employees.**

[2] However, **do not** apply for a new EIN if the existing entity only **(a)** changed its business name, **(b)** elected on Form 8832 to change the way it is taxed (or is covered by the default rules), or **(c)** terminated its partnership status because at least 50% of the total interests in partnership capital and profits were sold or exchanged within a 12-month period. (The EIN of the terminated partnership should continue to be used. See Regulations section 301.6109-1(d)(2)(iii).)

[3] Do not use the EIN of the prior business unless you became the "owner" of a corporation by acquiring its stock.

[4] However, IRA trusts that are required to file **Form 990-T,** Exempt Organization Business Income Tax Return, must have an EIN.

[5] A plan administrator is the person or group of persons specified as the administrator by the instrument under which the plan is operated.

[6] Entities applying to be a Qualified Intermediary (QI) need a QI-EIN even if they already have an EIN. **See Rev. Proc. 2000-12.**

[7] See also *Household employer* on page 4. (**Note:** State or local agencies may need an EIN for other reasons, e.g., hired employees.)

[8] Most LLCs **do not** need to file Form 8832. See **Limited liability company (LLC)** on page 4 for details on completing Form SS-4 for an LLC.

[9] An existing corporation that is electing or revoking S corporation status should use its previously-assigned EIN.

⊛

Instructions for Form SS-4

(Rev. December 2001)

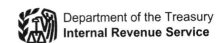
Department of the Treasury
Internal Revenue Service

Application for Employer Identification Number

Section references are to the Internal Revenue Code unless otherwise noted.

General Instructions

Use these instructions to complete **Form SS-4,** Application for Employer Identification Number. Also see **Do I Need an EIN?** on page 2 of Form SS-4.

Purpose of Form

Use Form SS-4 to apply for an employer identification number (EIN). An EIN is a nine-digit number (for example, 12-3456789) assigned to sole proprietors, corporations, partnerships, estates, trusts, and other entities for tax filing and reporting purposes. The information you provide on this form will establish your business tax account.

 *An EIN is for use in connection with your business activities only. Do **not** use your EIN in place of your social security number (SSN).*

File only one Form SS-4. Generally, a sole proprietor should file only one Form SS-4 and needs only one EIN, regardless of the number of businesses operated as a sole proprietorship or trade names under which a business operates. However, if the proprietorship incorporates or enters into a partnership, a new EIN is required. Also, each corporation in an affiliated group must have its own EIN.

EIN applied for, but not received. If you do not have an EIN by the time a **return** is due, write "Applied For" and the date you applied in the space shown for the number. **Do not** show your social security number (SSN) as an EIN on returns.

If you do not have an EIN by the time a **tax deposit** is due, send your payment to the Internal Revenue Service Center for your filing area as shown in the instructions for the form that you are are filing. Make your check or money order payable to the **"United States Treasury"** and show your name (as shown on Form SS-4), address, type of tax, period covered, and date you applied for an EIN.

Related Forms and Publications

The following **forms** and **instructions** may be useful to filers of Form SS-4:
• **Form 990-T,** Exempt Organization Business Income Tax Return
• **Instructions for Form 990-T**
• **Schedule C (Form 1040),** Profit or Loss From Business
• **Schedule F (Form 1040),** Profit or Loss From Farming
• **Instructions for Form 1041 and Schedules A, B, D, G, I, J, and K-1,** U.S. Income Tax Return for Estates and Trusts

• **Form 1042,** Annual Withholding Tax Return for U.S. Source Income of Foreign Persons
• **Instructions for Form 1065,** U.S. Return of Partnership Income
• **Instructions for Form 1066,** U.S. Real Estate Mortgage Investment Conduit (REMIC) Income Tax Return
• **Instructions for Forms 1120 and 1120-A**
• **Form 2553,** Election by a Small Business Corporation
• **Form 2848,** Power of Attorney and Declaration of Representative
• **Form 8821,** Tax Information Authorization
• **Form 8832,** Entity Classification Election
   For more **information** about filing Form SS-4 and related issues, see:
• **Circular A,** Agricultural Employer's Tax Guide (Pub. 51)
• **Circular E,** Employer's Tax Guide (Pub. 15)
• **Pub. 538,** Accounting Periods and Methods
• **Pub. 542,** Corporations
• **Pub. 557,** Exempt Status for Your Organization
• **Pub. 583,** Starting a Business and Keeping Records
• **Pub. 966,** EFTPS: Now a Full Range of Electronic Choices to Pay All Your Federal Taxes
• **Pub. 1635,** Understanding Your EIN
• **Package 1023,** Application for Recognition of Exemption
• **Package 1024,** Application for Recognition of Exemption Under Section 501(a)

How To Get Forms and Publications

Phone. You can order forms, instructions, and publications by phone 24 hours a day, 7 days a week. Just call 1-800-TAX-FORM (1-800-829-3676). You should receive your order or notification of its status within 10 workdays.

Personal computer. With your personal computer and modem, you can get the forms and information you need using the IRS Web Site at **www.irs.gov** or File Transfer Protocol at **ftp.irs.gov.**

CD-ROM. For small businesses, return preparers, or others who may frequently need tax forms or publications, a CD-ROM containing over 2,000 tax products (including many prior year forms) can be purchased from the National Technical Information Service (NTIS).

   To order **Pub. 1796,** Federal Tax Products on CD-ROM, call **1-877-CDFORMS** (1-877-233-6767) toll free or connect to **www.irs.gov/cdorders.**

Tax Help for Your Business

IRS-sponsored Small Business Workshops provide information about your Federal and state tax obligations. For information about workshops in your area, call 1-800-829-1040 and ask for your Taxpayer Education Coordinator.

How To Apply

You can apply for an EIN by telephone, fax, or mail depending on how soon you need to use the EIN.

Application by Tele-TIN. Under the Tele-TIN program, you can receive your EIN by telephone and use it immediately to file a return or make a payment. To receive an EIN by telephone, IRS suggests that you complete Form SS-4 so that you will have all relevant information available. Then call the Tele-TIN number at 1-866-816-2065. (International applicants must call 215-516-6999.) Tele-TIN hours of operation are 7:30 a.m. to 5:30 p.m. The person making the call must be authorized to sign the form or be an authorized designee. See **Signature** and **Third Party Designee** on page 6. Also see the **TIP** below.

An IRS representative will use the information from the Form SS-4 to establish your account and assign you an EIN. Write the number you are given on the upper right corner of the form and sign and date it. Keep this copy for your records.

If requested by an IRS representative, mail or fax (facsimile) the signed Form SS-4 (including any Third Party Designee authorization) **within 24 hours** to the Tele-TIN Unit at the service center address provided by the IRS representative.

 *Taxpayer representatives can use Tele-TIN to apply for an EIN on behalf of their client and request that the EIN be faxed to their **client** on the same day. (**Note:** By utilizing this procedure, you are authorizing the IRS to fax the EIN without a cover sheet.)*

Application by Fax-TIN. Under the Fax-TIN program, you can receive your EIN by fax within 4 business days. Complete and fax Form SS-4 to the IRS using the Fax-TIN number listed below for your state. A long-distance charge to callers outside of the local calling area will apply. Fax-TIN numbers can only be used to apply for an EIN. **The numbers may change without notice.** Fax-TIN is available 24 hours a day, 7 days a week.

Be sure to provide your fax number so that IRS can fax the EIN back to you. (**Note:** By utilizing this procedure, you are authorizing the IRS to fax the EIN without a cover sheet.)

Do not call Tele-TIN for the same entity because duplicate EINs may be issued. See **Third Party Designee** on page 6.

Application by mail. Complete Form SS-4 at least 4 to 5 weeks before you will need an EIN. Sign and date the application and mail it to the service center address for your state. You will receive your EIN in the mail in approximately 4 weeks. See also **Third Party Designee** on page 6.

Call 1-800-829-1040 to verify a number or to ask about the status of an application by mail.

If your principal business, office or agency, or legal residence in the case of an individual, is located in:	Call the Tele-TIN or Fax-TIN number shown or file with the "Internal Revenue Service Center" at:
Connecticut, Delaware, District of Columbia, Florida, Georgia, Maine, Maryland, Massachusetts, New Hampshire, New Jersey, New York, North Carolina, Ohio, Pennsylvania, Rhode Island, South Carolina, Vermont, Virginia, West Virginia	Attn: EIN Operation Holtsville, NY 00501 Tele-TIN 866-816-2065 Fax-TIN 631-447-8960
Illinois, Indiana, Kentucky, Michigan	Attn: EIN Operation Cincinnati, OH 45999 Tele-TIN 866-816-2065 Fax-TIN 859-669-5760
Alabama, Alaska, Arizona, Arkansas, California, Colorado, Hawaii, Idaho, Iowa, Kansas, Louisiana, Minnesota, Mississippi, Missouri, Montana, Nebraska, Nevada, New Mexico, North Dakota, Oklahoma, Oregon, Puerto Rico, South Dakota, Tennessee, Texas, Utah, Washington, Wisconsin, Wyoming	Attn: EIN Operation Philadelphia, PA 19255 Tele-TIN 866-816-2065 Fax-TIN 215-516-3990
If you have no legal residence, principal place of business, or principal office or agency in any state:	Attn: EIN Operation Philadelphia, PA 19255 Tele-TIN 215-516-6999 Fax-TIN 215-516-3990

Specific Instructions

Print or type all entries on Form SS-4. Follow the instructions for each line to expedite processing and to avoid unnecessary IRS requests for additional information. Enter "N/A" (nonapplicable) on the lines that do not apply.

Line 1—Legal name of entity (or individual) for whom the EIN is being requested. Enter the legal name of the entity (or individual) applying for the EIN exactly as it appears on the social security card, charter, or other applicable legal document.

Individuals. Enter your first name, middle initial, and last name. If you are a sole proprietor, enter your individual name, not your business name. Enter your business name on line 2. Do not use abbreviations or nicknames on line 1.

Trusts. Enter the name of the trust.

Estate of a decedent. Enter the name of the estate.

Partnerships. Enter the legal name of the partnership as it appears in the partnership agreement.

Corporations. Enter the corporate name as it appears in the corporation charter or other legal document creating it.

Plan administrators. Enter the name of the plan administrator. A plan administrator who already has an EIN should use that number.

Line 2—Trade name of business. Enter the trade name of the business if different from the legal name. The trade name is the "doing business as " (DBA) name.

 Use the full legal name shown on line 1 on all tax returns filed for the entity. (However, if you enter a trade name on line 2 and choose to use the trade name instead of the legal name, enter the trade name on all returns you file.) To prevent processing delays and errors, always use the legal name only (or the trade name only) on all tax returns.

Line 3—Executor, trustee, "care of" name. Trusts enter the name of the trustee. Estates enter the name of the executor, administrator, or other fiduciary. If the entity applying has a designated person to receive tax information, enter that person's name as the "care of" person. Enter the individual's first name, middle initial, and last name.

Lines 4a-b—Mailing address. Enter the mailing address for the entity's correspondence. If line 3 is completed, enter the address for the executor, trustee or "care of" person. Generally, this address will be used on all tax returns.

 File Form 8822, Change of Address, to report any subsequent changes to the entity's mailing address.

Lines 5a-b—Street address. Provide the entity's physical address **only** if different from its mailing address shown in lines 4a-b. **Do not** enter a P.O. box number here.

Line 6—County and state where principal business is located. Enter the entity's primary **physical** location.

Lines 7a-b—Name of principal officer, general partner, grantor, owner, or trustor. Enter the first name, middle initial, last name, and SSN of **(a)** the principal officer if the business is a corporation, **(b)** a general partner if a partnership, **(c)** the owner of an entity that is disregarded as separate from its owner (disregarded entities owned by a corporation enter the corporation's name and EIN), or **(d)** a grantor, owner, or trustor if a trust.

If the person in question is an **alien individual** with a previously assigned individual taxpayer identification number (ITIN), enter the ITIN in the space provided and submit a copy of an official identifying document. If necessary, complete **Form W-7,** Application for IRS Individual Taxpayer Identification Number, to obtain an ITIN.

You are **required** to enter an SSN, ITIN, or EIN unless the only reason you are applying for an EIN is to make an entity classification election (see Regulations section 301.7701-1 through 301.7701-3) and you are a nonresident alien with no effectively connected income from sources within the United States.

Line 8a—Type of entity. Check the box that best describes the type of entity applying for the EIN. If you are an alien individual with an ITIN previously assigned to you, enter the ITIN in place of a requested SSN.

 This is not an election for a tax classification of an entity. See "Limited liability company (LLC)" on page 4.

Other. If not specifically mentioned, check the "Other" box, enter the type of entity and the type of return, if any, that will be filed (for example, "Common Trust Fund, Form 1065" or "Created a Pension Plan"). Do not enter "N/A." If you are an alien individual applying for an EIN, see the **Lines 7a-b** instructions above.

● **Household employer.** If you are an individual, check the "Other" box and enter "Household Employer" and your SSN. If you are a state or local agency serving as a tax reporting agent for public assistance recipients who become household employers, check the "Other" box and enter "Household Employer Agent." If you are a trust that qualifies as a household employer, you do not need a separate EIN for reporting tax information relating to household employees; use the EIN of the trust.

● **QSub.** For a qualified subchapter S subsidiary (QSub) check the "Other" box and specify "QSub."

● **Withholding agent.** If you are a withholding agent required to file Form 1042, check the "Other" box and enter "Withholding Agent."

Sole proprietor. Check this box if you file Schedule C, C-EZ, or F (Form 1040) and have a qualified plan, or are required to file excise, employment, or alcohol, tobacco, or firearms returns, or are a payer of gambling winnings. Enter your SSN (or ITIN) in the space provided. If you are a nonresident alien with no effectively connected income from sources within the United States, you do not need to enter an SSN or ITIN.

Corporation. This box is for any corporation **other than a personal service corporation.** If you check this box, enter the income tax form number to be filed by the entity in the space provided.

 If you entered "1120S" after the "Corporation" checkbox, the corporation must file Form 2553 no later than the 15th day of the 3rd month of the tax year the election is to take effect. Until Form 2553 has been received and approved, you will be considered a Form 1120 filer. See the Instructions for Form 2553.

Personal service corp. Check this box if the entity is a personal service corporation. An entity is a personal service corporation for a tax year only if:
● The principal activity of the entity during the testing period (prior tax year) for the tax year is the performance of personal services substantially by employee-owners, and
● The employee-owners own at least 10% of the fair market value of the outstanding stock in the entity on the last day of the testing period.

Personal services include performance of services in such fields as health, law, accounting, or consulting. For more information about personal service corporations, see the Instructions for Forms 1120 and 1120-A and Pub. 542.

Other nonprofit organization. Check this box if the nonprofit organization is other than a church or church-controlled organization and specify the type of nonprofit organization (for example, an educational organization).

 *If the organization also seeks tax-exempt status, you **must** file either Package 1023 or Package 1024. See Pub. 557 for more information.*

If the organization is covered by a group exemption letter, enter the four-digit **group exemption number (GEN).** (Do not confuse the GEN with the nine-digit EIN.) If you do not know the GEN, contact the parent organization. Get Pub. 557 for more information about group exemption numbers.

Plan administrator. If the plan administrator is an individual, enter the plan administrator's SSN in the space provided.

REMIC. Check this box if the entity has elected to be treated as a real estate mortgage investment conduit (REMIC). See the Instructions for Form 1066 for more information.

Limited liability company (LLC). An LLC is an entity organized under the laws of a state or foreign country as a limited liability company. For Federal tax purposes, an LLC may be treated as a partnership or corporation or be disregarded as an entity separate from its owner.

By **default,** a domestic LLC with only one member is **disregarded** as an entity separate from its owner and must include all of its income and expenses on the owner's tax return (e.g., **Schedule C (Form 1040)**). Also by default, a domestic LLC with two or more members is treated as a partnership. A domestic LLC may file Form 8832 to avoid either default classification and elect to be classified as an association taxable as a corporation. For more information on entity classifications (including the rules for foreign entities), see the instructions for Form 8832.

 Do not** file Form 8832 if the LLC accepts the default classifications above. **However, if the LLC will be electing S Corporation status, it must timely file both Form 8832 and Form 2553.

Complete Form SS-4 for LLCs as follows:
• A single-member, domestic LLC that accepts the default classification (above) does not need an EIN and generally should not file Form SS-4. Generally, the LLC should use the name and EIN of its **owner** for all Federal tax purposes. However, the reporting and payment of employment taxes for employees of the LLC may be made using the name and EIN of **either** the owner or the LLC as explained in Notice 99-6, 1999-1 C.B. 321. You can find Notice 99-6 on page 12 of Internal Revenue Bulletin 1999-3 at **www.irs.gov. (Note:** If the LLC-applicant indicates in box 13 that it has employees or expects to have employees, the owner (whether an individual or other entity) of a single-member domestic LLC will also be assigned its own EIN (if it does not

already have one) even if the LLC will be filing the employment tax returns.)
• A single-member, domestic LLC that accepts the default classification (above) and wants an EIN for filing employment tax returns (see above) or non-Federal purposes, such as a state requirement, must check the "Other" box and write "Disregarded Entity" or, when applicable, "Disregarded Entity—Sole Proprietorship" in the space provided.
• A multi-member, domestic LLC that accepts the default classification (above) must check the "Partnership" box.
• A domestic LLC that will be filing Form 8832 to elect corporate status must check the "Corporation" box and write in "Single-Member" or "Multi-Member" immediately below the "form number" entry line.

Line 9—Reason for applying. Check only **one** box. Do not enter "N/A."

Started new business. Check this box if you are starting a new business that requires an EIN. If you check this box, enter the type of business being started. **Do not** apply if you already have an EIN and are only adding another place of business.

Hired employees. Check this box if the existing business is requesting an EIN because it has hired or is hiring employees and is therefore required to file employment tax returns. **Do not** apply if you already have an EIN and are only hiring employees. For information on employment taxes (e.g., for family members), see Circular E.

 You may be required to make electronic deposits of all depository taxes (such as employment tax, excise tax, and corporate income tax) using the Electronic Federal Tax Payment System (EFTPS). See section 11, Depositing Taxes, of Circular E and Pub. 966.

Created a pension plan. Check this box if you have created a pension plan and need an EIN for reporting purposes. Also, enter the type of plan in the space provided.

 Check this box if you are applying for a trust EIN when a new pension plan is established. In addition, check the "Other" box in line 8a and write "Created a Pension Plan" in the space provided.

Banking purpose. Check this box if you are requesting an EIN for banking purposes only, and enter the banking purpose (for example, a bowling league for depositing dues or an investment club for dividend and interest reporting).

Changed type of organization. Check this box if the business is changing its type of organization. For example, the business was a sole proprietorship and has been incorporated or has become a partnership. If you check this box, specify in the space provided (including available space immediately below) the type of change made. For example, "From Sole Proprietorship to Partnership."

Purchased going business. Check this box if you purchased an existing business. **Do not** use the former owner's EIN unless you became the "owner" of a corporation by acquiring its stock.

Created a trust. Check this box if you created a trust, and enter the type of trust created. For example, indicate if the trust is a nonexempt charitable trust or a split-interest trust.

Exception. Do **not** file this form for certain grantor-type trusts. The trustee does not need an EIN for the trust if the trustee furnishes the name and TIN of the grantor/owner and the address of the trust to all payors. See the Instructions for Form 1041 for more information.

 Do not check this box if you are applying for a trust EIN when a new pension plan is established. Check "Created a pension plan."

Other. Check this box if you are requesting an EIN for any other reason; and enter the reason. For example, a newly-formed state government entity should enter "Newly-Formed State Government Entity" in the space provided.

Line 10—Date business started or acquired. If you are starting a new business, enter the starting date of the business. If the business you acquired is already operating, enter the date you acquired the business. Trusts should enter the date the trust was legally created. Estates should enter the date of death of the decedent whose name appears on line 1 or the date when the estate was legally funded.

Line 11—Closing month of accounting year. Enter the last month of your accounting year or tax year. An accounting or tax year is usually 12 consecutive months, either a calendar year or a fiscal year (including a period of 52 or 53 weeks). A calendar year is 12 consecutive months ending on December 31. A fiscal year is either 12 consecutive months ending on the last day of any month other than December or a 52-53 week year. For more information on accounting periods, see Pub. 538.

Individuals. Your tax year generally will be a calendar year.

Partnerships. Partnerships must adopt one of the following tax years:
- The tax year of the majority of its partners,
- The tax year common to all of its principal partners,
- The tax year that results in the least aggregate deferral of income, or
- In certain cases, some other tax year.
 See the Instructions for Form 1065 for more information.

REMICs. REMICs must have a calendar year as their tax year.

Personal service corporations. A personal service corporation generally must adopt a calendar year unless:
- It can establish a business purpose for having a different tax year, or
- It elects under section 444 to have a tax year other than a calendar year.

Trusts. Generally, a trust must adopt a calendar year except for the following:
- Tax-exempt trusts,
- Charitable trusts, and
- Grantor-owned trusts.

Line 12—First date wages or annuities were paid or will be paid. If the business has or will have employees, enter the date on which the business began or will begin to pay wages. If the business does not plan to have employees, enter "N/A."

Withholding agent. Enter the date you began or will begin to pay income (including annuities) to a nonresident alien. This also applies to individuals who are required to file Form 1042 to report alimony paid to a nonresident alien.

Line 13—Highest number of employees expected in the next 12 months. Complete each box by entering the number (including zero ("-0-")) of "Agricultural," "Household," or "Other" employees expected by the applicant in the next 12 months. For a definition of agricultural labor (farmwork), see Circular A.

Lines 14 and 15. Check the **one** box in line 14 that best describes the principal activity of the applicant's business. Check the "Other" box (and specify the applicant's principal activity) if none of the listed boxes applies.

Use line 15 to describe the applicant's principal line of business in more detail. For example, if you checked the "Construction" box in line 14, enter additional detail such as "General contractor for residential buildings" in line 15.

 Do not complete lines 14 and 15 if you entered zero "(-0-)" in line 13.

Construction. Check this box if the applicant is engaged in erecting buildings or other structures, (e.g., streets, highways, bridges, tunnels). The term "Construction" also includes special trade contractors, (e.g., plumbing, HVAC, electrical, carpentry, concrete, excavation, etc. contractors).

Real estate. Check this box if the applicant is engaged in renting or leasing real estate to others; managing, selling, buying or renting real estate for others; or providing related real estate services (e.g., appraisal services).

Rental and leasing. Check this box if the applicant is engaged in providing tangible goods such as autos, computers, consumer goods, or industrial machinery and equipment to customers in return for a periodic rental or lease payment.

Manufacturing. Check this box if the applicant is engaged in the mechanical, physical, or chemical transformation of materials, substances, or components into new products. The assembling of component parts of manufactured products is also considered to be manufacturing.

Transportation & warehousing. Check this box if the applicant provides transportation of passengers or cargo; warehousing or storage of goods; scenic or sight-seeing transportation; or support activities related to these modes of transportation.

Finance & insurance. Check this box if the applicant is engaged in transactions involving the creation, liquidation, or change of ownership of financial assets and/or facilitating such financial transactions;

underwriting annuities/insurance policies; facilitating such underwriting by selling insurance policies; or by providing other insurance or employee-benefit related services.

Health care and social assistance. Check this box if the applicant is engaged in providing physical, medical, or psychiatric care using licensed health care professionals or providing social assistance activities such as youth centers, adoption agencies, individual/family services, temporary shelters, etc.

Accommodation & food services. Check this box if the applicant is engaged in providing customers with lodging, meal preparation, snacks, or beverages for immediate consumption.

Wholesale–agent/broker. Check this box if the applicant is engaged in arranging for the purchase or sale of goods owned by others or purchasing goods on a commission basis for goods traded in the wholesale market, usually between businesses.

Wholesale–other. Check this box if the applicant is engaged in selling goods in the wholesale market generally to other businesses for resale on their own account.

Retail. Check this box if the applicant is engaged in selling merchandise to the general public from a fixed store; by direct, mail-order, or electronic sales; or by using vending machines.

Other. Check this box if the applicant is engaged in an activity not described above. Describe the applicant's principal business activity in the space provided.

Lines 16a-c. Check the applicable box in line 16a to indicate whether or not the entity (or individual) applying for an EIN was issued one previously. Complete lines 16b and 16c **only** if the "Yes" box in line 16a is checked. If the applicant previously applied for **more than one** EIN, write "See Attached" in the empty space in line 16a and attach a separate sheet providing the line 16b and 16c information for each EIN previously requested.

Third Party Designee. Complete this section **only** if you want to authorize the named individual to receive the entity's EIN and answer questions about the completion of Form SS-4. The designee's authority terminates at the time the EIN is assigned and released to the designee. **You must complete the signature area for the authorization to be valid.**

Signature. When required, the application must be signed by **(a)** the individual, if the applicant is an individual, **(b)** the president, vice president, or other principal officer, if the applicant is a corporation, **(c)** a responsible and duly authorized member or officer having knowledge of its affairs, if the applicant is a partnership, government entity, or other unincorporated organization, or **(d)** the fiduciary, if the applicant is a trust or an estate. Foreign applicants may have any duly-authorized person, (e.g., division manager), sign Form SS-4.

Privacy Act and Paperwork Reduction Act Notice. We ask for the information on this form to carry out the Internal Revenue laws of the United States. We need it to comply with section 6109 and the regulations thereunder which generally require the inclusion of an employer identification number (EIN) on certain returns, statements, or other documents filed with the Internal Revenue Service. If your entity is required to obtain an EIN, you are required to provide all of the information requested on this form. Information on this form may be used to determine which Federal tax returns you are required to file and to provide you with related forms and publications.

We disclose this form to the Social Security Administration for their use in determining compliance with applicable laws. We may give this information to the Department of Justice for use in civil and criminal litigation, and to the cities, states, and the District of Columbia for use in administering their tax laws. We may also disclose this information to Federal, state, or local agencies that investigate or respond to acts or threats of terrorism or participate in intelligence or counterintelligence activities concerning terrorism.

We will be unable to issue an EIN to you unless you provide all of the requested information which applies to your entity. Providing false information could subject you to penalties.

You are not required to provide the information requested on a form that is subject to the Paperwork Reduction Act unless the form displays a valid OMB control number. Books or records relating to a form or its instructions must be retained as long as their contents may become material in the administration of any Internal Revenue law. Generally, tax returns and return information are confidential, as required by section 6103.

The time needed to complete and file this form will vary depending on individual circumstances. The estimated average time is:

Recordkeeping	6 min.
Learning about the law or the form	22 min.
Preparing the form	46 min.
Copying, assembling, and sending the form to the IRS	20 min.

If you have comments concerning the accuracy of these time estimates or suggestions for making this form simpler, we would be happy to hear from you. You can write to the Tax Forms Committee, Western Area Distribution Center, Rancho Cordova, CA 95743-0001. **Do not** send the form to this address. Instead, see **How To Apply** on page 2.

WAIVER OF NOTICE

OF THE ORGANIZATIONAL MEETING

OF

_____

We, the undersigned incorporators named in the certificate of incorporation of the above-named corporation hereby agree and consent that the organization meeting of the corporation be held on the date and time and place stated below and hereby waive all notice of such meeting and of any adjournment thereof.

Place of meeting: _____

Date of Meeting: _____

Time of meeting: _____

Dated: _____

_____
Incorporator

_____
Incorporator

_____
Incorporator

MINUTES OF THE ORGANIZATIONAL MEETING OF

INCORPORATORS AND DIRECTORS OF

_____

The organization meeting of the above corporation was held on _____,
_____ at _____
at _____ o'clock ___m.

The following persons were present:

_____   _____
_____   _____
_____   _____

The Waiver of notice of this meeting was signed by all directors and incorporators named in the Articles of Incorporation and filed in the minute book.

The meeting was called to order by _____ an Incorporator named in the Articles of Incorporation. _____ was nominated and elected Chairperson and acted as such until relieved by the president. _____ was nominated and elected temporary secretary, and acted as such until relieved by the permanent secretary.

A copy of the Articles of Incorporation which was filed with the Secretary of State of the State of _____ on _____, _____ was examined by the Directors and Incorporators and filed in the minute book.

The election of officers for the coming year was then held and the following were duly nominated and elected by the Board of Directors to be the officers of the corporation, to serve until such time as their successors are elected and qualified:

President: _____
Vice President: _____
Secretary: _____
Treasurer: _____

The proposed Bylaws for the corporation were then presented to the meeting and discussed. Upon motion duly made, seconded and carried, the Bylaws were adopted and added to the minute book.

A corporate seal for the corporation was then presented to the meeting and upon motion duly made, seconded and carried, it was adopted as the seal of the corporation. An impression thereof was then made in the margin of these minutes

The necessity of opening a bank account was then discussed and upon motion duly made, seconded and carried, the following resolution was adopted:

RESOLVED that the corporation open bank accounts with _____ _____ and that the officers of the corporation are authorized to take such action as is necessary to open such accounts; that the bank's printed form of resolution is hereby adopted and incorporated into these minutes by reference and shall be placed in the minute book; that any _____ of the following persons shall have signature authority over the account:

_____   _____
_____   _____
_____   _____

Proposed stock certificates and stock transfer ledger were then presented to the meeting and examined. Upon motion duly made, seconded and carried the stock certificates and ledger were adopted as the certificates and transfer book to be used by the corporation. A sample stock certificate marked "VOID" and the stock transfer ledger were then added to the minute book. Upon motion duly made, seconded and carried, it was then resolved that the stock certificates, when issued, would be signed by the President and the Secretary of the corporation.

The tax status of the corporation was then discussed and it was moved, seconded and carried that the stock of the corporation be issued under §1244 of the Internal Revenue Code and that the officers of the corporation take the necessary action to:

1.   Obtain an employer tax number by filing form SS-4,

2.   ❑   Become an S-Corporation for tax purposes,
        ❑   Remain a C-Corporation for tax purposes,

The expenses of organizing the corporation were then discussed and it was moved, seconded and carried that the corporation pay in full from the corporate funds the expenses and reimburse any advances made by the incorporators upon proof of payment.

The Directors named in the Articles of Incorporation then tendered their resignations, effective upon the adjournment of this meeting. Upon motion duly made, seconded and carried, the following named persons were elected as Directors of the corporation, each to hold office until the first annual meeting of shareholders, and until a successor of each shall have been elected and qualified.

_____

_____

_____

There were presented to the corporation, the following offer(s) to purchase shares of capital stock:

FROM	NO. OF SHARES	CONSIDERATION
_____	_____	_____
_____	_____	_____
_____	_____	_____
_____	_____	_____

The offers were discussed and after motion duly made, seconded and carried were approved. It was further resolved that the Board of Directors has determined that the consideration was valued at least equal to the value of the shares to be issued and that upon tender of the consideration, fully paid nonassessable shares of the corporation be issued.

There being no further business before the meeting, on motion duly made, seconded and carried, the meeting adjourned.

DATED: _____

_____

President

_____

Secretary

BYLAWS OF

_____

A FLORIDA CORPORATION

ARTICLE I - OFFICES

The principal office of the Corporation shall be located in the City of _____ and the State of _____. The Corporation may also maintain offices at such other places as the Board of Directors may, from time to time, determine.

ARTICLE II - SHAREHOLDERS

Section 1 - Annual Meetings: The annual meeting of the shareholders of the Corporation shall be held each year on at _____m. at the principal office of the Corporation or at such other places, within or without the State of Florida, as the Board may authorize, for the purpose of electing directors, and transacting such other business as may properly come before the meeting.

Section 2 - Special Meetings: Special meetings of the shareholders may be called at any time by the Board, the President, or by the holders of twenty-five percent (25%) of the shares then outstanding and entitled to vote.

Section 3 - Place of Meetings: All meetings of shareholders shall be held at the principal office of the Corporation, or at such other places as the board shall designate in the notice of such meetings.

Section 4 - Notice of Meetings: Written or printed notice stating the place, day, and hour of the meeting and, in the case of a special meeting, the purpose of the meeting, shall be delivered personally or by mail not less than ten days, nor more than sixty days, before the date of the meeting. Notice shall be given to each Member of record entitled to vote at the meeting. If mailed, such notice shall be deemed to have been delivered when deposited in the United States Mail with postage paid and addressed to the Member at his address as it appears on the records of the Corporation.

Section 5 - Waiver of Notice: A written waiver of notice signed by a Member, whether before or after a meeting, shall be equivalent to the giving of such notice. Attendance of a Member at a meeting shall constitute a waiver of notice of such meeting, except when the Member attends for the express purpose of objecting, at the beginning of the meeting, to the transaction of any business because the meeting is not lawfully called or convened.

Section 6 - Quorum: Except as otherwise provided by Statute, or the Articles of Incorporation, at all meetings of share-holders of the Corporation, the presence at the commencement of such meetings in person or by proxy of shareholders of record holding a majority of the total number of shares of the Corporation then issued and outstanding and entitled to vote, but in no event less than one-third of the shares entitled to vote at the meeting, shall constitute a quorum for the transaction of any business. If any shareholder leaves after the commencement of a meeting, this shall have no effect on the existence of a quorum, after a quorum has been established at such meeting.

Despite the absence of a quorum at any annual or special meeting of shareholders, the shareholders, by a major-ity of the votes cast by the holders of shares entitled to vote thereon, may adjourn the meeting. At any such adjourned meeting at which a quorum is present, any business may be transacted at the meeting as originally called as if a quorum had been present.

Section 7 - Voting: Except as otherwise provided by Statute or by the Articles of Incorporation, any corporate action, other than the election of directors, to be taken by vote of the shareholders, shall be authorized by a majority of votes cast at a meeting of shareholders by the holders of shares entitled to vote thereon.

Except as otherwise provided by Statute or by the Articles of Incorporation, at each meeting of shareholders, each holder of record of stock of the Corporation entitled to vote thereat, shall be entitled to one vote for each share of stock registered in his name on the stock transfer books of the corporation.

Each shareholder entitled to vote may do so by proxy; provided, however, that the instrument authorizing such proxy to act shall have been executed in writing by the shareholder himself. No proxy shall be valid after the expiration of eleven months from the date of its execution, unless the person executing it shall have specified therein, the length of time it is to continue in force. Such instrument shall be exhibited to the Secretary at the meeting and shall be filed with the records of the corporation.

Any resolution in writing, signed by all of the shareholders entitled to vote thereon, shall be and constitute action by such shareholders to the effect therein expressed, with the same force and effect as if the same had been duly passed by unanimous vote at a duly called meeting of shareholders and such resolution so signed shall be inserted in the Minute Book of the Corporation under its proper date.

ARTICLE III - BOARD OF DIRECTORS

Section 1 - Number, Election and Term of Office: The number of the directors of the Corporation shall be (_____) This number may be increased or decreased by the amendment of these bylaws by the Board but shall in no case be less than _____ director(s). The members of the Board, who need not be shareholders, shall be elected by a majority of the votes cast at a meeting of shareholders entitled to vote in the election. Each director shall hold office until the annual meeting of the shareholders next succeeding his election, and until his successor is elected and qualified, or until his prior death, resignation or removal.

Section 2 - Vacancies: Any vacancy in the Board shall be filled for the unexpired portion of the term by a majority vote of the remaining directors, though less than a quorum, at any regular meeting or special meeting of the Board called for that purpose. Any such director so elected may be replaced by the shareholders at a regular or special meeting of shareholders.

Section 3 - Duties and Powers: The Board shall be responsible for the control and management of the affairs, property and interests of the Corporation, and may exercise all powers of the Corporation, except as limited by statute.

Section 4 - Annual Meetings: An annual meeting of the Board shall be held immediately following the annual meeting of the shareholders, at the place of such annual meeting of shareholders. The Board from time to time, may provide by resolution for the holding of other meetings of the Board, and may fix the time and place thereof.

Section 5 - Special Meetings: Special meetings of the Board shall be held whenever called by the President or by one of the directors, at such time and place as may be specified in the respective notice or waivers of notice thereof.

Section 6 - Notice and Waiver: Notice of any special meeting shall be given at least five days prior thereto by written notice delivered personally, by mail or by telegram to each Director at his address. If mailed, such notice shall be deemed to be delivered when deposited in the United States Mail with postage prepaid. If notice is given by telegram, such notice shall be deemed to be delivered when the telegram is delivered to the telegraph company.

Any Director may waive notice of any meeting, either before, at, or after such meeting, by signing a waiver of notice. The attendance of a Director at a meeting shall constitute a waiver of notice of such meeting and a waiver of any and all objections to the place of such meeting, or the manner in which it has been called or convened, except when a Director states at the beginning of the meeting any objection to the transaction of business because the meeting is not lawfully called or convened.

Section 7 - Chairman: The Board may, at its discretion, elect a Chairman. At all meetings of the Board, the Chairman of the Board, if any and if present, shall preside. If there is no Chairman, or he is absent, then the President shall preside, and in his absence, a Chairman chosen by the directors shall preside.

Section 8 - Quorum and Adjournments: At all meetings of the Board, the presence of a majority of the entire Board shall be necessary and sufficient to constitute a quorum for the transaction of business, except as otherwise provided by law, by the Articles of Incorporation, or by these bylaws. A majority of the directors present at the time and place of any regular or special meeting, although less than a quorum, may adjourn the same from time to time without notice, until a quorum shall be present.

Section 9 - Board Action: At all meetings of the Board, each director present shall have one vote, irrespective of the number of shares of stock, if any, which he may hold. Except as otherwise provided by Statute, the action of a majority of the directors present at any meeting at which a quorum is present shall be the act of the Board. Any action authorized, in writing, by all of the Directors entitled to vote thereon and filed with the minutes of the Corporation shall be the act of the Board with the same force and effect as if the same had been passed by unanimous vote at a duly called meeting of the Board. Any action taken by the Board may be taken without a meeting if agreed to in writing by all members before or after the action is taken and if a record of such action is filed in the minute book.

Section 10 - Telephone Meetings: Directors may participate in meetings of the Board through use of a telephone if such can be arranged so that all Board members can hear all other members. The use of a telephone for participation shall constitute presence in person.

Section 11 - Resignation and Removal: Any director may resign at any time by giving written notice to another Board member, the President or the Secretary of the Corporation. Unless otherwise specified in such written notice, such resignation shall take effect upon receipt thereof by the Board or by such officer, and the acceptance of such resignation shall not be necessary to make it effective. Any director may be removed with or without cause at any time by the affirmative vote of shareholders holding of record in the aggregate at least a majority of the outstanding shares of the Corporation at a special meeting of the shareholders called for that purpose, and may be removed for cause by action of the Board.

Section 12 - Compensation: No stated salary shall be paid to directors, as such for their services, but by resolution of the Board a fixed sum and/or expenses of attendance, if any, may be allowed for attendance at each regular or special meeting of the Board. Nothing herein contained shall be construed to preclude any director from serving the Corporation in any other capacity and receiving compensation therefor.

ARTICLE IV - OFFICERS

Section 1 - Number, Qualification, Election and Term: The officers of the Corporation shall consist of a President, a Secretary, a Treasurer, and such other officers, as the Board may from time to time deem advisable. Any officer may be, but is not required to be, a director of the Corporation. The officers of the Corporation shall be elected by the Board at the regular annual meeting of the Board. Each officer shall hold office until the annual meeting of the Board next succeeding his election, and until his successor shall have been elected and qualified, or until his death, resignation or removal.

Section 2 - Resignation and Removal: Any officer may resign at any time by giving written notice of such resignation to the President or the Secretary of the Corporation or to a member of the Board. Unless otherwise specified in such written notice, such resignation shall take effect upon receipt thereof by the Board member or by such officer, and the acceptance of such resignation shall not be necessary to make it effective. Any officer may be removed, either with or without cause, and a successor elected by a majority vote of the Board at any time.

Section 3 - Vacancies: A vacancy in any office may at any time be filled for the unexpired portion of the term by a majority vote of the Board.
Section 4 - Duties of Officers: Officers of the Corporation shall, unless otherwise provided by the Board, each have such powers and duties as generally pertain to their respective offices as well as such powers and duties as may from time to time be specifically decided by the Board. The President shall be the chief executive officer of the Corporation.

Section 5 - Compensation: The officers of the Corporation shall be entitled to such compensation as the Board shall from time to time determine.

Section 6 - Delegation of Duties: In the absence or disability of any Officer of the Corporation or for any other reason deemed sufficient by the Board of Directors, the Board may delegate his powers or duties to any other Officer or to any other Director.

Section 7 - Shares of Other Corporations: Whenever the Corporation is the holder of shares of any other Corporation, any right or power of the Corporation as such shareholder (including the attendance, acting and voting at shareholders' meetings and execution of waivers, consents, proxies or other instruments) may be exercised on behalf of the Corporation by the President, any Vice President, or such other person as the Board may authorize.

ARTICLE V - COMMITTEES

The Board of Directors may, by resolution, designate an Executive Committee and one or more other committees. Such committees shall have such functions and may exercise such power of the Board of Directors as can be lawfully delegated, and to the extent provided in the resolution or resolutions creating such committee or committees. Meetings of committees may be held without notice at such time and at such place as shall from time to time be determined by the committees. The committees of the corporation shall keep regular minutes of their proceedings, and report these minutes to the Board of Directors when required.

ARTICLE VI - BOOKS, RECORDS AND REPORTS

Section 1 - Annual Report: The Corporation shall send an annual report to the Members of the Corporation not later than _____ months after the close of each fiscal year of the Corporation. Such report shall include a balance sheet as of the close of the fiscal year of the Corporation and a revenue and disbursement statement for the year ending on such closing date. Such financial statements shall be prepared from and in accordance with the books of the Corporation, and in conformity with generally accepted accounting principles applied on a consistent basis.

Section 2 - Permanent Records: The corporation shall keep current and correct records of the accounts, minutes of the meetings and proceedings and membership records of the corporation. Such records shall be kept at the registered office or the principal place of business of the corporation. Any such records shall be in written form or in a form capable of being converted into written form.

Section 3 - Inspection of Corporate Records: Any person who is a Voting Member of the Corporation shall have the right at any reasonable time, and on written demand stating the purpose thereof, to examine and make copies from the relevant books and records of accounts, minutes, and records of the Corporation. Upon the written request of any Voting Member, the Corporation shall mail to such Member a copy of the most recent balance sheet and revenue and disbursement statement.

ARTICLE VII- SHARES OF STOCK

Section 1 - Certificates: Each shareholder of the corporation shall be entitled to have a certificate representing all shares which he or she owns. The form of such certificate shall be adopted by a majority vote of the Board of Directors and shall be signed by the President and Secretary of the Corporation and sealed with the seal of the corporation. No certificate representing shares shall be issued until the full amount of consideration therefore has been paid.

Section 2 - Stock Ledger: The corporation shall maintain a ledger of the stock records of the Corporation. Transfers of shares of the Corporation shall be made on the stock ledger of the Corporation only at the direction of the holder of record upon surrender of the outstanding certificate(s). The Corporation shall be entitled to treat the holder of record of any share or shares as the absolute owner thereof for all purposes and, accordingly, shall not be bound to recognize any legal, equitable or other claim to, or interest in, such share or shares on the part of any other person, whether or not it shall have express or other notice thereof, except as otherwise expressly provided by law.

ARTICLE VIII - DIVIDENDS

Upon approval by the Board of Directors the corporation may pay dividends on its shares in the form of cash, property or additional shares at any time that the corporation is solvent and if such dividends would not render the corporation insolvent.

ARTICLE IX - FISCAL YEAR

The fiscal year of the Corporation shall be the period selected by the Board of Directors as the tax year of the Corporation for federal income tax purposes.

ARTICLE X - CORPORATE SEAL

The Board of Directors may adopt, use and modify a corporate seal. Failure to affix the seal to corporate documents shall not affect the validity of such document.

ARTICLE XI - AMENDMENTS

The Articles of Incorporation may be amended by the Shareholders as provided by _____ statutes. These Bylaws may be altered, amended, or replaced by the Board of Directors; provided, however, that any Bylaws or amendments thereto as adopted by the Board of Directors may be altered, amended, or repealed by vote of the Shareholders. Bylaws adopted by the Members may not be amended or repealed by the Board.

ARTICLE XII - INDEMNIFICATION

Any officer, director or employee of the Corporation shall be indemnified to the full extent allowed by the laws of the State of _____.

Certified to be the Bylaws of the corporation adopted by the Board of Directors on _____, _____.

_____
Secretary

BYLAWS OF

_____

A FLORIDA SERVICE CORPORATION

ARTICLE I - OFFICES

The principal office of the Corporation shall be located in the City of _____ and the State of Florida. The Corporation may also maintain offices at such other places as the Board of Directors may, from time to time, determine.

ARTICLE II - PURPOSES

The business purpose of the Corporation shall be to engage in all aspects of the practice of _____ and its fields of specialization. The Corporation shall render professional services only through its legally authorized officers, agents and employees.

ARTICLE III - SHAREHOLDERS

Section 1 - Qualifications: Only persons who are duly licensed and in good standing in the profession by the State of Florida may be shareholders of the Corporation. Neither the Corporation nor the shareholders may transfer any shares to persons who are not duly licensed. All share certificates of the corporation shall contain a notice that the transfer is restricted by the bylaws of the Corporation. If any shareholder shall become disqualified to practice the profession, he or she shall immediately make arrangements to transfer his or her shares to a qualified person or to the Corporation and shall no longer participate in the profits of the Corporation related to the profession.

Section 2 - Annual Meetings: The annual meeting of the shareholders of the Corporation shall be held each year on_____ at _____ m. at the principal office of the Corporation or at such other places, within or without the State of Florida, as the Board may authorize, for the purpose of electing directors, and transacting such other business as may properly come before the meeting.

Section 3 - Special Meetings: Special meetings of the shareholders may be called at any time by the Board, the President, or by the holders of twenty-five percent (25%) of the shares then outstanding and entitled to vote.

Section 4 - Place of Meetings: All meetings of shareholders shall be held at the principal office of the Corporation, or at such other places as the Board shall designate in the notice of such meetings.

Section 5 - Notice of Meetings: Written or printed notice stating the place, day, and hour of the meeting and, in the case of a special meeting, the purpose of the meeting, shall be delivered personally or by mail not less than ten days, nor more than sixty days, before the date of the meeting. Notice shall be given to each Member of record entitled to vote at the meeting. If mailed, such notice shall be deemed to have been delivered when deposited in the United States Mail with postage paid and addressed to the Member at his address as it appears on the records of the Corporation.

Section 6 - Waiver of Notice: A written waiver of notice signed by a Member, whether before or after a meeting, shall be equivalent to the giving of such notice. Attendance of a Member at a meeting shall constitute a waiver of notice of such meeting, except when the Member attends for the express purpose of objecting, at the beginning of the meeting, to the transaction of any business because the meeting is not lawfully called or convened.

Section 7 - Quorum: Except as otherwise provided by Statute, or the by Articles of Incorporation, at all meetings of shareholders of the Corporation, the presence at the commencement of such meetings of shareholders of record holding a majority of the total number of shares of the Corporation then issued and outstanding and entitled to vote, but in no event less than one-third of the shares entitled to vote at the meeting, shall constitute a quorum for the transaction of any business. If any shareholder leaves after the commencement of a meeting, this shall have no effect on the existence of a quorum, after a quorum has been established at such meeting.

Despite the absence of a quorum at any annual or special meeting of shareholders, the shareholders, by a majority of the votes cast by the holders of shares entitled to vote thereon, may adjourn the meeting. At any such adjourned meeting at which a quorum is present, any business may be transacted at the meeting as originally called as if a quorum had been present.

Section 8 - Voting: Except as otherwise provided by Statute or by the Articles of Incorporation, any corporate action, other than the election of directors, to be taken by vote of the shareholders, shall be authorized by a majority of votes cast at a meeting of shareholders by the holders of shares entitled to vote thereon.

Except as otherwise provided by Statute or by the Articles of Incorporation, at each meeting of shareholders, each holder of record of stock of the Corporation entitled to vote thereat, shall be entitled to one vote for each share of stock registered in his name on the stock transfer books of the corporation.

Any resolution in writing, signed by all of the shareholders entitled to vote thereon, shall be and constitute action by such shareholders to the effect therein expressed, with the same force and effect as if the same had been duly passed by unanimous vote at a duly called meeting of shareholders and such resolution so signed shall be inserted in the Minute Book of the Corporation under its proper date.

Section 9 - Proxies: Shareholders may not at any time vote by proxy or enter into any voting trust or other agreement vesting another person with the voting power of his stock.

ARTICLE IV - BOARD OF DIRECTORS

Section 1 Qualifications: Only persons who are duly licensed and in good standing in the profession by the State of Florida may be directors of the Corporation. If any director shall become disqualified from practicing the profession, he or she shall immediately resign his or her directorship and any other employment with the Corporation.

Section 2 - Number, Election and Term of Office: The number of the directors of the Corporation shall be (____) This number may be increased or decreased by the amendment of these bylaws by the Board but shall in no case be less than one director. The members of the Board, who need not be shareholders, shall be elected by a majority of the votes cast at a meeting of shareholders entitled to vote in the election. Each director shall hold office until the annual meeting of the shareholders next succeeding his election, and until his successor is elected and qualified, or until his prior death, resignation or removal.

Section 3 - Vacancies: Any vacancy in the Board shall be filled for the unexpired portion of the term by a majority vote of the remaining directors, though less than a quorum, at any regular meeting or special meeting of the Board called for that purpose. Any such director so elected may be replaced by the shareholders at a regular or special meeting of shareholders.

Section 4 - Duties and Powers: The Board shall be responsible for the control and management of the affairs, property and interests of the Corporation, and may exercise all powers of the Corporation, except as limited by statute.

Section 5 - Annual Meetings: An annual meeting of the Board shall be held immediately following the annual meeting of the shareholders, at the place of such annual meeting of shareholders. The Board, from time to time, may provide by resolution for the holding of other meetings of the Board, and may fix the time and place thereof.

Section 6 - Special Meetings: Special meetings of the Board shall be held whenever called by the President or by one of the directors, at such time and place as may be specified in the respective notice or waivers of notice thereof.

Section 7 - Notice and Waiver: Notice of any special meeting shall be given at least five days prior thereto by written notice delivered personally, by mail or by telegram to each director at his address. If mailed, such notice shall be deemed to be delivered when deposited in the United States Mail with postage prepaid. If notice is given by telegram, such notice shall be deemed to be delivered when the telegram is delivered to the telegraph company.

Any director may waive notice of any meeting, either before, at, or after such meeting, by signing a waiver of notice. The attendance of a director at a meeting shall constitute a waiver of notice of such meeting and a waiver of any and all objections to the place of such meeting, or the manner in which it has been called or convened, except when a director states at the beginning of the meeting any objection to the transaction of business because the meeting is not lawfully called or convened.

Section 8 - Chairman: The Board may, at its discretion, elect a Chairman. At all meetings of the Board, the Chairman of the Board, if any and if present, shall preside. If there is no Chairman, or he is absent, then the President shall preside, and in his absence, a Chairman chosen by the directors shall preside.

Section 9 - Quorum and Adjournments: At all meetings of the Board, the presence of a majority of the entire Board shall be necessary and sufficient to constitute a quorum for the transaction of business, except as otherwise provided by law, by the Articles of Incorporation, or by these bylaws. A majority of the directors present at the time and place of any regular or special meeting, although less than a quorum, may adjourn the same from time to time without notice, until a quorum shall be present.

Section 10 - Board Action: At all meetings of the Board, each director present shall have one vote, irrespective of the number of shares of stock, if any, which he may hold. Except as otherwise provided by Statute, the action of a majority of the directors present at any meeting at which a quorum is present shall be the act of the Board. Any action authorized, in writing, by all of the Directors entitled to vote thereon and filed with the minutes of the Corporation shall be the act of the Board with the same force and effect as if the same had been passed by unanimous vote at a duly called meeting of the Board. Any action taken by the Board may be taken without a meeting if agreed to in writing by all members before or after the action is taken and if a record of such action is filed in the Minute Book.

Section 11 - Telephone Meetings: Directors may participate in meetings of the Board through use of a telephone if such can be arranged so that all Board members can hear all other members. The use of a telephone for participation shall constitute presence in person.

Section 12 - Resignation and Removal: Any director may resign at any time by giving written notice to another Board member, the President or the Secretary of the Corporation. Unless otherwise specified in such written notice, such resignation shall take effect upon receipt thereof by the Board or by such officer, and the acceptance of such resignation shall not be necessary to make it effective. Any director may be removed with or without cause at any time by the affirmative vote of shareholders holding of record in the aggregate at least a majority of the outstanding shares of the Corporation at a special meeting of the shareholders called for that purpose, and may be removed for cause by action of the Board.

Section 13 - Compensation: No stated salary shall be paid to directors, as such for their services, but by resolution of the Board a fixed sum and/or expenses of attendance, if any, may be allowed for attendance at each regular or special meeting of the Board. Nothing herein contained shall be construed to preclude any director from serving the Corporation in any other capacity and receiving compensation therefor.

ARTICLE V - OFFICERS

Section 1 Qualifications: Only persons who are duly licensed and in good standing in the profession by the State of Florida may be officers of the Corporation. If any director shall become disqualified from practicing the profession, he or she shall immediately resign his or her directorship and any other employment with the corporation.

Section 2 - Number, Election and Term: The officers of the Corporation shall consist of a President, a Secretary, a Treasurer, and such other officers, as the Board may from time to time deem advisable. Any officer may be, but is not required to be, a director of the Corporation. Any two or more offices may be held by the same person. The officers of the Corporation shall be elected by the Board at the regular annual meeting of the Board. Each officer shall hold office until the annual meeting of the Board next succeeding his election, and until his successor shall have been elected and qualified, or until his death, resignation or removal.

Section 3 - Resignation and Removal: Any officer may resign at any time by giving written notice of such resignation to the President or the Secretary of the Corporation or to a member of the Board. Unless otherwise specified in such written notice, such resignation shall take effect upon receipt thereof by the Board member or by such officer, and the acceptance of such resignation shall not be necessary to make it effective. Any officer may be removed, either with or without cause, and a successor elected by a majority vote of the Board at any time.

Section 4 - Vacancies: A vacancy in any office may at any time be filled for the unexpired portion of the term by a majority vote of the Board.

Section 5 - Duties of Officers: The officers of the Corporation shall, unless otherwise provided by the Board, each have such powers and duties as generally pertain to their respective offices as well as such powers and duties as may from time to time be specifically decided by the Board. The President shall be the chief executive officer of the Corporation.

Section 6 - Compensation: The officers of the Corporation shall be entitled to such compensation as the Board shall from time to time determine.

Section 7 - Delegation of Duties: In the absence or disability of any Officer of the Corporation or for any other reason deemed sufficient by the Board of Directors, the Board may delegate his powers or duties to any other Officer or to any other director.

Section 8 - Shares of Other Corporations: Whenever the Corporation is the holder of shares of any other Corporation, any right or power of the Corporation as such shareholder (including the attendance, acting and voting at shareholders' meetings and execution of waivers, consents, proxies or other instruments) may be exercised on behalf of the Corporation by the President, any Vice President, or such other person as the Board may authorize.

ARTICLE VI - COMMITTEES

The Board of Directors may, by resolution, designate an Executive Committee and one or more other committees. Such committees shall have such functions and may exercise such power of the Board of Directors as can be lawfully delegated, and to the extent provided in the resolution or resolutions creating such committee or committees. Meetings of committees may be held without notice at such time and at such place as shall from time to time be determined by the committees. The committees of the corporation shall keep regular minutes of their proceedings, and report these minutes to the Board of Directors when required.

ARTICLE VII - BOOKS, RECORDS AND REPORTS

Section 1 - Annual Report: The Corporation shall send an annual report to the Members of the Corporation not later than four months after the close of each fiscal year of the Corporation. Such report shall include a balance sheet as of the close of the fiscal year of the Corporation and a revenue and disbursement statement for the year ending on such closing date. Such financial statements shall be prepared from and in accordance with the books of the Corporation, and in conformity with generally accepted accounting principles applied on a consistent basis.

Section 2 - Permanent Records: The Corporation shall keep current and correct records of the accounts, minutes of the meetings and proceedings and membership records of the Corporation. Such records shall be kept at the registered office or the principal place of business of the Corporation. Any such records shall be in written form or in a form capable of being converted into written form.

Section 3 - Inspection of Corporate Records: Any person who is a Voting Member of the Corporation shall have the right at any reasonable time, and on written demand stating the purpose thereof, to examine and make copies from the relevant books and records of accounts, minutes, and records of the Corporation. Upon the written request of any Voting Member, the Corporation shall mail to such Member a copy of the most recent balance sheet and revenue and disbursement statement.

ARTICLE VIII- SHARES OF STOCK

<u>Section 1 - Authorized shares</u>: The Corporation shall be authorized to issue _____ shares of stock in one class only, each with a par value of $_____.

<u>Section 2 - Certificates</u>: Each shareholder of the Corporation shall be entitled to have a certificate representing all shares which he or she owns. The form of such certificate shall be adopted by a majority vote of the Board of Directors and shall be signed by the President and Secretary of the Corporation and sealed with the seal of the Corporation. No certificate representing shares shall be issued until the full amount of consideration therefore has been paid.

<u>Section 3 - Stock Ledger</u>: The Corporation shall maintain a ledger of the stock records of the Corporation. Transfers of shares of the Corporation shall be made on the stock ledger of the Corporation only at the direction of the holder of record upon surrender of the outstanding certificate(s). The Corporation shall be entitled to treat the holder of record of any share or shares as the absolute owner thereof for all purposes and, accordingly, shall not be bound to recognize any legal, equitable or other claim to, or interest in, such share or shares on the part of any other person, whether or not it shall have express or other notice thereof, except as otherwise expressly provided by law.

ARTICLE IX - DIVIDENDS

Upon approval by the Board of Directors the corporation may pay dividends on its shares in the form of cash, property or additional shares at any time that the Corporation is solvent and if such dividends would not render the Corporation insolvent.

ARTICLE X - FISCAL YEAR

The fiscal year of the Corporation shall be the period selected by the Board of Directors as the tax year of the Corporation for federal income tax purposes.

ARTICLE XI - CORPORATE SEAL

The Board of Directors may adopt, use and modify a corporate seal. Failure to affix the seal to corporate documents shall not affect the validity of such document.

ARTICLE XII - AMENDMENTS

The Articles of Incorporation may be amended by the shareholders as provided by Florida statutes. These bylaws may be altered, amended, or replaced by the Board of Directors; provided, however, that any bylaws or amendments thereto as adopted by the Board of Directors may be altered, amended, or repealed by vote of the shareholders. Bylaws adopted by the Members may not be amended or repealed by the Board.

ARTICLE XIII - INDEMNIFICATION

Any officer, director or employee of the Corporation shall be indemnified to the full extent allowed by the laws of the State of Florida.

Certified to be the bylaws of the corporation adopted by the Board of Directors on _____, _____.

_____
Secretary

Banking Resolution of

_____

The undersigned, being the corporate secretary of the above corporation, hereby certifies that on the _____ day of _____, _____ the Board of Directors of the corporation adopted the following resolution:

RESOLVED that the corporation open bank accounts with _____ _____ and that the officers of the corporation are authorized to take such action as is necessary to open such accounts; that the bank's printed form of resolution is hereby adopted and incorporated into these minutes by reference and shall be placed in the minute book; that any _____ of the following persons shall have signature authority over the account:

_____

_____

_____

_____

and that said resolution has not been modified or rescinded.

Date: _____

_____
Corporate Secretary

(Seal)

This page intentionally left blank.

Offer to Purchase Stock

Part A: Offer to Purchase Stock

Date: _____

To the Board of Directors of

_____

    The undersigned, hereby offers to purchase _____ shares of the _____ stock of your corporation at a total purchase price of _____.

                                        Very truly yours,

                                       _____

Part B: Offer to Sell Stock
Pursuant to Sec. 1244 I.R.C.

Date: _____

To: _____

Dear

    The corporation hereby offers to sell to you _____ shares of its common stock at a price of $_____ per share. These shares are issued pursuant to Section 1244 of the Internal Revenue Code.

    Your signature below shall constitute an acceptance of our offer as of the date it is received by the corporation.

                                         Very truly yours,

                                       _____

                                    By:_____

Accepted:

_____

This page intentionally left blank.

Resolution

of

_____

a Florida Corporation

RESOLVED that the corporation shall reimburse the following parties for the organizational expenses of the organizers of this corporation and that the corporation shall amortize or deduct these expenses as allowed by IRS regulations.

Name	Expense	Amount
_____	_____	$_____
_____	_____	$_____
_____	_____	$_____
_____	_____	$_____
_____	_____	$_____

Date:_____

_____

_____

_____

_____

_____

This page intentionally left blank.

Bill of Sale

The undersigned, in consideration of the issuance of _____ shares of common stock of _____, a Florida corporation, hereby grants, bargains, sells, transfers and delivers unto said corporation the following goods and chattels:

To have and to hold the same forever.

And the undersigned, their heirs, successors and administrators, covenant and warrant that they are the lawful owners of the said goods and chattels and that they are free from all encumbrances. That the undersigned have the right to sell this property and that they will warrant and defend the sale of said property against the lawful claims and demands of all persons.

IN WITNESS whereof the undersigned have executed this Bill of Sale this _____ day of _____, _____.

_____

_____

_____

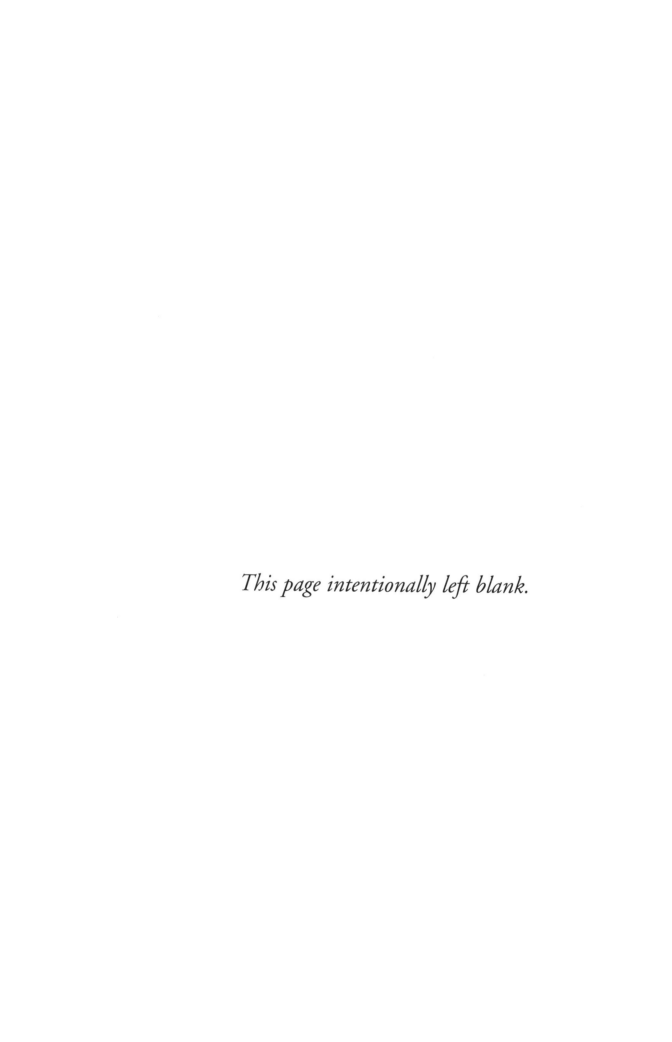

This page intentionally left blank.

Form 2553
(Rev. December 2002)

Department of the Treasury
Internal Revenue Service

Election by a Small Business Corporation
(Under section 1362 of the Internal Revenue Code)
► See Parts II and III on back and the separate instructions.
► The corporation may either send or fax this form to the IRS. See page 2 of the instructions.

OMB No. 1545-0146

Notes:
1. *Do not file Form 1120S, U.S. Income Tax Return for an S Corporation, for any tax year before the year the election takes effect.*
2. *This election to be an S corporation can be accepted only if all the tests are met under Who May Elect on page 1 of the instructions; all shareholders have signed the consent statement; and the exact name and address of the corporation and other required form information are provided.*
3. *If the corporation was in existence before the effective date of this election, see Taxes an S Corporation May Owe on page 1 of the instructions.*

Part I — Election Information

Please Type or Print

Name of corporation (see instructions)

A Employer identification number

Number, street, and room or suite no. (If a P.O. box, see instructions.)

B Date incorporated

City or town, state, and ZIP code

C State of incorporation

D Check the applicable box(es) if the corporation, after applying for the EIN shown in **A** above, changed its name ☐ or address ☐

E Election is to be effective for tax year beginning (month, day, year) . . . . ▶ / /

F Name and title of officer or legal representative who the IRS may call for more information

G Telephone number of officer or legal representative ( )

H If this election takes effect for the first tax year the corporation exists, enter month, day, and year of the **earliest** of the following: (1) date the corporation first had shareholders, (2) date the corporation first had assets, or (3) date the corporation began doing business . . . . ▶ / /

I Selected tax year: Annual return will be filed for tax year ending (month and day) ▶
If the tax year ends on any date other than December 31, except for a 52–53-week tax year ending with reference to the month of December, you **must** complete Part II on the back. If the date you enter is the ending date of a 52–53-week tax year, write "52–53-week year" to the right of the date.

J Name and address of each shareholder; shareholder's spouse having a community property interest in the corporation's stock; and each tenant in common, joint tenant, and tenant by the entirety. (A husband and wife (and their estates) are counted as one shareholder in determining the number of shareholders without regard to the manner in which the stock is owned.)	K Shareholders' Consent Statement. Under penalties of perjury, we declare that we consent to the election of the above-named corporation to be an S corporation under section 1362(a) and that we have examined this consent statement, including accompanying schedules and statements, and to the best of our knowledge and belief, it is true, correct, and complete. We understand our consent is binding and may not be withdrawn after the corporation has made a valid election. (Shareholders sign and date below.)		L Stock owned		M Social security number or employer identification number (see instructions)	N Shareholder's tax year ends (month and day)
	Signature	Date	Number of shares	Dates acquired		

Under penalties of perjury, I declare that I have examined this election, including accompanying schedules and statements, and to the best of my knowledge and belief, it is true, correct, and complete.

Signature of officer ▶   Title ▶   Date ▶

For Paperwork Reduction Act Notice, see page 4 of the instructions.   Cat. No. 18629R   Form **2553** (Rev. 12-2002)

178 ◆

Part II   Selection of Fiscal Tax Year (All corporations using this part must complete item O and item P, Q, or R.)

O   Check the applicable box to indicate whether the corporation is:

1. ☐ A new corporation adopting the tax year entered in item I, Part I.

2. ☐ An existing corporation retaining the tax year entered in item I, Part I.

3. ☐ An existing corporation changing to the tax year entered in item I, Part I.

P   Complete item P if the corporation is using the automatic approval provisions of Rev. Proc. 2002-38, 2002-22 I.R.B. 1037, to request **(1)** a natural business year (as defined in section 5.05 of Rev. Proc. 2002-38) or **(2)** a year that satisfies the ownership tax year test (as defined in section 5.06 of Rev. Proc. 2002-38). Check the applicable box below to indicate the representation statement the corporation is making.

1. Natural Business Year ▶ ☐ I represent that the corporation is adopting, retaining, or changing to a tax year that qualifies as its natural business year as defined in section 5.05 of Rev. Proc. 2002-38 and has attached a statement verifying that it satisfies the 25% gross receipts test (see instructions for content of statement). I also represent that the corporation is not precluded by section 4.02 of Rev. Proc. 2002-38 from obtaining automatic approval of such adoption, retention, or change in tax year.

2. Ownership Tax Year ▶ ☐ I represent that shareholders (as described in section 5.06 of Rev. Proc. 2002-38) holding more than half of the shares of the stock (as of the first day of the tax year to which the request relates) of the corporation have the same tax year or are concurrently changing to the tax year that the corporation adopts, retains, or changes to per item I, Part I, and that such tax year satisfies the requirement of section 4.01(3) of Rev. Proc. 2002-38. I also represent that the corporation is not precluded by section 4.02 of Rev. Proc. 2002-38 from obtaining automatic approval of such adoption, retention, or change in tax year.

Note: *If you do not use item P and the corporation wants a fiscal tax year, complete either item Q or R below. Item Q is used to request a fiscal tax year based on a business purpose and to make a back-up section 444 election. Item R is used to make a regular section 444 election.*

Q   Business Purpose- To request a fiscal tax year based on a business purpose, you must check box Q1. See instructions for details including payment of a user fee. You may also check box Q2 and/or box Q3.

1. Check here ▶ ☐ if the fiscal year entered in item I, Part I, is requested under the prior approval provisions of Rev. Proc. 2002-39, 2002-22 I.R.B. 1046. Attach to Form 2553 a statement describing the relevant facts and circumstances and, if applicable, the gross receipts from sales and services necessary to establish a business purpose. See the instructions for details regarding the gross receipts from sales and services. If the IRS proposes to disapprove the requested fiscal year, do you want a conference with the IRS National Office?
☐ Yes   ☐ No

2. Check here ▶ ☐ to show that the corporation intends to make a back-up section 444 election in the event the corporation's business purpose request is not approved by the IRS. (See instructions for more information.)

3. Check here ▶ ☐ to show that the corporation agrees to adopt or change to a tax year ending December 31 if necessary for the IRS to accept this election for S corporation status in the event (1) the corporation's business purpose request is not approved and the corporation makes a back-up section 444 election, but is ultimately not qualified to make a section 444 election, or (2) the corporation's business purpose request is not approved and the corporation did not make a back-up section 444 election.

R   Section 444 Election- To make a section 444 election, you must check box R1 and you may also check box R2.

1. Check here ▶ ☐ to show the corporation will make, if qualified, a section 444 election to have the fiscal tax year shown in item I, Part I. To make the election, you must complete **Form 8716,** Election To Have a Tax Year Other Than a Required Tax Year, and either attach it to Form 2553 or file it separately.

2. Check here ▶ ☐ to show that the corporation agrees to adopt or change to a tax year ending December 31 if necessary for the IRS to accept this election for S corporation status in the event the corporation is ultimately not qualified to make a section 444 election.

Part III   Qualified Subchapter S Trust (QSST) Election Under Section 1361(d)(2)*

Income beneficiary's name and address	Social security number
Trust's name and address	Employer identification number

Date on which stock of the corporation was transferred to the trust (month, day, year) . . . . ▶   /   /

In order for the trust named above to be a QSST and thus a qualifying shareholder of the S corporation for which this Form 2553 is filed, I hereby make the election under section 1361(d)(2). Under penalties of perjury, I certify that the trust meets the definitional requirements of section 1361(d)(3) and that all other information provided in Part III is true, correct, and complete.

Signature of income beneficiary or signature and title of legal representative or other qualified person making the election   Date

*Use Part III to make the QSST election only if stock of the corporation has been transferred to the trust on or before the date on which the corporation makes its election to be an S corporation. The QSST election must be made and filed separately if stock of the corporation is transferred to the trust after the date on which the corporation makes the S election.

Instructions for Form 2553

(Rev. December 2002)

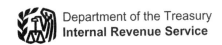
Department of the Treasury
Internal Revenue Service

Election by a Small Business Corporation

Section references are to the Internal Revenue Code unless otherwise noted.

General Instructions

Purpose

To elect to be an S corporation, a corporation must file Form 2553. The election permits the income of the S corporation to be taxed to the shareholders of the corporation rather than to the corporation itself, except as noted below under **Taxes an S Corporation May Owe.**

Who May Elect

A corporation may elect to be an S corporation only if it meets all of the following tests:

1. It is a domestic corporation.

Note: *A limited liability company (LLC)* **must** *file* **Form 8832**, *Entity Classification Election, to elect to be treated as an association taxable as a corporation in order to elect to be an S corporation.*

2. It has no more than 75 shareholders. A husband and wife (and their estates) are treated as one shareholder for this requirement. All other persons are treated as separate shareholders.

3. Its only shareholders are individuals, estates, exempt organizations described in section 401(a) or 501(c)(3), or certain trusts described in section 1361(c)(2)(A). See the instructions for Part III regarding qualified subchapter S trusts (QSSTs).

A trustee of a trust wanting to make an election under section 1361(e)(3) to be an electing small business trust (ESBT) should see Notice 97-12, 1997-1 C.B. 385. However, in general, for tax years beginning after May 13, 2002, Notice 97-12 is superseded by Regulations section 1.1361-1(c)(1). Also see Rev. Proc. 98-23, 1998-1 C.B. 662, for guidance on how to convert a QSST to an ESBT. However, in general, for tax years beginning after May 13, 2002, Rev. Proc. 98-23 is superseded by Regulations section 1.1361-1(j)(12). If there was an inadvertent failure to timely file an ESBT election, see the relief provisions under Rev. Proc. 98-55, 1998-2 C.B. 643.

4. It has no nonresident alien shareholders.

5. It has only one class of stock (disregarding differences in voting rights). Generally, a corporation is treated as having only one class of stock if all outstanding shares of the corporation's stock confer identical rights to distribution and liquidation proceeds. See Regulations section 1.1361-1(l) for details.

6. It is not one of the following ineligible corporations:

a. A bank or thrift institution that uses the reserve method of accounting for bad debts under section 585,

b. An insurance company subject to tax under the rules of subchapter L of the Code,

c. A corporation that has elected to be treated as a possessions corporation under section 936, or

d. A domestic international sales corporation (DISC) or former DISC.

7. It has a permitted tax year as required by section 1378 or makes a section 444 election to have a tax year other than a permitted tax year. Section 1378 defines a permitted tax year as a tax year ending December 31, or any other tax year for which the corporation establishes a business purpose to the satisfaction of the IRS. See Part II for details on requesting a fiscal tax year based on a business purpose or on making a section 444 election.

8. Each shareholder consents as explained in the instructions for column K.

See sections 1361, 1362, and 1378 for additional information on the above tests.

A parent S corporation can elect to treat an eligible wholly-owned subsidiary as a qualified subchapter S subsidiary (QSub). If the election is made, the assets, liabilities, and items of income, deduction, and credit of the QSub are treated as those of the parent. To make the election, get **Form 8869,** Qualified Subchapter S Subsidiary Election. If the QSub election was not timely filed, the corporation may be entitled to relief under Rev. Proc. 98-55.

Taxes an S Corporation May Owe

An S corporation may owe income tax in the following instances:

1. If, at the end of any tax year, the corporation had accumulated earnings and profits, and its passive investment income under section 1362(d)(3) is more than 25% of its gross receipts, the corporation may owe tax on its excess net passive income.

2. A corporation with net recognized built-in gain (as defined in section 1374(d)(2)) may owe tax on its built-in gains.

3. A corporation that claimed investment credit before its first year as an S corporation will be liable for any investment credit recapture tax.

4. A corporation that used the LIFO inventory method for the year immediately preceding its first year as an S corporation may owe an additional tax due to LIFO recapture. The tax is paid in four equal installments, the first of which must be paid by the due date (not including extensions) of the corporation's income tax return for its last tax year as a C corporation.

For more details on these taxes, see the Instructions for Form 1120S.

Where To File

Send the original election (no photocopies) or fax it to the Internal Revenue Service Center listed below. If the corporation files this election by fax, keep the original Form 2553 with the corporation's permanent records.

If the corporation's principal business, office, or agency is located in ▼	Use the following Internal Revenue Service Center address or fax number ▼
Connecticut, Delaware, District of Columbia, Illinois, Indiana, Kentucky, Maine, Maryland, Massachusetts, Michigan, New Hampshire, New Jersey, New York, North Carolina, Ohio, Pennsylvania, Rhode Island, South Carolina, Vermont, Virginia, West Virginia, Wisconsin	Cincinnati, OH 45999 (859) 669-5748
Alabama, Alaska, Arizona, Arkansas, California, Colorado, Florida, Georgia, Hawaii, Idaho, Iowa, Kansas, Louisiana, Minnesota, Mississippi, Missouri, Montana, Nebraska, Nevada, New Mexico, North Dakota, Oklahoma, Oregon, South Dakota, Tennessee, Texas, Utah, Washington, Wyoming	Ogden, UT 84201 (801) 620-7116

When To Make the Election

Complete and file Form 2553 **(a)** at any time before the 16th day of the 3rd month of the tax year, if filed during the tax year the election is to take effect, or **(b)** at any time during the preceding tax year. An election made no later than 2 months and 15 days after the beginning of a tax year that is less than 2½ months long is treated as timely made for that tax year. **An election made after the 15th day of the 3rd month but before the end of the tax year is effective for the next year.** For example, if a calendar tax year corporation makes the election in April 2002, it is effective for the corporation's 2003 calendar tax year.

However, an election made after the due date will be accepted as timely filed if the corporation can show that the failure to file on time was due to reasonable cause. To request relief for a late election, the corporation generally must request a private letter ruling and pay a user fee in accordance with Rev. Proc. 2002-1, 2002-1 I.R.B. 1 (or its successor). But if the election is filed within 12 months of its due date and the original due date for filing the corporation's initial Form 1120S has not passed, the ruling and user fee requirements do not apply. To

request relief in this case, write "FILED PURSUANT TO REV. PROC. 98-55" at the top of page 1 of Form 2553, attach a statement explaining the reason for failing to file the election on time, and file Form 2553 as otherwise instructed. See Rev. Proc. 98-55 for more details.

See Regulations section 1.1362-6(b)(3)(iii) for how to obtain relief for an inadvertent invalid election if the corporation filed a timely election, but one or more shareholders did not file a timely consent.

Acceptance or Nonacceptance of Election

The service center will notify the corporation if its election is accepted and when it will take effect. The corporation will also be notified if its election is not accepted. The corporation should generally receive a determination on its election within 60 days after it has filed Form 2553. If box Q1 in Part II is checked on page 2, the corporation will receive a ruling letter from the IRS in Washington, DC, that either approves or denies the selected tax year. When box Q1 is checked, it will generally take an additional 90 days for the Form 2553 to be accepted.

Care should be exercised to ensure that the IRS receives the election. If the corporation is not notified of acceptance or nonacceptance of its election within 3 months of the date of filing (date mailed), or within 6 months if box Q1 is checked, take follow-up action by corresponding with the service center where the corporation filed the election.

If the IRS questions whether Form 2553 was filed, an acceptable proof of filing is **(a)** certified or registered mail receipt (timely postmarked) from the U.S. Postal Service, or its equivalent from a designated private delivery service (see Notice 2002-62, 2002-39 I.R.B. 574 (or its successor)); **(b)** Form 2553 with accepted stamp; **(c)** Form 2553 with stamped IRS received date; or **(d)** IRS letter stating that Form 2553 has been accepted.

 *Do not file Form 1120S for any tax year before the year the election takes effect. If the corporation is now required to file **Form 1120**, U.S. Corporation Income Tax Return, or any other applicable tax return, continue filing it until the election takes effect.*

End of Election

Once the election is made, it stays in effect until it is terminated. If the election is terminated in a tax year beginning after 1996, IRS consent is generally required for another election by the corporation (or a successor corporation) on Form 2553 for any tax year before the 5th tax year after the first tax year in which the termination took effect. See Regulations section 1.1362-5 for details.

Specific Instructions

Part I (*All corporations must complete.*)

Name and Address of Corporation

Enter the true corporate name as stated in the corporate charter or other legal document creating it. If the corporation's mailing address is the same as someone else's, such as a shareholder's, enter "c/o" and this person's name following the name of the corporation. Include the suite, room, or other unit number after the street address. If the Post Office does not deliver to the street address and the corporation has a P.O. box, show the box number instead of the street address. If the corporation changed its name or address after applying for its employer identification number, be sure to check the box in item D of Part I.

Item A. Employer Identification Number (EIN)

If the corporation has applied for an EIN but has not received it, enter "applied for." If the corporation does not have an EIN, it should apply for one on **Form SS-4,** Application for Employer Identification Number. You can order Form SS-4 by calling 1-800-TAX-FORM (1-800-829-3676) or by accessing the IRS Web Site **www.irs.gov**.

Item E. Effective Date of Election

Enter the beginning effective date (month, day, year) of the tax year requested for the S corporation. Generally, this will be the beginning date of the tax year for which the ending effective date is required to be shown in item I, Part I. For a new corporation (first year the corporation exists) it will generally be the date required to be shown in item H, Part I. The tax year of a new corporation starts on the date that it has shareholders, acquires assets, or begins doing business, whichever happens first. If the effective date for item E for a newly formed corporation is later than the date in item H, the corporation should file Form 1120 or Form 1120-A for the tax period between these dates.

Column K. Shareholders' Consent Statement

Each shareholder who owns (or is deemed to own) stock at the time the election is made must consent to the election. If the election is made during the corporation's tax year for which it first takes effect, any person who held stock at any time during the part of that year that occurs before the election is made, must consent to the election, even though the person may have sold or transferred his or her stock before the election is made.

An election made during the first 2½ months of the tax year is effective for the following tax year if any person who held stock in the corporation during the part of the tax year before the election was made, and who did not hold stock at the time the election was made, did not consent to the election.

Note: *Once the election is made, a new shareholder is not required to consent to the election; a new Form 2553 will not be required.*

Each shareholder consents by signing and dating in column K or signing and dating a separate consent statement described below. The following special rules apply in determining who must sign the consent statement.
- If a husband and wife have a community interest in the stock or in the income from it, both must consent.
- Each tenant in common, joint tenant, and tenant by the entirety must consent.
- A minor's consent is made by the minor, legal representative of the minor, or a natural or adoptive parent of the minor if no legal representative has been appointed.
- The consent of an estate is made by the executor or administrator.
- The consent of an electing small business trust is made by the trustee.
- If the stock is owned by a trust (other than an electing small business trust), the deemed owner of the trust must consent. See section 1361(c)(2) for details regarding trusts that are permitted to be shareholders and rules for determining who is the deemed owner.

Continuation sheet or separate consent statement. If you need a continuation sheet or use a separate consent statement, attach it to Form 2553. The separate consent statement must contain the name, address, and EIN of the corporation and the shareholder information requested in columns J through N of Part I. If you want, you may combine all the shareholders' consents in one statement.

Column L

Enter the number of shares of stock each shareholder owns and the dates the stock was acquired. If the election is made during the corporation's tax year for which it first takes effect, do not list the shares of stock for those shareholders who sold or transferred all of their stock before the election was made. However, these shareholders must still consent to the election for it to be effective for the tax year.

Column M

Enter the social security number of each shareholder who is an individual. Enter the EIN of each shareholder that is an estate, a qualified trust, or an exempt organization.

Column N

Enter the month and day that each shareholder's tax year ends. If a shareholder is changing his or her tax year, enter the tax year the shareholder is changing to, and attach an explanation indicating the present tax year and the basis for the change (e.g., automatic revenue procedure or letter ruling request).

Signature

Form 2553 must be signed by the president, treasurer, assistant treasurer, chief accounting officer, or other corporate officer (such as tax officer) authorized to sign.

Part II

Complete Part II if you selected a tax year ending on any date other than December 31 (other than a 52-53-week tax year ending with reference to the month of December).

Note: *In certain circumstances the corporation may not obtain automatic approval of a fiscal year under the natural business year (Box P1) or ownership tax year (Box P2) provisions if it is under examination, before an area office, or before a federal court with respect to any income tax issue and the annual accounting period is under consideration. For details, see section 4.02 of Rev. Proc. 2002-38, 2002-22 I.R.B. 1037.*

Box P1

Attach a statement showing separately for each month the amount of gross receipts for the most recent 47 months. A corporation that does not have a 47-month period of gross receipts cannot automatically establish a natural business year.

Box Q1

For examples of an acceptable business purpose for requesting a fiscal tax year, see section 5.02 of Rev. Proc. 2002-39, 2002-22 I.R.B. 1046, and Rev. Rul. 87-57, 1987-2 C.B. 117.

Attach a statement showing the relevant facts and circumstances to establish a business purpose for the requested fiscal year. For details on what is sufficient to establish a business purpose, see section 5.02 of Rev. Proc. 2002-39.

If your business purpose is based on one of the natural business year tests provided in section 5.03 of Rev. Proc. 2002-39, identify if you are using the 25% gross receipts, annual business cycle, or seasonal business test. For the 25% gross receipts test, provide a schedule showing the amount of gross receipts for each month for the most recent 47 months. For either the annual business cycle or seasonal business test, provide the gross receipts from sales and services (and inventory costs, if applicable) for each month of the short period, if any, and the three immediately preceding tax years. If the corporation has been in existence for less than three tax years, submit figures for the period of existence.

If you check box Q1, you will be charged a user fee of up to $600 (subject to change—see Rev. Proc. 2002-1 or its successor). Do not pay the fee when filing Form 2553. The service center will send Form 2553 to the IRS in Washington, DC, who, in turn, will notify the corporation that the fee is due.

Box Q2

If the corporation makes a back-up section 444 election for which it is qualified, then the election will take effect in the event the business purpose request is not approved. In some cases, the tax year requested under the back-up section 444 election may be different than the tax year requested under business purpose. See **Form 8716,** Election To Have a Tax Year Other Than a Required Tax Year, for details on making a back-up section 444 election.

Boxes Q2 and R2

If the corporation is not qualified to make the section 444 election after making the item Q2 back-up section 444 election or indicating its intention to make the election in item R1, and therefore it later files a calendar year return, it should write "Section 444 Election Not Made" in the top left corner of the first calendar year Form 1120S it files.

Part III

Certain qualified subchapter S trusts (QSSTs) may make the QSST election required by section 1361(d)(2) in Part III. Part III may be used to make the QSST election only if corporate stock has been transferred to the trust on or before the date on which the corporation makes its election to be an S corporation. However, a statement can be used instead of Part III to make the election. If there was an inadvertent failure to timely file a QSST election, see the relief provisions under Rev. Proc. 98-55.

Note: *Use Part III **only** if you make the election in Part I (i.e., Form 2553 cannot be filed with only Part III completed).*

The deemed owner of the QSST must also consent to the S corporation election in column K, page 1, of Form 2553. See section 1361(c)(2).

Paperwork Reduction Act Notice. We ask for the information on this form to carry out the Internal Revenue laws of the United States. You are required to give us the information. We need it to ensure that you are complying with these laws and to allow us to figure and collect the right amount of tax.

You are not required to provide the information requested on a form that is subject to the Paperwork Reduction Act unless the form displays a valid OMB control number. Books or records relating to a form or its instructions must be retained as long as their contents may become material in the administration of any Internal Revenue law. Generally, tax returns and return information are confidential, as required by section 6103.

The time needed to complete and file this form will depend on individual circumstances. The estimated average time is:

Recordkeeping	9 hr., 34 min.
Learning about the law or the form	3 hr., 28 min.
Preparing, copying, assembling, and sending the form to the IRS	3 hr., 47 min.

If you have comments concerning the accuracy of these time estimates or suggestions for making this form simpler, we would be happy to hear from you. You can write to the Tax Forms Committee, Western Area Distribution Center, Rancho Cordova, CA 95743-0001. **Do not** send the form to this address. Instead, see **Where To File** on page 2.

Resolution

of

_____

a Florida Corporation

RESOLVED that the corporation elects "S-Corporation" status for tax purposes under the Internal Revenue Code and that the officers of the corporation are directed to file IRS Form 2553 and to take any further action necessary for the corporation to qualify for S-corporation status.

Shareholders' Consent

The undersigned shareholders being all of the shareholders of the above corporation, a _____ corporation hereby consent to the election of the corporation to obtain S-corporation status

Name and Address of Shareholder	Shares Owned	Date Acquired
_____	_____	_____
_____	_____	_____
_____	_____	_____

Date:_____

_____

_____

_____

_____

_____

WAIVER OF NOTICE OF THE ANNUAL MEETING OF
THE BOARD OF DIRECTORS OF

_____

The undersigned, being all the Directors of the Corporation, hereby agree and consent that an annual meeting of the Board of Directors of the Corporation be held on the _____ day of _____, _____ at ____ o'clock ___m at _____ _____ and do hereby waive all notice whatsoever of such meeting and of any adjournment or adjournments thereof.

We do further agree and consent that any and all lawful business may be transacted at such meeting or at any adjournment or adjournments thereof as may be deemed advisable by the Directors present. Any business transacted at such meeting or at any adjournment or adjournments thereof shall be as valid and legal as if such meeting or adjourned meeting were held after notice.

Date: _____

_____
Director

_____
Director

_____
Director

_____
Director

MINUTES OF THE ANNUAL MEETING OF
THE BOARD OF DIRECTORS OF

_____

The annual meeting of the Board of Directors of the Corporation was held on the date and at the time and place set forth in the written waiver of notice signed by the directors, and attached to the minutes of this meeting.

The following were present, being all the directors of the Corporation:

_____   _____

_____   _____

The meeting was called to order and it was moved, seconded and unanimously carried that _____ act as Chairman and that _____ act as Secretary.

The minutes of the last meeting of the Board of Directors which was held on _____, _____ were read and approved by the Board.

Upon motion duly made, seconded and carried, the following were elected officers for the following year and until their successors are elected and qualify:

President:
Vice President:
Secretary
Treasurer:

There being no further business to come before the meeting, upon motion duly made, seconded and unanimously carried, it was adjourned.

                                        _____
                                        Secretary

Directors:

_____

_____

_____

_____

WAIVER OF NOTICE OF THE ANNUAL MEETING OF
THE SHAREHOLDERS OF

_____

The undersigned, being all the shareholders of the Corporation, hereby agree and consent that an annual meeting of the shareholders of the Corporation be held on the ____ day of _____, _____ at ____ o'clock ___m at _____ _____ and do hereby waive all notice whatsoever of such meeting and of any adjournment or adjournments thereof.

We do further agree and consent that any and all lawful business may be transacted at such meeting or at any adjournment or adjournments thereof. Any business transacted at such meeting or at any adjournment or adjournments thereof shall be as valid and legal as if such meeting or adjourned meeting were held after notice.

Date: _____

_____
Shareholder

_____
Shareholder

_____
Shareholder

_____
Shareholder

MINUTES OF THE ANNUAL MEETING OF
SHAREHOLDERS OF

_____

The annual meeting of Shareholders of the Corporation was held on the date and at the time and place set forth in the written waiver of notice signed by the shareholders, and attached to the minutes of this meeting.

There were present the following shareholders:

Shareholder   No. of Shares

_____   _____

_____   _____

_____   _____

_____   _____

The meeting was called to order and it was moved, seconded and unanimously carried that _____ act as Chairman and that _____ act as Secretary.

A roll call was taken and the Chairman noted that all of the outstanding shares of the Corporation were represented in person or by proxy. Any proxies were attached to these minutes.

The minutes of the last meeting of the shareholders which was held on _____, _____ were read and approved by the shareholders.

Upon motion duly made, seconded and carried, the following were elected directors for the following year:

_____   _____

_____   _____

There being no further business to come before the meeting, upon motion duly made, seconded and unanimously carried, it was adjourned.

_____
Secretary

Shareholders:

_____

_____

_____

_____

WAIVER OF NOTICE OF SPECIAL MEETING OF
THE BOARD OF DIRECTORS OF

_____

The undersigned, being all the Directors of the Corporation, hereby agree and consent that a special meeting of the Board of Directors of the Corporation be held on the _____ day of _____, _____ at ____ o'clock ___m at _____ _____ and do hereby waive all notice whatsoever of such meeting and of any adjournment or adjournments thereof.

The purpose of the meeting is:

We do further agree and consent that any and all lawful business may be transacted at such meeting or at any adjournment or adjournments thereof as may be deemed advisable by the Directors present. Any business transacted at such meeting or at any adjournment or adjournments thereof shall be as valid and legal as if such meeting or adjourned meeting were held after notice.

Date: _____

_____
Director

_____
Director

_____
Director

_____
Director

MINUTES OF SPECIAL MEETING OF
THE BOARD OF DIRECTORS OF

_____

A special meeting of the Board of Directors of the Corporation was held on the date and at the time and place set forth in the written waiver of notice signed by the directors, and attached to the minutes of this meeting.

The following were present, being all the directors of the Corporation:

_____   _____

_____   _____

The meeting was called to order and it was moved, seconded and unanimously carried that _____ act as Chairman and that _____ act as Secretary.

The minutes of the last meeting of the Board of Directors which was held on _____, _____ were read and approved by the Board.

Upon motion duly made, seconded and carried, the following resolution was adopted:

There being no further business to come before the meeting, upon motion duly made, seconded and unanimously carried, it was adjourned.

_____
Secretary

Directors:

_____

_____

_____

_____

WAIVER OF NOTICE OF SPECIAL MEETING OF
THE SHAREHOLDERS OF

_____

The undersigned, being all the shareholders of the Corporation, hereby agree and consent that a special meeting of the shareholders of the Corporation be held on the _____ day of _____, _____ at _____ o'clock ____m at _____ _____ and do hereby waive all notice whatsoever of such meeting and of any adjournment or adjournments thereof.

The purpose of the meeting is

We do further agree and consent that any and all lawful business may be transacted at such meeting or at any adjournment or adjournments thereof. Any business transacted at such meeting or at any adjournment or adjournments thereof shall be as valid and legal as if such meeting or adjourned meeting were held after notice.

Date: _____

_____
Shareholder

_____
Shareholder

_____
Shareholder

_____
Shareholder

MINUTES OF SPECIAL MEETING OF
SHAREHOLDERS OF

_____

A special meeting of Shareholders of the Corporation was held on the date and at the time and place set forth in the written waiver of notice signed by the shareholders, and attached to the minutes of this meeting.

There were present the following shareholders:

Shareholder	No. of Shares
_____	_____
_____	_____
_____	_____
_____	_____

The meeting was called to order and it was moved, seconded and unanimously carried that _____ act as Chairman and that _____ act as Secretary.

A roll call was taken and the Chairman noted that all of the outstanding shares of the Corporation were represented in person or by proxy. Any proxies were attached to these minutes.

The minutes of the last meeting of the shareholders which was held on _____, _____ were read and approved by the shareholders.

Upon motion duly made, seconded and carried, the following resolution was adopted:

There being no further business to come before the meeting, upon motion duly made, seconded and unanimously carried, it was adjourned.

_____
Secretary

Shareholders:

_____

_____

_____

_____

This page intentionally left blank.

ARTICLES OF DISSOLUTION

Pursuant to 607.1401, Florida Statutes, this Florida profit corporation submits the following articles of dissolution:

FIRST: The name of the corporation is:_____

_____

SECOND: The filing date of the articles of incorporation was:_____

THIRD: (CHECK ONE)

       ❏ None of the corporation's shares have been issued.

       ❏ The corporation has not commenced business.

FOURTH: No debt of the corporation remains unpaid.

FIFTH: The net assets of the corporation remaining after winding up have been distributed to the shareholders, if shares were issued.

SIXTH: Adoption of Dissolution (CHECK ONE)

       ❏ A majority of the incorporators authorized the dissolution.

       ❏ A majority of the directors authorized the dissolution.

    Signed this _____ day of _____, _____.

Signature _____
          (By the chairman or vice chairman of the board, president, or other officer - if there are no officers or directors, by an incorporator.)

_____
(Typed or printed name)

_____
(Title)

This page intentionally left blank.

ARTICLES OF DISSOLUTION

Pursuant to section 607.1403, Florida Statutes, this Florida profit corporation submits the following articles of dissolution:

FIRST: The name of the corporation is:_____

_____

SECOND: The date dissolution was authorized:_____

THIRD: Adoption of Dissolution   (CHECK ONE)

❑ Dissolution was approved by the shareholders. The number of votes cast for dissolution was sufficient for approval.

❑ Dissolution was approved by vote of the shareholders through voting groups.

The following statement must be separately provided for each voting group entitled to vote separately on the plan to dissolve:

The number of votes cast for dissolution was sufficient for approval by

_____
(voting group)

Signed this _____ day of _____, _____.

Signature _____
(By the Chairman or Vice Chairman of the Board, President, or other officer)

_____
(Typed or printed name)

_____
(Title)

This page intentionally left blank.

TRANSMITTAL LETTER

TO: Amendment Section
            Division of Corporations

SUBJECT:_____
                            (Name of Corporation)

DOCUMENT NUMBER:_____

The enclosed Officer/Director Resignation for a Corporation and fee are submitted for filing.

Please return all correspondence concerning this matter to the following:

_____
                    (Name of Person)

_____
                (Name of Firm/Company)

_____
                        (Address)

_____
                (City/State and Zip Code)

For further information concerning this matter, please call:

_____ at (_____)_____
            (Name of Person)   (Area Code & Daytime Telephone Number)

Enclosed is a check for $35.00 made payable to the Florida Department of State.

Mailing Address: **Street Address:**
Amendment Section   Amendment Section
Division of Corporations   Division of Corporations
P.O. Box 6327   409 E. Gaines Street
Tallahassee, FL 32314   Tallahassee, FL 32399

OFFICER / DIRECTOR RESIGNATION
FOR A CORPORATION

I, _____ , hereby resign as_____

(Title)

of_____ ,

(Name of Corporation)

_____ , a corporation organized under the laws of the State of

(Document Number, if known)

_____ .

_____

(Signature of resigning officer/director)

FILING FEE IS $35.00

Make checks payable to Florida Department of State and mail to:

Amendment Section
Division of Corporations
P.O. Box 6327
Tallahassee, Florida 32314

TRANSMITTAL LETTER

TO: Amendment Section
Division of Corporations

SUBJECT:_____
(Name of Corporation)

DOCUMENT NUMBER:_____

The enclosed Resignation of Registered Agent for a Corporation and fee are submitted for filing.

Please return all correspondence concerning this matter to the following:

_____
(Name of Person)

_____
(Name of Firm/Company)

_____
(Address)

_____
(City/State and Zip Code)

For further information concerning this matter, please call:

_____ at (_____)_____
(Name of Person)   (Area Code & Daytime Telephone Number)

Enclosed is a check made payable to the Florida Department of State for $87.50 for an active corporation or $35.00 for an administratively dissolved, voluntarily dissolved or withdrawn corporation.

Mailing Address:
Amendment Section
Division of Corporations
P.O. Box 6327
Tallahassee, FL 32314

Street Address:
Amendment Section
Division of Corporations
409 E. Gaines Street
Tallahassee, FL 32399

CR2E046(11/02)

RESIGNATION OF REGISTERED AGENT
FOR A CORPORATION

Pursuant to the provisions of sections 607.0502(2), 617.0502(2), 607.1509, or 617.1509,

Florida Statutes, the undersigned, _____

(Name of Registered Agent)

hereby resigns as Registered Agent for _____,

(Name of Corporation)

_____

(Document Number, if known)

A copy of this resignation was mailed to the above listed corporation at its last known address.

The agency is terminated and the office discontinued on the 31st day after the date on which this statement is filed.

_____

(Signature of Resigning Agent)

If signing on behalf of an entity:

_____

(Typed or Printed Name)

_____

(Capacity)

Fee for filing this document:
$87.50 - Active corporation
$35.00 - Administratively dissolved/voluntarily dissolved/
withdrawn corporation

Make checks payable to Florida Department of State and mail to:
Division of Corporations
P.O. Box 6327
Tallahassee, FL 32314

TRANSMITTAL LETTER

TO: Amendment Section
Division of Corporations

SUBJECT:_____
(Name of corporation)

DOCUMENT NUMBER:_____

The enclosed Statement of Change of Registered Office/Agent and fee are submitted for filing.

Please return all correspondence concerning this matter to the following:

_____
(Name of person)

_____
(Name of firm/company)

_____
(Address)

_____
(City/state and zip code)

For further information concerning this matter, please call:

_____ at (_____)_____
(Name of person)   (Area code & daytime telephone number)

Enclosed is a $35.00 check made payable to the Department of State.

Mailing Address:
Amendment Section
Division of Corporations
P.O. Box 6327
Tallahassee, FL 32314

Street Address:
Amendment Section
Division of Corporations
409 E. Gaines Street
Tallahassee, FL 32399

STATEMENT OF CHANGE OF REGISTERED OFFICE OR REGISTERED AGENT OR BOTH FOR CORPORATIONS

Pursuant to the provisions of sections 607.0502, 617.0502, 607.1508, or 617.1508, Florida Statutes, this statement of change is submitted for a corporation organized under the laws of the State of _____ in order to change its registered office or registered agent, or both, in the State of Florida.

1. The name of the corporation:_____

2. The principal office address:_____

_____

3. The mailing address (if different):_____

_____

4. Date of incorporation/qualification: _____ Document number: _____

5. The name and street address of the current registered agent and registered office on file with the Florida Department of State:

_____

_____

_____

6. The name and street address of the new registered agent (if changed) and /or registered office (if changed):

_____

(P.O. Box or personal mailbox **NOT** acceptable)

_____

The street address of its registered office and the street address of the business office of its registered agent, as changed will be identical.

Such change was authorized by resolution duly adopted by its board of directors or by an officer so authorized by the board, or the corporation has been notified in writing of the change.

_____   _____
(Signature of an officer, chairman or vice chairman of the board)   (Printed or typed name and title)

I hereby accept the appointment as registered agent and agree to act in this capacity. I further agree to comply with the provisions of all statutes relative to the proper and complete performance of my duties, and I am familiar with and accept the obligation of my position as registered agent. Or, if this document is being filed merely to reflect a change in the registered office address, I hereby confirm that the corporation has been notified in writing of this change.

_____   _____
(Signature of Registered Agent)   (Date)

If signing on behalf of an entity:

_____   _____
(Typed or Printed Name)   (Capacity)

* * * FILING FEE: $35.00 * * *

Stock Ledger

Certificates Issued

Transfer of Shares

Cert. No.	No. of Shares	Date of Acquisition	Shareholder Name and Address	From Whom Transferred	Amount Paid	Date of Transfer	To Whom Transferred	Cert. No. Surrendered	No. of Shares Transferred	Cert. No.

This page intentionally left blank.

Certificate No. _____
No. of shares _____
Dated _____
Issued to: _____
_____
_____

☐ Original issue
Documentary stamp tax paid:
$ _____
(Attach stamps to this stub.)

☐ Transferred from: _____
_____

Date: _____

Original Cert. No.	Original No. Shares	No. of Shares Transferred
_____	_____	_____

Received Cert. No. _____
No. of shares _____
New certificates issued:

Cert. No.	No. of Shares
_____	_____
_____	_____

Certificate No. _____
No. of shares _____
Dated _____
Issued to: _____
_____
_____

☐ Original issue
Documentary stamp tax paid:
$ _____
(Attach stamps to this stub.)

☐ Transferred from: _____
_____

Date: _____

Original Cert. No.	Original No. Shares	No. of Shares Transferred
_____	_____	_____

Received Cert. No. _____
No. of shares _____
New certificates issued:

Cert. No.	No. of Shares
_____	_____
_____	_____

Certificate No. _____
No. of shares _____
Dated _____
Issued to: _____
_____
_____

☐ Original issue
Documentary stamp tax paid:
$ _____
(Attach stamps to this stub.)

☐ Transferred from: _____
_____

Date: _____

Original Cert. No.	Original No. Shares	No. of Shares Transferred
_____	_____	_____

Received Cert. No. _____
No. of shares _____
New certificates issued:

Cert. No.	No. of Shares
_____	_____
_____	_____

Certificate No. _____
No. of shares _____
Dated _____
Issued to: _____

☐ Original issue
Documentary stamp tax paid:
$_____
(Attach stamps to this stub.)

☐ Transferred from:
_____
Date: _____

Original Cert. No.	Original No. Shares	No. of Shares Transferred
_____	_____	_____

Received Cert. No. _____
No. of shares _____
New certificates issued:

Cert. No.	No. of Shares
_____	_____
_____	_____

Certificate No. _____
No. of shares _____
Dated _____
Issued to: _____

☐ Original issue
Documentary stamp tax paid:
$_____
(Attach stamps to this stub.)

☐ Transferred from:
_____
Date: _____

Original Cert. No.	Original No. Shares	No. of Shares Transferred
_____	_____	_____

Received Cert. No. _____
No. of shares _____
New certificates issued:

Cert. No.	No. of Shares
_____	_____
_____	_____

Certificate No. _____
No. of shares _____
Dated _____
Issued to: _____

☐ Original issue
Documentary stamp tax paid:
$_____
(Attach stamps to this stub.)

☐ Transferred from:
_____
Date: _____

Original Cert. No.	Original No. Shares	No. of Shares Transferred
_____	_____	_____

Received Cert. No. _____
No. of shares _____
New certificates issued:

Cert. No.	No. of Shares
_____	_____
_____	_____

The shares represented by this certificate have not been registered under state or federal securities laws. Therefore, they may not be transferred until the corporation determines that such transfer will not adversely affect the exemptions relied upon.

Shares

Certificate No.

Organized under the laws of the State of Florida

This certifies that

_____ shares of _____

is the holder of record of _____ stock of

transferable only on the books of the corporation by the holder hereof in person or by Attorney upon surrender of this certificate properly endorsed.

In witness whereof, the said corporation has caused this certificate to be signed by its duly authorized officers and its corporate seal to be hereto affixed this _____ day of _____.

_____

_____

For value received, _____ hereby sell, assign and transfer unto _____
_____,
_____ shares
represented by this certificate and do hereby irrevocably constitute and appoint
_____ attorney to transfer the said shares
on the books of the corporation with full power of substitution in the premises.

Dated _____

_____

Witness:

_____

Certificate No.

Shares

The shares represented by this certificate have not been registered under state or federal securities laws. Therefore, they may not be transferred until the corporation determines that such transfer will not adversely affect the exemptions relied upon.

Organized under the laws of the State of Florida

This certifies that _____ is the holder of record of

_____ shares of _____ stock of

transferable only on the books of the corporation by the holder hereof in person or by Attorney upon surrender of this certificate properly endorsed.

In witness whereof, the said corporation has caused this certificate to be signed by its duly authorized officers and its corporate seal to be hereto affixed this _____ day of _____.

_____

_____

For value received, _____ hereby sell, assign and transfer unto _____

_____,

_____ *shares*

represented   by   this   certificate   and   do   hereby   irrevocably   constitute   and   appoint

_____ *attorney to transfer the said shares*

on the books of the corporation with full power of substitution in the premises.

Dated _____

_____

Witness:

_____

The shares represented by this certificate have not been registered under state or federal securities laws. Therefore, they may not be transferred until the corporation determines that such transfer will not adversely affect the exemptions relied upon.

Shares

Certificate No.

Organized under the laws of the State of Florida

This certifies that _____ *is the holder of record of*

_____ *shares of* _____ *stock of*

transferable only on the books of the corporation by the holder hereof in person or by Attorney upon surrender of this certificate properly endorsed.

In witness whereof, the said corporation has caused this certificate to be signed by its duly authorized officers and its corporate seal to be hereto affixed this _____ day of _____.

For value received, _____ hereby sell, assign and transfer unto _____
_____,
_____ shares
represented by this certificate and do hereby irrevocably constitute and appoint
_____ attorney to transfer the said shares
on the books of the corporation with full power of substitution in the premises.

Dated _____

_____

Witness:

_____

The shares represented by this certificate have not been registered under state or federal securities laws. Therefore, they may not be transferred until the corporation determines that such transfer will not adversely affect the exemptions relied upon.

Shares

Certificate No.

Organized under the laws of the State of Florida

This certifies that _____ is the holder of record of

_____ shares of _____ stock of

transferable only on the books of the corporation by the holder hereof in person or by Attorney upon surrender of this certificate properly endorsed.

In witness whereof, the said corporation has caused this certificate to be signed by its duly authorized officers and its corporate seal to be hereto affixed this _____

_____ day of _____, _____.

_____

For value received, _____ hereby sell, assign and transfer unto _____ ,

_____ *shares* *represented by this certificate and do hereby irrevocably constitute and appoint* _____ *attorney to transfer the said shares* *on the books of the corporation with full power of substitution in the premises.*

Dated _____

_____

Witness:

_____

The shares represented by this certificate have not been registered under state or federal securities laws. Therefore, they may not be transferred until the corporation determines that such transfer will not adversely affect the exemptions relied upon.

Shares

Certificate No.

Organized under the laws of the State of Florida

This certifies that _____ is the holder of record of

_____ shares of _____ stock of

transferable only on the books of the corporation by the holder hereof in person or by Attorney upon surrender of this certificate properly endorsed.

In witness whereof, the said corporation has caused this certificate to be signed by its duly authorized officers and its corporate seal to be hereto affixed this _____ day of _____.

_____

_____

For value received, _____ hereby sell, assign and transfer unto _____

_____,

_____ shares
represented   by   this   certificate   and   do   hereby   irrevocably   constitute   and   appoint
_____ attorney to transfer the said shares
on the books of the corporation with full power of substitution in the premises.

Dated _____

_____

Witness:

_____

SHAREHOLDER AGREEMENT

WHEREAS the undersigned shareholders are forming a Corporation and wish to protect their interests and those of the Corporation, in consideration of the mutual promises and conditions set out below, the parties agree as follows:

1. *Best Efforts.* Each shareholder agrees to devote his or her best efforts to the development of the Corporation. No shareholder shall participate in any enterprise which competes in any way with the activities of the Corporation.

2. *Right to Serve as Director or Officer.* Each shareholder shall, so long as he owns shares in the Corporation, have the right to serve as a director of the Corporation or to designate some responsible person to serve as his nominee.

The officers of the Corporation shall be the following shareholders, each of whom shall continue to serve as long as he owns shares:

President _____

Vice President _____

Treasurer _____

Secretary _____

Any officer or director who ceases to be a shareholder shall no longer be an officer or director upon the transfer of shares.

3. *Salary.* The Corporation shall employ the shareholders and pay salaries to them as follows:

Name of Shareholder and initial salary

_____ $_____

_____ $_____

_____ $_____

The salary received by any shareholder as an officer or employee or in any other function or for any other service shall serve as compensation for all services or functions the shareholder performs for the Corporation. The directors may increase or decrease the salaries from time to time, upon unanimous vote.

4. *Additional Shares.* The Corporation shall not, without consent of all of the shareholders, do any of the following: (a) issue additional shares of any class or any securities convertible into shares of any

class; (b) merge or participate in a share exchange with any other Corporation; or (c) transfer all or substantially all of the assets of the Corporation for any consideration other than cash.

In the event the shareholders agree to issue additional shares or securities convertible into shares, then each of the shareholders shall have the right to purchase any such securities so offered at a future date in proportion to his then respective interest in the Corporation at the time of such offer.

5. *Transfer of Shares.* No shares shall be transferred in any manner or by any means except upon unanimous consent of the shareholders. If a proposed sale is not agreed to by unanimous consent, a shareholder may resign from his positions with the corporation and be bought out by the corporation as provided below.

6. *Buyout.* Upon the death, resignation, adjudication of incompetency, or bankruptcy by any shareholder, or the transfer, agreement to transfer, or attachment of any shares, the Corporation shall purchase all of the shares of the shareholder so affected at the value of shares described below. Payment by the corporation for such buyout shall be within thirty days of the determination of value and the transferring shareholder shall execute all documents necessary to transfer his or her shares.

7. *Value of Shares.* The parties agree that upon execution of this agreement the value of each share of stock is $_____. This value shall be reviewed and updated once each year and at any time that a sale of shares is contemplated. New value shall be set by a unanimous vote of the shareholders. If the shareholders cannot agree, then the corporation's accountant shall be asked to set a value. If any shareholder disagrees with the corporation's accountant's value, he or she may get the value of another accountant. If the two accountants cannot agree to an acceptable value, they shall choose a third accountant to set the final value.

8. *S Corporation Status.* If the Corporation is an S corporation and if it reasonably determines that any proposed transferee is not eligible as a shareholder of a Subchapter S Corporation or that such transfer would cause the Corporation to lose its qualification as a Subchapter S Corporation, then the Corporation may so notify the shareholder of that determination and thereby forbid the consummation of the transfer.

9. *Endorsement.* The certificates for shares of the Corporation shall be endorsed as follows: "The shares represented by this certificate are subject to and are transferable only on compliance with a Shareholders Agreement a copy of which is on file in the office of the Secretary of the Corporation."

10. *Formalities.* Whenever under this Agreement notice is required to be given, it shall be given in writing served in person or by certified or registered mail, return receipt requested, to the address of the shareholder listed in the stock ledger of the corporation, and it shall be deemed to have been given upon personal delivery or on the date notice is posted.

11. *Termination.* This Agreement shall terminate and all rights and obligations hereunder shall cease upon the happening of any one of the following events:

(a) The adjudication of the Corporation as bankrupt, the execution by it of any assignment for the benefit of creditors, or the appointment of a receiver for the Corporation;

(b) The voluntary or involuntary dissolution of the Corporation;

(c) By a written Agreement signed by all the shareholders to terminate this Agreement.

12. *Entire Agreement.* This Agreement embodies the entire representations, Agreements and conditions in relation to the subject matter hereof and no representations, understandings or Agreements, oral or otherwise, in relation thereto exist between the parties except as herein expressly set forth. The Agreement may not be amended or terminated orally but only as expressly provided herein or by an instrument in writing duly executed by the parties hereto.

13. *Heirs and Assigns.* This Agreement and the various rights and obligations arising under it shall inure to the benefit of and be binding upon the parties hereto and their respective heirs, successors and assigns.

14. *Severability.* The invalidity or unenforceability of any term or provision of this Agreement or the non-application of such term or provision to any person or circumstance shall not impair or affect the remainder of this Agreement, and its application to other persons and circumstances and the remaining terms and provisions hereof shall not be invalidated but shall remain in full force and effect.

15. *Gender.* Whenever in this Agreement any pronoun is used in reference to any shareholder, purchaser or other person or entity, natural or otherwise, the singular shall include the plural, and the masculine shall include the feminine or the neuter, as required by context.

16. *Arbitration.* All disputes between shareholders or between the corporation and a shareholder shall be settled by arbitration and the parties hereto specifically waive they rights to bring action in any court, except to enforce an arbitration decision.

17. *Choice of Law.* This Agreement shall be governed by and construed in accordance with the laws of the State of Florida.

IN WITNESS WHEREOF, the parties hereto have executed this Agreement the date and place first above mentioned.

_____ (Name of Corporation)

By: _____,
President

                                           _____ Shareholder

                                           _____ Shareholder

                                           _____ Shareholder

                                           _____ Shareholder

INDEX

Your #1 Source for Real World Legal Information...

SPHINX® PUBLISHING
An Imprint of Sourcebooks, Inc.®

- Written by lawyers
- Simple English explanation of the law
- Forms and instructions included

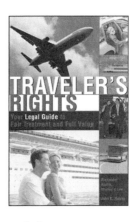

THE MOST VALUABLE BUSINESS LEGAL FORMS YOU'LL EVER NEED, 3RD ED.

This book contains more than fifty valuable documents, including completed, sample forms and blank, ready-to-use forms. Performance reviews and employee warning notices are alos included.

216 pages; $21.95;
ISBN 1-57248-167-6

PROFIT FROM INTELLECTUAL PROPERTY

Understaind the differences among the types of intellectual property in order to distinguish specific protection that may be legally afforded. Avoid problems with a licensing agreement by understanding various clauses and provisions. Maximize the profitability of your IP through real world sample licenses.

288 pages; $28.95;
ISBN 1-57248-332-6

TRAVELER'S RIGHTS

Lear specifics relating to air, car rental, hotels/motels, cruises, and tour packages in order to determine your various options. Protect yourself by understanding various federal laws that regulate both the industry and the traveler.

304 pages; $21.95;
ISBN 1-57248-335-0

See the following order form for books written specifically for California, the District of Columbia, Florida, Georgia, Illinois, Maryland, Massachusetts, Michigan, Minnesota, New Jersey, New York, North Carolina, Ohio, Pennsylvania, Texas, and Virginia!

What our customers say about our books:

"It couldn't be more clear for the lay person." —R.D.

"I want you to know I really appreciate your book. It has saved me a lot of time and money." —L.T.

"Your real estate contracts book has saved me nearly $12,000.00 in closing costs over the past year." —A.B.

"...many of the legal questions that I have had over the years were answered clearly and concisely through your plain English interpretation of the law." —C.E.H.

"If there weren't people out there like you I'd be lost. You have the best books of this type out there." —S.B.

"...your forms and directions are easy to follow." —C.V.M.

Sphinx Publishing's Legal Survival Guides
are directly available from Sourcebooks, Inc., or from your local bookstores.

For credit card orders call 1–800–432–7444, write P.O. Box 4410, Naperville, IL 60567-4410,
or fax 630-961-2168

Find more legal information at: www.SphinxLegal.com

SPHINX® PUBLISHING'S NATIONAL TITLES
Valid in All 50 States

LEGAL SURVIVAL IN BUSINESS

The Complete Book of Corporate Forms	$24.95
The Complete Patent Book	$26.95
The Entrepreneur's Internet Handbook	$21.95
How to Form a Limited Liability Company (2E)	$24.95
Incorporate in Delaware from Any State	$24.95
Incorporate in Nevada from Any State	$24.95
How to Form a Nonprofit Corporation (2E)	$24.95
How to Form Your Own Corporation (4E)	$26.95
How to Form Your Own Partnership (2E)	$24.95
How to Register Your Own Copyright (4E)	$24.95
How to Register Your Own Trademark (3E)	$21.95
Most Valuable Business Legal Forms You'll Ever Need (3E)	$21.95
Profit from Intellectual Property	$28.95
Protect Your Patent	$24.95
The Small Business Owner's Guide to Bankruptcy	$21.95

LEGAL SURVIVAL IN COURT

Crime Victim's Guide to Justice (2E)	$21.95
Grandparents' Rights (3E)	$24.95
Help Your Lawyer Win Your Case (2E)	$14.95
Jurors' Rights (2E)	$12.95
Legal Research Made Easy (3E)	$21.95
Winning Your Personal Injury Claim (2E)	$24.95
Your Rights When You Owe Too Much	$16.95

LEGAL SURVIVAL IN REAL ESTATE

Essential Guide to Real Estate Contracts (2E)	$18.95
Essential Guide to Real Estate Leases	$18.95
How to Buy a Condominium or Townhome (2E)	$19.95
How to Buy Your First Home	$18.95
Working with Your Homeowners Association	$19.95

LEGAL SURVIVAL IN PERSONAL AFFAIRS

The 529 College Savings Plan	$16.95
The Antique and Art Collector's Legal Guide	$24.95
Cómo Hacer su Propio Testamento	$16.95
Cómo Restablecer su propio Crédito y Renegociar sus Deudas	$21.95
Cómo Solicitar su Propio Divorcio	$24.95
The Complete Legal Guide to Senior Care	$21.95
Family Limited Partnership	$26.95
Gay & Lesbian Rights	$26.95
Guía de Inmigración a Estados Unidos (3E)	$24.95
Guía de Justicia para Víctimas del Crimen	$21.95
How to File Your Own Bankruptcy (5E)	$21.95
How to File Your Own Divorce (5E)	$26.95
How to Make Your Own Simple Will (3E)	$18.95
How to Write Your Own Living Will (3E)	$18.95
How to Write Your Own Premarital Agreement (3E)	$24.95
Inmigración a los EE. UU. Paso a Paso	$22.95
Living Trusts and Other Ways to Avoid Probate (3E)	$24.95
Manual de Beneficios para el Seguro Social	$18.95
Mastering the MBE	$16.95
Most Valuable Personal Legal Forms You'll Ever Need (2E)	$26.95
Neighbor v. Neighbor (2E)	$16.95
The Nanny and Domestic Help Legal Kit	$22.95
The Power of Attorney Handbook (4E)	$19.95
Repair Your Own Credit and Deal with Debt (2E)	$18.95
El Seguro Social Preguntas y Respuestas	$14.95
Sexual Harassment:Your Guide to Legal Action	$18.95
The Social Security Benefits Handbook (3E)	$18.95
Social Security Q&A	$12.95
Teen Rights	$22.95
Traveler's Rights	$21.95
Unmarried Parents' Rights (2E)	$19.95
U.S. Immigration Step by Step	$21.95
U.S.A. Immigration Guide (4E)	$24.95
The Visitation Handbook	$18.95
The Wills, Estate Planning and Trusts Legal Kit	&26.95
Win Your Unemployment Compensation Claim (2E)	$21.95
Your Right to Child Custody, Visitation and Support (2E)	$24.95

Legal Survival Guides are directly available from Sourcebooks, Inc., or from your local bookstores.

SPHINX® PUBLISHING ORDER FORM

<table>
<tr><td>BILL TO:</td><td>SHIP TO:</td></tr>
</table>

<table>
<tr><td>Phone #</td><td>Terms</td><td>F.O.B. Chicago, IL</td><td>Ship Date</td></tr>
</table>

Charge my: ☐ VISA ☐ MasterCard ☐ American Express

☐ **Money Order or Personal Check**

Credit Card Number   Expiration Date

Qty	ISBN	Title	Retail	Ext.	Qty	ISBN	Title	Retail	Ext.
		SPHINX PUBLISHING NATIONAL TITLES				1-57248-169-2	The Power of Attorney Handbook (4E)	$19.95	
						1-57248-332-6	Profit from Intellectual Property	$28.95	
	1-57248-238-9	The 529 College Savings Plan	$16.95			1-57248-329-6	Protect Your Patent	$24.95	
	1-57248-349-0	The Antique and Art Collector's Legal Guide	$24.95			1-57248-344-X	Repair Your Own Credit and Deal with Debt (2E)	$18.95	
	1-57248-148-X	Cómo Hacer su Propio Testamento	$16.95			1-57248-350-4	El Seguro Social Preguntas y Respuestas	$14.95	
	1-57248-226-5	Cómo Restablecer su propio Crédito y Renegociar sus Deudas	$21.95			1-57248-217-6	Sexual Harassment: Your Guide to Legal Action	$18.95	
	1-57248-147-1	Cómo Solicitar su Propio Divorcio	$24.95			1-57248-219-2	The Small Business Owner's Guide to Bankruptcy	$21.95	
	1-57248-166-8	The Complete Book of Corporate Forms	$24.95			1-57248-168-4	The Social Security Benefits Handbook (3E)	$18.95	
	1-57248-229-X	The Complete Legal Guide to Senior Care	$21.95			1-57248-216-8	Social Security Q&A	$12.95	
	1-57248-201-X	The Complete Patent Book	$26.95			1-57248-221-4	Teen Rlghts	$22.95	
	1-57248-163-3	Crime Victim's Guide to Justice (2E)	$21.95			1-57248-335-0	Traveler's Rights	$21.95	
	1-57248-251-6	The Entrepreneur's Internet Handbook	$21.95			1-57248-236-2	Unmarried Parents' Rights (2E)	$19.95	__ __
	1-57248-346-6	Essential Guide to Real Estate Contracts (2E)	$18.95			1-57248-218-4	U.S. Immigration Step by Step	$21.95	
	1-57248-160-9	Essential Guide to Real Estate Leases	$18.95			1-57248-161-7	U.S.A. Immigration Guide (4E)	$24.95	
	1-57248-254-0	Family Limited Partnership	$26.95			1-57248-192-7	The Visitation Handbook	$18.95	
	1-57248-331-8	Gay & Lesbian Rights	$26.95			1-57248-225-7	Win Your Unemployment Compensation Claim (2E)	$21.95	
	1-57248-139-0	Grandparents' Rights (3E)	$24.95			1-57248-330-X	The Wills, Estate Planning and Trusts Legal Kit	&26.95	
	1-57248-188-9	Guía de Inmigración a Estados Unidos (3E)	$24.95			1-57248-138-2	Winning Your Personal Injury Claim (2E)	$24.95	
	1-57248-187-0	Guía de Justicia para Víctimas del Crimen	$21.95			1-57248-333-4	Working with Your Homeowners Association	$19.95	
	1-57248-103-X	Help Your Lawyer Win Your Case (2E)	$14.95			1-57248-162-5	Your Right to Child Custody, Visitation and Support (2E)	$24.95	
	1-57248-164-1	How to Buy a Condominium or Townhome (2E)	$19.95			1-57248-157-9	Your Rights When You Owe Too Much	$16.95	
	1-57248-328-8	How to Buy Your First Home	$18.95				**CALIFORNIA TITLES**		
	1-57248-191-9	How to File Your Own Bankruptcy (5E)	$21.95						
	1-57248-343-1	How to File Your Own Divorce (5E)	$26.95			1-57248-150-1	CA Power of Attorney Handbook (2E)	$18.95	
	1-57248-222-2	How to Form a Limited Liability Company (2E)	$24.95			1-57248-337-7	How to File for Divorce in CA (4E)	$26.95	
	1-57248-231-1	How to Form a Nonprofit Corporation (2E)	$24.95			1-57248-145-5	How to Probate and Settle an Estate in CA	$26.95	
	1-57248-345-8	How to Form Your Own Corporation (4E)	$26.95			1-57248-336-9	How to Start a Business in CA (2E)	$21.95	
	1-57248-224-9	How to Form Your Own Partnership (2E)	$24.95			1-57248-194-3	How to Win in Small Claims Court in CA (2E)	$18.95	
	1-57248-232-X	How to Make Your Own Simple Will (3E)	$18.95			1-57248-246-X	Make Your Own CA Will	$18.95	
	1-57248-200-1	How to Register Your Own Copyright (4E)	$24.95			1-57248-196-X	The Landlord's Legal Guide in CA	$24.95	
	1-57248-104-8	How to Register Your Own Trademark (3E)	$21.95			1-57248-241-9	Tenants' Rights in CA	$21.95	
	1-57248-233-8	How to Write Your Own Living Will (3E)	$18.95				**FLORIDA TITLES**		
	1-57248-156-0	How to Write Your Own Premarital Agreement (3E)	$24.95						
	1-57248-230-3	Incorporate in Delaware from Any State	$24.95			1-57071-363-4	Florida Power of Attorney Handbook (2E)	$16.95	
	1-57248-158-7	Incorporate in Nevada from Any State	$24.95			1-57248-176-5	How to File for Divorce in FL (7E)	$26.95	
	1-57248-250-8	Inmigración a los EE.UU. Paso a Paso	$22.95			1-57248-356-3	How to Form a Corporation in FL (6E)	$24.95	
	1-57071-333-2	Jurors' Rights (2E)	$12.95			1-57248-203-6	How to Form a Limited Liability Co. in FL (2E)	$24.95	
	1-57248-223-0	Legal Research Made Easy (3E)	$21.95			1-57071-401-0	How to Form a Partnership in FL	$22.95	
	1-57248-165-X	Living Trusts and Other Ways to Avoid Probate (3E)	$24.95			1-57248-113-7	How to Make a FL Will (6E)	$16.95	
	1-57248-186-2	Manual de Beneficios para el Seguro Social	$18.95			1-57248-088-2	How to Modify Your FL Divorce Judgment (4E)	$24.95	
	1-57248-220-6	Mastering the MBE	$16.95			1-57248-144-7	How to Probate and Settle an Estate in FL (4E)	$26.95	
	1-57248-167-6	Most Val. Business Legal Forms You'll Ever Need (3E)	$21.95			1-57248-339-3	How to Start a Business in FL (7E)	$21.95	
	1-57248-360-1	Most Val. Personal Legal Forms You'll Ever Need (2E)	$26.95			1-57248-204-4	How to Win in Small Claims Court in FL (7E)	$18.95	
	1-57248-098-X	The Nanny and Domestic Help Legal Kit	$22.95			1-57248-202-8	Land Trusts in Florida (6E)	$29.95	
	1-57248-089-0	Neighbor v. Neighbor (2E)	$16.95			1-57248-338-5	Landlords' Rights and Duties in FL (9E)	$22.95	
							Form Continued on Following Page	**SUBTOTAL**	

To order, call Sourcebooks at 1-800-432-7444 or FAX (630) 961-2168 (Bookstores, libraries, wholesalers—please call for discount)

Prices are subject to change without notice.

Find more legal information at: **www.SphinxLegal.com**

Lantana Public Library SPHINX® PUBLISHING ORDER FORM

Qty	ISBN	Title	Retail	Ext.
		GEORGIA TITLES		
_____	1-57248-340-7	How to File for Divorce in GA (5E)	$21.95	_____
_____	1-57248-180-3	How to Make a GA Will (4E)	$21.95	_____
_____	1-57248-341-5	How to Start a Business in Georgia (3E)	$21.95	_____
		ILLINOIS TITLES		
_____	1-57248-244-3	Child Custody, Visitation, and Support in IL	$24.95	_____
_____	1-57248-206-0	How to File for Divorce in IL (3E)	$24.95	_____
_____	1-57248-170-6	How to Make an IL Will (3E)	$16.95	_____
_____	1-57248-247-8	How to Start a Business in IL (3E)	$21.95	_____
_____	1-57248-252-4	The Landlord's Legal Guide in IL	$24.95	_____
		MARYLAND, VIRGINIA AND THE DISTRICT OF COLUMBIA		
_____	1-57248-240-0	How to File for Divorce in MD, VA and DC	$28.95	_____
		MASSACHUSETTS TITLES		
_____	1-57248-128-5	How to File for Divorce in MA (3E)	$24.95	_____
_____	1-57248-115-3	How to Form a Corporation in MA	$24.95	_____
_____	1-57248-108-0	How to Make a MA Will (2E)	$16.95	_____
_____	1-57248-248-6	How to Start a Business in MA (3E)	$21.95	_____
_____	1-57248-209-5	The Landlord's Legal Guide in MA	$24.95	_____
		MICHIGAN TITLES		
_____	1-57248-215-X	How to File for Divorce in MI (3E)	$24.95	_____
_____	1-57248-182-X	How to Make a MI Will (3E)	$16.95	_____
_____	1-57248-183-8	How to Start a Business in MI (3E)	$18.95	_____
		MINNESOTA TITLES		
_____	1-57248-142-0	How to File for Divorce in MN	$21.95	_____
_____	1-57248-179-X	How to Form a Corporation in MN	$24.95	_____
_____	1-57248-178-1	How to Make a MN Will (2E)	$16.95	_____
		NEW JERSEY TITLES		
_____	1-57248-239-7	How to File for Divorce in NJ	$24.95	_____
		NEW YORK TITLES		
_____	1-57248-193-5	Child Custody, Visitation and Support in NY	$26.95	_____
_____	1-57248-351-2	File for Divorce in NY	$26.95	_____
_____	1-57248-249-4	How to Form a Corporation in NY (2E)	$24.95	_____
_____	1-57248-095-5	How to Make a NY Will (2E)	$16.95	_____
_____	1-57248-199-4	How to Start a Business in NY (2E)	$18.95	_____
_____	1-57248-198-6	How to Win in Small Claims Court in NY (2E)	$18.95	_____
_____	1-57248-197-8	Landlords' Legal Guide in NY	$24.95	_____
_____	1-57071-188-7	New York Power of Attorney Handbook	$19.95	_____
_____	1-57248-122-6	Tenants' Rights in NY	$21.95	_____

Qty	ISBN	Title	Retail	E
		NORTH CAROLINA TITLES		
_____	1-57248-185-4	How to File for Divorce in NC (3E)	$22.95	_
_____	1-57248-129-3	How to Make a NC Will (3E)	$16.95	_
_____	1-57248-184-6	How to Start a Business in NC (3E)	$18.95	_
_____	1-57248-091-2	Landlords' Rights & Duties in NC	$21.95	_
		OHIO TITLES		
_____	1-57248-190-0	How to File for Divorce in OH (2E)	$24.95	_
_____	1-57248-174-9	How to Form a Corporation in OH	$24.95	_
_____	1-57248-173-0	How to Make an OH Will	$16.95	_
		PENNSYLVANIA TITLES		
_____	1-57248-242-7	Child Custody, Visitation and Support in PA	$26.95	_
_____	1-57248-211-7	How to File for Divorce in PA (3E)	$26.95	_
_____	1-57248-094-3	How to Make a PA Will (2E)	$16.95	_
_____	1-57248-357-1	How to Start a Business in PA (3E)	$21.95	_
_____	1-57248-245-1	The Landlord's Legal Guide in PA	$24.95	_
		TEXAS TITLES		
_____	1-57248-171-4	Child Custody, Visitation, and Support in TX	$22.95	_
_____	1-57248-172-2	How to File for Divorce in TX (3E)	$24.95	_
_____	1-57248-114-5	How to Form a Corporation in TX (2E)	$24.95	_
_____	1-57248-255-9	How to Make a TX Will (3E)	$16.95	_
_____	1-57248-214-1	How to Probate and Settle an Estate in TX (3E)	$26.95	_
_____	1-57248-228-1	How to Start a Business in TX (3E)	$18.95	_
_____	1-57248-111-0	How to Win in Small Claims Court in TX (2E)	$16.95	_
_____	1-57248-355-5	the Landlord's Legal Guide in TX	$24.95	_

SUBTOTAL THIS PAGE _____

SUBTOTAL PREVIOUS PAGE _____

Shipping — $5.00 for 1st book, $1.00 each additional _____

Illinois residents add 6.75% sales tax _____

Connecticut residents add 6.00% sales tax _____

TOTAL _____

To order, call Sourcebooks at 1-800-432-7444 or FAX (630) 961-2168 (Bookstores, libraries, wholesalers—please call for discount)
Prices are subject to change without notice.
Find more legal information at: **www.SphinxLegal.com**